Photographer's Guide to the Sony DSC-RX100 III

Photographer's Guide to the Sony DSC-RX100 III

Getting the Most from Sony's Pocketable Digital Camera

Alexander S. White

WHITE KNIGHT PRESS
HENRICO, VIRGINIA

Published by
White Knight Press
9704 Old Club Trace
Henrico, Virginia 23238
www.whiteknightpress.com
contact@whiteknightpress.com

ISBN: 978-1-937986-51-3 (paperback)
            978-1-937986-27-8 (e-book)

Printed in the United States of America

To my wife, Clenise.

Contents

CHAPTER 5: OTHER CONTROLS   92

Chapter 6: Playback and Printing   108

Chapter 7: Custom and Setup Menus   119

CHAPTER 8: MOTION PICTURES   154

CHAPTER 9: WI-FI, APPLICATIONS, AND OTHER TOPICS   172

Introduction

This book is a guide to the operation of the Sony Cyber-shot DSC-RX100 III digital camera. It contains much of the same information as my earlier guides for the RX100 and RX100 II models, but I have revised it for the RX100 III with new illustrations and new or revised text where needed.

When Sony announced this camera model, I had no hesitation in deciding to write a new book for it. The RX100 III continues in the tradition of the earlier models with great portability, excellent image quality, and advanced features for taking stills and videos. It adds several enhancements, including a pop-up electronic viewfinder and an improved lens with a wide-angle setting of 24mm, a bright f/1.8 aperture at the wide-angle end, and an f/2.8 aperture at the telephoto end. The camera also adds a tilting LCD screen, an advanced video format, a built-in neutral density filter, and the ability to download camera apps that can add features and functions.

Of course, it's not possible to provide every desirable feature in a single camera of this size, and the enhancements resulted in the loss of a couple of features from the previous model. Most significantly, the RX100 III has no hot shoe for attaching an external flash or viewfinder. Of course, the shoe is not needed for a viewfinder, which is now built into the camera. The other noticeable change is the reduction of the maximum optical zoom range from 100mm to 70mm. In exchange for this reduction, though, the new model's lens offers a wide-angle focal length of 24mm, which improves the camera's ability to photograph subjects such as wide landscapes, groups of people, and interiors of rooms.

My goal with this book is to provide a thorough guide to the camera's features, explaining how they work and when you might want to use them. The book is aimed largely at beginning and intermediate photographers who are not satisfied with the official documentation and prefer a more user-friendly explanation of the camera's controls and menus. For those seeking more advanced information, I discuss some topics that go beyond the basics, and I include in the appendices information about additional resources. I will provide updates and other information at my website, whiteknightpress.com, as warranted.

Finally, one note on the scope of this guide: I live in the United States, and I bought my camera here. I am not very familiar with the variations for cameras sold in Europe or elsewhere, such as different battery chargers. The photographic functions are generally not different, so this guide should be useful to photographers in all locations. I should note that the frame rates for HD video are different in different areas: the version of the RX100 III sold in the U.S. uses the 30 frames per second (fps) standard for video, whereas cameras sold in Europe use 25 fps. The video functions and operations are not different, just the frame rates. I have stated measurements of distance and weight in both the Imperial and metric systems, for the benefit of readers in various countries around the world.

CHAPTER 1: PRELIMINARY SETUP

Setting Up the Camera

When you purchase your Sony DSC-RX100 III, the box should contain the camera itself, battery, charger, wrist strap, two adapters for attaching a shoulder strap (though no shoulder strap is supplied), micro USB cable, and brief instruction pamphlet. There is no CD with software or user's guide; the software programs supplied by Sony are accessible through the Internet.

To install PlayMemories Home, the Sony software for viewing and working with images and videos on computers, go to the following Internet address: http://www.sony.net/pm. If you have a Macintosh computer, you can get the Sony software at http://www.sony.co.jp/imsoft/Mac/.

You also can install Sony's Image Data Converter software, which converts the camera's Raw images so you can edit them on a computer. That software is available for both Windows-based computers and Macs at the web addresses listed above.

You might want to attach the wrist strap as soon as possible to help you keep a tight grip on the camera. The strap can be attached to the small mounting lug on either the left or right side of the camera. I have never attached the strap, though, because the camera is so small that I can hold it firmly without much risk of dropping it, even without a strap. See Appendix A for a discussion of custom grips that can also be of use.

CHARGING AND INSERTING THE BATTERY

The Sony battery for the DSC-RX100 III is the NP-BX1. The standard procedure is to charge the battery while it's inside the camera. To do this, you use the supplied USB cable, which plugs into the camera and into the Sony charger or a USB port on your computer. There are pluses and minuses to charging the battery while it is inside the camera. On the positive side, you don't need an external charger, and the camera can charge automatically when it's connected to your computer. You also can find portable charging devices with USB ports; many automobiles have USB slots where you can plug in your RX100 III to keep up its charge.

One of the main drawbacks is that you cannot effectively use the camera while the battery is being charged with the Sony charger. If you try, the camera will display a message saying you cannot operate the camera, though, oddly enough, the camera will still shoot and save images, but they will be blocked from view by the error screen. You can view them later, after the charger is unplugged. To add to the mix of possibilities, when I charged the camera by plugging the USB cable into an Anker 40-watt desktop USB charger rather than using the Sony charger, I found that I could operate the camera normally. However, I mention these oddities only to give a complete account of the situation. In practical terms, you probably will not want to use the camera while it's plugged in for charging.

The other problem with the standard charging system is that the Sony charger does not let you charge another battery outside of the camera. One solution to this situation is to purchase at least one extra battery and a device that will charge your batteries externally. I'll discuss batteries, chargers, and other accessories in Appendix A.

For now, get the battery charged by inserting it into the camera and connecting the charger. You first need to open the battery compartment door on the bottom of the camera and put in the battery. You can only insert it fully into the camera one way; what I do is look for the 4 gold-colored metal contact squares on the end of the battery and insert the battery so those 4 squares are positioned close to the front of the camera as the battery goes into the compartment, as shown in Figure 1-1 and Figure 1-2. You may have to nudge aside the small blue latch that holds the battery in place, which is seen in Figure 1-3.

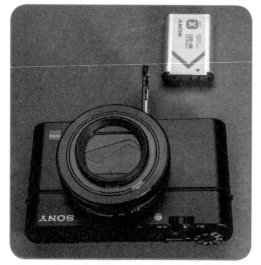

Figure 1-1. Battery Lined Up to Go into Camera

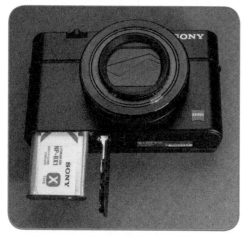

Figure 1-2. Battery Going into Camera

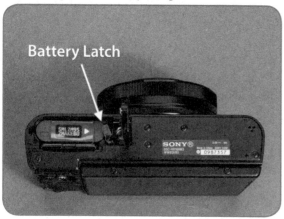

Figure 1-3. Battery Secured by Latch

With the battery inserted and secured by the latch, close the battery compartment door and slide the ridged latch on the door to the closed position. Then plug the larger, rectangular end of the USB cable into the corresponding slot on the provided AC charger,

which is model number AC-UB10 in the United States. Plug the smaller end of the cable into the micro USB port on the upper part of the camera's right side as you hold it in shooting position, as shown in Figure 1-4.

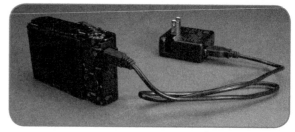

Figure 1-4. Sony USB Charger Attached to Camera

Plug the charger's prongs into a standard electrical outlet. An orange lamp in the center of the power (On/Off) button on top of the camera will light up steadily while the battery is charging; when it goes out, the battery is fully charged. The full charging cycle should take about 230 minutes. If the charging lamp flashes, that indicates a problem with the charger or a problem with the temperature of the camera's environment.

CHOOSING AND INSERTING A MEMORY CARD

The RX100 III does not ship with a memory card. If you turn the camera on with no card inserted, you will see the message "NO CARD" in the upper left corner of the screen. If you ignore this message and press the shutter button to take a picture, don't be fooled into thinking that the camera is storing it in internal memory. The camera will temporarily store the image and play it back if you press the Playback button, but the image will not be permanently saved. Some camera models have a small amount of built-in memory so you can take and store a few pictures even without a card, but the RX100 III does not have that safety net. (In an emergency, if you took one important picture with no card, you might be able to save it. First, don't turn off the camera. Second, play the image, and connect one end of a micro-HDMI cable to the camera's HDMI port and the other end to a video capture device. Then capture the image to that device or to a computer connected to that device. I have done this using a Blackmagic Intensity Pro device, which saved the image to Photoshop. But that process is for emergencies only.)

To avoid the frustration of having a great camera that can't save images, you need to use a memory card. The RX100 III uses 2 types of memory storage. First, it can use all varieties of SD cards, which are about the size of a postage stamp. These cards come in several varieties; some examples are shown in Figure 1-5.

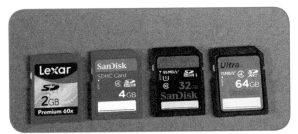

Figure 1-5. Card Types: SD 2GB, SDHC 4GB, SDHC 32GB, SDXC 64 GB

The standard card, called simply SD, comes in capacities from 8 megabytes (MB) to 2 gigabytes (GB). A higher-capacity card, SDHC, comes in sizes from 4 GB to 32 GB. The newest, and highest-capacity card, SDXC (for extended capacity) comes in sizes of 48 GB, 64 GB, 128 GB, and 256 GB; this version of the card can have a capacity up to 2 terabytes (TB), theoretically, and SDXC cards generally have faster transfer speeds than the smaller-capacity cards. There also is a special variety of SD card called an Eye-Fi card, which I will discuss a bit later in this chapter.

The RX100 III also can use micro-SD cards, which are often used in smartphones and other small devices. These smaller cards operate the same as SD cards, but you need an adapter to use this tiny card in the RX100 III camera, as shown in Figure 1-6.

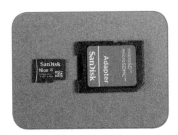

Figure 1-6. Micro-SD Card and Adapter

In addition to using SD cards, the RX100 III, being a Sony camera, also can use Sony's proprietary storage devices, known as Memory Stick cards. These cards are similar in size and capacity to SD cards, but with a slightly different shape, as shown in Figure 1-7.

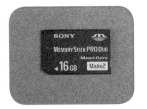

Figure 1-7. Memory Stick PRO Duo

Memory Stick cards come in various types, according to their capacities. The ones that can be used in the RX100 III are the Memory Stick PRO Duo, Memory Stick PRO-HG Duo, Memory Stick XC-HG Duo, and Memory Stick Micro (M2). The Memory Stick Micro, like the micro-SD card, requires an adapter.

There is one major limitation on your choice of a memory card. If you want to record video using the XAVC S format, which provides the highest quality, you have to use either an SDXC card with a capacity of 64 GB or more and speed of Class 10, UHS-I, or faster, or a Memory Stick XC-HG Duo. The XAVC S format is worth using if you want high-quality video, and it is a good idea to get one of the high-powered cards that can support its use.

If you do not care about using the XAVC S video format, the factors to consider in choosing a card are capacity and speed. If you're planning to record a good deal of HD video or a large number of Raw-format photos, you should get a large-capacity card, but don't get carried away—the largest cards have such huge capacities that you may be wasting money purchasing them.

There are several variables to consider in computing how many images or videos you can store on a particular size of card, such as which aspect ratio you're using (16:9, 3:2, 4:3, or 1:1), image size, and quality. Here are a few examples of what can be stored on a 64 GB SDXC card. If you're using the standard 3:2 aspect ratio, you can store about 2,900 Raw images (the highest quality), 4,300 high-quality JPEG images (Large size and Extra Fine quality), or about 9,900 of the lower-quality Standard images (Large size).

Here are some guidelines for video. You can fit about 2 hours 40 minutes of the highest-quality XAVC S video on a 64 GB card. That same card will hold about 41 hours 30 minutes of video at the lowest MP4 setting of 640 x 480 pixels, also known as VGA quality. Note, though, that the camera is limited to recording no more than about 29 minutes of video in any format in any one sequence. The higher-quality MP4 format can be recorded only for 15 minutes in one sequence, because of the 2 GB file size limit.

The other major consideration is the speed of the card. High speed is important to get good results for recording continuous bursts of images and the highest-quality video with this camera. You should try to find a card that writes data at a rate of 6 MB/second or faster to record HD video. If you go by the class designation, a Class 4 card should be sufficient for shooting stills, and a Class 6 card should suffice for recording AVCHD video.

Newer cards, such as the SanDisk Extreme Pro and the Lexar Professional, shown in Figure 1-8, come with the UHS designation, for ultra high speed.

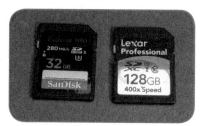

Figure 1-8. High-speed SD Cards

There are currently 2 designations: UHS-I and UHS-II. The fastest cards, such as the SanDisk Extreme PRO UHS-II card, are rated to write data at a speed up to 280 MB/s.

If you know you will never need to record XAVC S video, then you can use a card such as the 32 GB Lexar Professional SDHC card, rated in Class 10 for speed. However, if there is any chance you will want to use the XAVC S format, you should choose a card such as the 64 GB SanDisk Extreme Pro UHS-II.

If you have an older computer with a built-in card reader, or just an older external reader, there is a chance it will not read newer SDHC cards. In that case, you would have to either get a new reader that will accept SDHC cards or download images from the camera to your computer using the USB cable. Using the newest variety of card, SDXC, also can be problematic with older computers. If your computer has a recent version of its operating system, it will be able to read SDXC cards if you use a compatible card reader.

You also may want to consider using an Eye-Fi card. This special type of device looks like an ordinary SDHC card, but it includes a tiny transmitter that lets it connect to a Wi-Fi network and send your images to

your computer on that network as soon as the images are recorded by the camera. You also may be able to use Direct Mode, which lets the Eye-Fi card send your images directly to a computer, smartphone, tablet, or other device without needing a network, though Direct Mode can be tricky to set up.

I have tested an 8 GB Pro X2 Eye-Fi card with the RX100 III, and it worked as expected. Within a few seconds after I snap a picture with this card in the camera, a thumbnail image appears in the upper right corner of my computer screen showing the progress of the upload. When all images have been uploaded, they are available in the Pictures/Eye-Fi folder on my computer. The Pro X2 models, shown in Figure 1-9, can handle Raw files and video files as well as the smaller JPEG files.

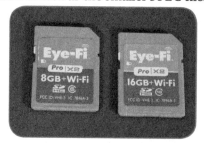

Figure 1-9. Eye-Fi Pro X2 SDHC Memory Cards

Of course, with the RX100 III Sony has included built-in Wi-Fi capability, as discussed in Chapter 9, so you do not need to use an Eye-Fi card or the equivalent to transfer images wirelessly. If you already have one or more wireless SD cards, you should be able to use them in your RX100 III, but there are other options for wireless transfer that may make more sense.

If you decide to use a Memory Stick card and want to use it with a card reader, be sure you have a reader that can accept those cards, which, as noted above, are not the same shape as SD cards.

Once you have chosen a card, open the same door on the bottom of the camera that covers the battery compartment, and slide the card in until it catches. An SD card is inserted with its label pointing toward the back of the camera, as shown in Figure 1-10; a Memory Stick card is inserted with its label pointing toward the front of the camera.

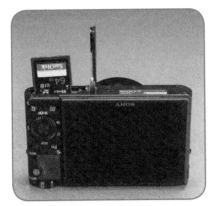

Figure 1-10. SD Card Going into Camera

Once the card has been pushed down until it catches, close the compartment door and slide the latch to the outside position. To remove a card, push down on its edge until it releases and springs up, so you can grab it.

Although the card may work well when newly inserted in the camera, it's a good idea to format a card when first using it in a camera, so it will have the correct file structure and will have any bad areas blocked off from use. To do this, turn on the camera by pressing the power button, then press the Menu button at the center right of the camera's back. Next, press the Right button (right edge of the Control wheel on the camera's back) multiple times until the small orange line near the top of the screen is positioned under the number 4, while the menu's highlight lines are on the toolbox icon, as shown in Figure 1-11.

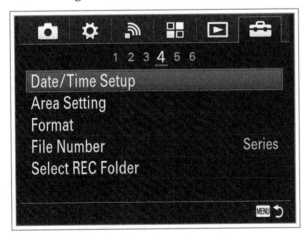

Figure 1-11. Screen 4 of Setup Menu

That icon is for the Setup menu. The orange highlight bar should be on the top line of the menu, on the Date/Time Setup command; press the Down button (bottom edge of the Control wheel), or turn the wheel, until the Format command is highlighted.

Press the button in the center of the Control wheel (called the "Center button" in this book) when the Format line is highlighted. On the next screen, seen in Figure 1-12, highlight Enter and press the button again to carry out the command.

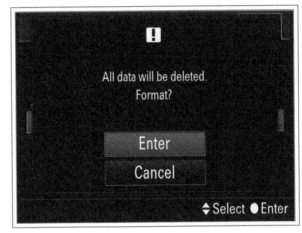

Figure 1-12. Format Confirmation Screen

SETTING THE LANGUAGE, DATE, AND TIME

Next, you need to make sure the date and time are set correctly before you start taking pictures because the camera records that information invisibly with each image and displays it later if you want. It is, of course, important to have the date (and the time of day) correctly recorded with your archives of digital images. The camera may prompt you to set the date and time the first time you turn it on, but if not, carry out this procedure.

First, follow the same steps with the menu as noted above, but this time select the Date/Time Setup item at the top of screen 4 of the Setup menu. Then press the Center button to move to the next screen. On that screen, select the Date/Time item, as shown in Figure 1-13, and press the Center button.

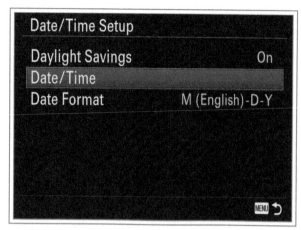

Figure 1-13. Date/Time Option Highlighted on Menu Screen

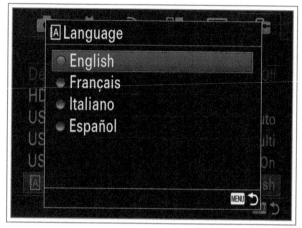

Figure 1-15. Language Selection Screen

By pressing the Left and Right buttons or by turning the Control wheel, move through the month, day, year, and time settings, and change them by pressing the Up and Down buttons. When these settings have been made, press the Center button to confirm. You can adjust the Daylight Savings Time and Date Format settings on the previous screen if you need to. Then press the Menu button to exit from the menu system.

If you need to change the language the camera uses for menus and other messages, press the Menu button as discussed above to enter the menu system, and navigate to screen 3 of the Setup menu, as shown in Figure 1-14.

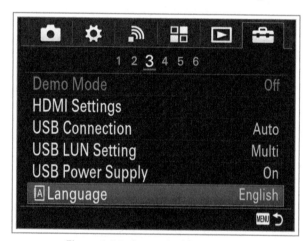

Figure 1-14. Screen 3 of Setup Menu

Then navigate with the direction buttons, if necessary, to the Language item at the bottom of the screen and press the Center button to select it. You then can select from the available languages on the menu, as shown in Figure 1-15.

Chapter 2: Basic Operations

Overview of Shooting Still Images

Now that the Sony RX100 III has the correct time and date set and a charged battery inserted along with a memory card, I'll discuss a setup for basic picture taking. For now, I won't discuss details about various options and why you might choose one over another. I'll just describe a reasonable set of steps that will get your camera into action and will record a usable image on your memory card.

Introduction to Main Controls

Before I discuss options for setting up the camera using the menu system and controls, I will introduce the main physical features of the camera. I won't discuss all of the controls here; I will cover them in more detail in Chapter 5. For now, I will include a series of images showing the main items on the camera. As I mention each item for the first time, I will describe its position and function; you may want to refer back to these images for a reminder about each control.

Top of Camera

On top of the camera are some of the most important controls and other features, as shown in Figure 2-1. You use the Mode dial to select a shooting mode for stills or video. For basic shooting without having to make other settings, turn the dial so the green or tan camera icon is next to the white marker; this will set the camera to one of its most automatic modes. The large, black shutter button is used to take pictures. Press it halfway to evaluate focus and exposure; press it all the way to take a picture. The zoom lever, surrounding the shutter button, is used to zoom the lens in and out between its telephoto and wide-angle settings. The lever also is used to change the views of images in playback mode.

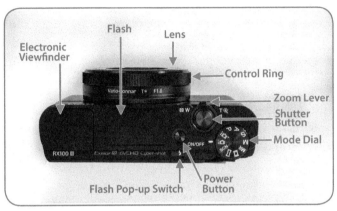

Figure 2-1. Controls on Top of Camera

The power button turns the camera on and off. An orange light in the center of the button glows when the battery is being charged in the camera. The flash is normally stored inside the top of the camera; if you want it to be available for use, you have to pop it up using the flash pop-up switch behind the power button. The built-in electronic viewfinder (EVF) is stored inside the camera's top at the far left side until you pop it up using the Finder switch on the camera's left side.

Back of Camera

Figure 2-2 shows the controls on the camera's back.

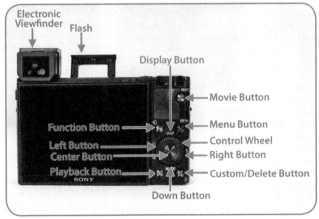

Figure 2-2. Controls on Back of Camera

The Movie button starts and stops a video recording. The Menu button calls up the system of menu screens with settings for shooting and other values, such as control button functions, audio features, and others. In shooting mode, the Function (Fn) button calls up a menu of camera settings for easy access. In playback mode, it activates the Send to Smartphone command, if the command is available. The Playback button puts the camera into playback mode so you can view your recorded images, and it also can turn the camera on. The Custom/Delete button, marked with a C, can be programmed to call up any one of numerous functions. By default, in shooting mode it calls up help screens with information about menu options. In playback mode, it always serves as the Delete button for erasing images.

The Control wheel is a rotary dial for setting values such as aperture and shutter speed and for navigating through menu screens. In addition, each of its 4 edges acts as a button when you press it in, for controlling items including flash mode, exposure compensation, continuous shooting, and the display screen. The Center button is used to confirm selections and for some other operations. The LCD screen—which displays the scene viewed by the camera along with the camera's settings and plays back recorded images—tilts up or down to allow you to hold the camera in a high or low position to view a scene from unusual angles. It also can rotate 180 degrees forward to let you take a self-portrait.

Front of Camera

Figure 2-3 shows the items of interest on the camera's front.

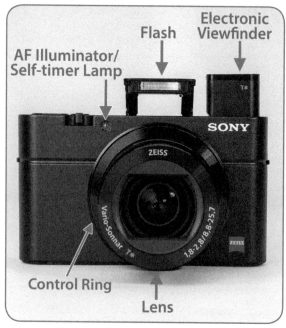

Figure 2-3. Items on Front of Camera

The AF Illuminator/Self-timer Lamp signals operation of the self-timer and provides illumination so the camera can use its autofocus system in dark areas. The Control ring, around the lens, can adjust items such as aperture, shutter speed, manual focus, and others, depending on the shooting mode and menu options in effect. The lens has a 35mm equivalent focal length range of 24mm to 70mm and an aperture range of f/1.8 to f/11.0. (The actual focal length of the lens is 8.8mm to 25.7mm; the "35mm equivalent" range is commonly used to state the focal length in a way that can easily be compared to lenses of other cameras.)

Right Side of Camera

On the right side of the camera are 2 small flaps, marked Multi and HDMI, as seen in Figure 2-4. Under those flaps are 2 ports, as shown in Figure 2-5.

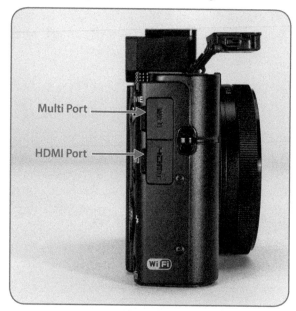

Figure 2-4. Port Covers on Right Side of Camera

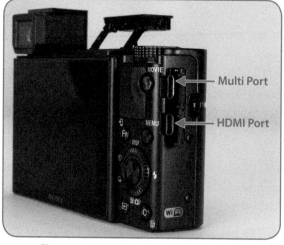

Figure 2-5. Ports on Right Side of Camera

The Multi port is where you connect the USB cable that is supplied with the camera to charge the battery, to connect the RX100 III to a computer to manage images, or to connect to a printer to print images directly from the camera. You also can connect a Sony wired remote control to this port, as discussed in Appendix A. The HDMI port is for connecting the camera to an HDTV to view images and videos. You can also use this port to output a "clean" video signal as discussed in Chapter 7, or to view the shooting information from the camera in shooting mode.

Left Side of Camera

The left side of the camera, shown in Figure 2-6, has 2 items of interest. The first is the Finder switch, which you press down to release the electronic viewfinder so it will pop up. You then have to pull the viewfinder eyepiece out of its housing so you can see the live view through the camera's lens. When you are finished with the viewfinder, press the eyepiece back into the housing. You can then press the viewfinder down into the camera's body. If you do this, the camera will turn off, so don't push the viewfinder down until you are ready to power off the camera.

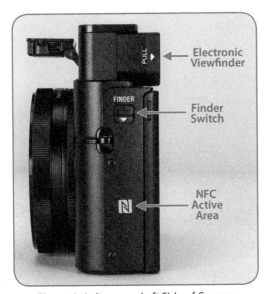

Figure 2-6. Items on Left Side of Camera

The second item of interest on the left side is the NFC (near field communication) area, where you touch the camera against a smartphone or tablet with NFC capability to establish a Wi-Fi connection automatically. I will discuss this feature in Chapter 9.

Bottom of Camera

Finally, as shown in Figure 2-7, on the bottom of the camera are the tripod socket, the battery/memory card compartment, and the speaker that produces sound for videos. There also is a notation on the camera's label stating whether this camera is set up for the 60i or 50i video standard. The 60i models are for use in the United States, Japan, Canada, and other countries that use the NTSC video standard; the 50i models are for use in European and other countries that use the PAL standard.

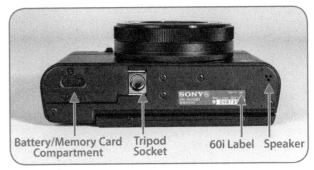

Figure 2-7. Items on Bottom of Camera

There also is one other item that can't be seen unless the battery compartment is open—the access lamp, located at the outside edge of the compartment, as shown in Figure 2-8. That red lamp lights up when the camera is writing data to the memory card. When the camera has taken a long series of continuous shots, the lamp may stay illuminated for several seconds. During that time, be sure you do not remove the battery or the memory card.

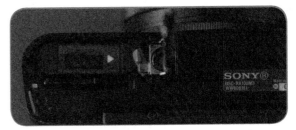

Figure 2-8. Access Lamp Inside Battery Compartment

FULLY AUTOMATIC: INTELLIGENT AUTO MODE

Now I'll discuss how to use these controls to take pictures and videos. Here's a list of steps to take if you want to set the camera to one of its most automatic modes and let it make (almost) all decisions for you. This is a good approach if you need to grab a quick shot without fiddling with too many settings.

1. Press the power button on top of the camera. The LCD screen will illuminate to show that the camera has turned on.

2. Turn the Mode dial so the green camera icon with a letter "i" is next to the white indicator line, as shown in Figure 2-9.

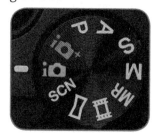

Figure 2-9. Intelligent Auto Mode

This sets the camera to the Intelligent Auto shooting mode. If you see the help screen that describes the mode (called the Mode Dial Guide), as seen in Figure 2-10, press the Center button to dismiss it. (I'll explain how to dispense with that help screen altogether in Chapter 7.)

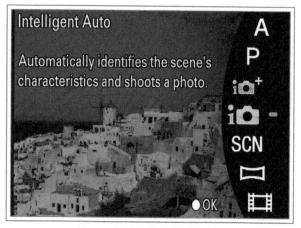

Figure 2-10. Mode Dial Guide

3. Press the Menu button to activate the menu system. As I discussed in Chapter 1, navigate through the menu screens by pressing the Right and Left buttons. You can tell which menu screen is active by looking at the small orange line (cursor) beneath the numbers. When a given screen is selected, navigate up and down through the options on that screen by pressing the Up and Down buttons or by turning the Control wheel right or left. When the orange selection bar is on the option you want, press the Center button to select that item. Then, pressing the Up and Down buttons or turning the Control wheel, highlight the value you want to set for that option, and press the Center

button to confirm it. You can then continue making menu settings; when you are finished with the menu system, press the Menu button to go back to the live view, so you can take pictures.

4. Using the procedure described in Step 3, make the settings shown in Table 2-1 using the menu system.

Table 2-1. **Suggested Settings for Intelligent Auto Mode**

Image Size	L: 20M
Aspect Ratio	3:2
Quality	Extra Fine
File Format	AVCHD
Record Setting	60p 28M (PS)
Drive Mode	Single shooting
Flash Mode	Autoflash
Red Eye Reduction	Off
Focus Mode	Single-shot AF
AF Illuminator	Auto
Center Lock-on AF	Off
Smile/Face Detection	Off
Soft Skin Effect	Off
Auto Object Framing	Off
SteadyShot (Stills)	On
SteadyShot (Movies)	Standard
Color Space	sRGB
Auto Slow Shutter	On
Audio Recording	On
Micref Level	Normal
Wind Noise Reduction	Off
Memory	No setting needed

5. If you don't want to go through the steps to make all of these settings, don't worry; you are likely to get good images even if you don't adjust most of these settings at this point. Several of the settings apply only to video recording, but I have listed settings for them anyway, in case a video opportunity arises and you need to press the red button to make a recording.

6. Press the Menu button again to make the menu disappear, if it hasn't done so already.

7. If you are shooting in dark conditions, press the flash pop-up switch, located on top of the camera behind the power button, to the right. Then press the Right button on the Control wheel, marked with a lightning bolt. A vertical menu will appear at the left side of the screen, as shown in Figure 2-11.

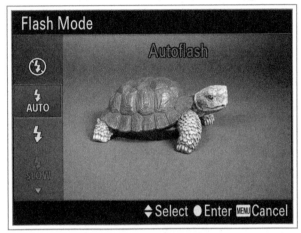

Figure 2-11. Flash Mode Menu

8. Make sure Autoflash is highlighted with the orange selection block. If it is not, press the direction buttons or turn the Control wheel to highlight it, so the Flash Mode is set to Autoflash. Press the Center button to dismiss this menu.

9. Using a procedure like that in Step 8, press the Left button, marked with a timer dial and an icon for a stack of images, and make sure the top option, showing a single rectangular frame, is selected, as shown in Figure 2-12. This sets the camera to take single shots, rather than continuous bursts.

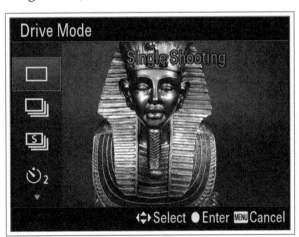

Figure 2-12. Drive Mode Menu

10. Aim the camera and compose the picture. Locate the zoom lever and push it to the left, toward the letter "W" on the camera, for a wider-angle shot, or to the right, toward the letter "T," to get a telephoto, zoomed-in shot.

11. Once the picture looks good, gently press the shutter button halfway and pause there. You should hear a beep and see one or more green focus brackets on the LCD indicating sharp focus. You also can look for a green disc in the extreme lower left corner of the screen. If that green disc lights up steadily, the image is in focus; if it flashes, the camera was unable to focus. In that case, you can re-aim and see if the autofocus system does better from a different distance or angle.

12. After you have made sure the focus is sharp, push the shutter button all the way to take the picture.

VARIATIONS FROM FULLY AUTOMATIC

Although the RX100 III takes care of the basic settings for you when it's set to Intelligent Auto mode, the camera lets you make a number of adjustments to fine-tune the shooting process when it's in this automatic mode or the Superior Auto shooting mode (designated on the Mode dial by the tan-colored camera icon).

Photo Creativity Feature

The Photo Creativity feature, available only in the Intelligent Auto and Superior Auto modes, is a simple way to make adjustments to the appearance of still images and videos. I can understand why Sony presents these adjustments in this way, making them easy to use and giving them non-technical names such as "Background Defocus" and "Brightness," rather than "aperture control" and "exposure compensation." However, it is somewhat confusing (to me, at least) that these same adjustments are made using different controls in the other, less-automatic shooting modes.

In any event, for now I will discuss how to make these adjustments in Intelligent Auto and Superior Auto mode. In Chapter 3, I will discuss all of the shooting modes, and in Chapters 4 and 5 I will discuss how to make similar settings in the more advanced shooting modes. For example, I will discuss aperture control in Chapter 3 in connection with Aperture Priority mode, and I will discuss exposure compensation in Chapter 5, in connection with the button that controls that function (the Down button, in the bottom position on the Control wheel).

With that introduction, here are details about how to make various settings in the 2 most automatic shooting modes using the Photo Creativity feature.

First, it's important to note that the Photo Creativity feature is not available if the Quality option on the Shooting menu is set to Raw or Raw & JPEG. So make sure that Quality is set to Extra Fine or Fine. (If you try to use Photo Creativity with Raw in effect, you will get an error message.) To use the Photo Creativity feature, press the Down button on the Control wheel—the button marked with the plus and minus icon and the camera icon with 3 plus signs at its right side, as shown in Figure 2-2. When you press that button, you will see some new icons and virtual controls appear on the LCD screen, as shown in Figure 2-13.

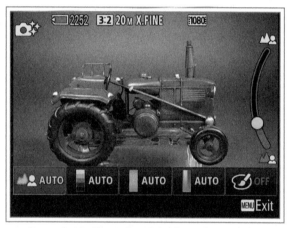

Figure 2-13. Photo Creativity Controls on Screen

At the bottom of the screen are 5 blocks, each with an icon for a setting. When the blocks first appear, each of the 4 blocks at the left should show the word AUTO, and the block at the far right, with an icon of an artist's palette and brush, should say OFF. Use the Right and Left buttons to move through these 5 blocks; each one will be highlighted in orange when it is selected. You can keep pressing the Right or Left button to wrap around to the other side of the group of icons if you want. For example, when the artist's palette is highlighted, you can press the Right button one more time to move directly to the block at the far left of the screen.

When one of the blocks is highlighted in orange, you can change the value for that setting by turning the Control wheel or by pressing the Up or Down button to move an indicator disc or icon along a curved scale at the right

side of the display. The display will change as appropriate to show the effect of your adjustment. For example, if you move the Color slider to the top of the curved scale, the image will appear more reddish, or "warm."

With the first 4 blocks, as you turn the wheel, a disc will move along a scale at the right of the screen. The disc will be green at first, but it will turn orange once the setting is changed. Also, the appearance of the icon for that block will change to show how the setting is changing, as seen in Figure 2-14.

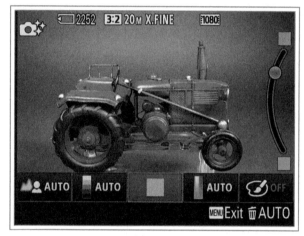

Figure 2-14. Photo Creativity Adjustment in Effect

When a block is first selected, a label for its setting will appear briefly on the screen and then disappear. The settings that are controlled by the 5 blocks are as follows, from left to right:

Background Defocus. This first setting is designed to leave the foreground sharp while the background is blurry. This effect, sometimes called "bokeh," can help separate the main subject from a background that might be distracting or unpleasant.

In technical terms, the camera's aperture (its opening to let in light) is opened up wider, which causes the depth of field to be shallower, allowing the background to go out of focus. When the disc is at the bottom of the scale, the aperture is opened as much as possible, resulting in a blurrier background; as the disc nears the top of the scale, the background should become sharper as the aperture narrows and depth of field increases. I will talk about this effect again in Chapter 3, in the discussion of the Aperture Priority shooting mode. Figure 2-15 is an example of an image with a defocused background.

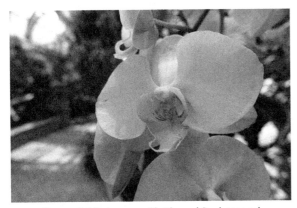

Figure 2-15. Image with Blurred Background

Brightness. This setting controls the brightness of images. The indicator disc starts in the middle of the scale. As you turn the Control wheel to move the disc higher, the image gets brighter; as it moves lower, the image darkens. In technical terms, this setting controls exposure compensation, which can be used in situations when the normal exposure calculated by the camera would not be ideal. For example, if a light-colored object, such as an eagle's head, is photographed against a dark background, the camera's automatic exposure control is likely to overexpose the light object, because the camera takes into account the broad expanse of dark tones in the image and increases the exposure level. With the Brightness control, you can decrease the brightness level so the subject will appear properly exposed, as shown in Figure 2-16.

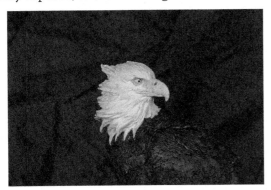

Figure 2-16. Image with Exposure Compensation Applied

Color. This third setting from the left lets you adjust the white balance of images, though Sony uses the term "Color" to simplify things. As I will discuss in Chapter 4, the white balance setting adjusts the camera's processing of colors according to the color temperature of the light source. For example, light from incandescent bulbs has a lower color temperature than light from a bright blue sky. The lower color temperatures are considered "warmer," with a reddish or yellowish cast, and the higher ones yield colors that are considered "cooler," with a more bluish appearance. (In this case, "warm" and "cool" have to do with the appearance, rather than the actual temperature, of the subjects.)

With this setting, again, the normal value is in the center of the curved scale. To make the colors of the scene appear cooler, or more bluish, turn the Control wheel to the left to move the indicator disc toward the bottom of the scale; reverse that process to make the colors warmer, or more reddish. Figure 2-17 shows the Color setting adjusted to the bluish side.

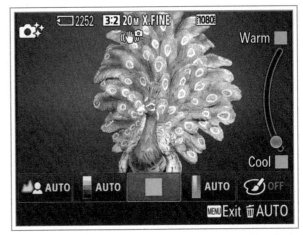

Figure 2-17. Photo Creativity Color Adjustment at Blue End of Scale

This adjustment does not change the actual white balance setting, which is fixed at Auto White Balance (AWB) for the automatic shooting modes; it merely tweaks the setting toward the warm or cool end of the scale. In some other shooting modes, as discussed in Chapter 4, you can make more precise adjustments to the camera's white balance through the White Balance menu option.

Vividness. The fourth setting from the left lets you adjust the intensity, or saturation, of colors in your images.

Again, the standard setting is in the middle of the scale; move the disc upward for more intense colors and downward for softer, less-saturated colors. In the more advanced shooting modes, you can adjust saturation in finer detail, along with contrast and sharpness, using the Creative Style menu option, as discussed in Chapter 4. Figure 2-18 shows Vividness set to its maximum.

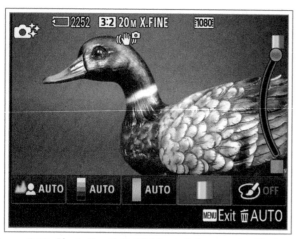

Figure 2-18. Photo Creativity Vividness Adjustment at Maximum

Picture Effect. The final option at the right, marked with an artist's palette, gives you access to the following settings: Toy Camera, Pop Color, Posterization Color, Posterization B/W, Retro Photo, Soft High-key, Partial Color: Red, Partial Color: Green, Partial Color: Blue, Partial Color: Yellow, and High Contrast Monochrome. These settings can produce dramatic effects, as indicated by their labels. The same settings are available through the Picture Effect item on the Shooting menu in advanced shooting modes, though there are some settings available through that menu item that cannot be made from the Photo Creativity system, such as different varieties of the Toy Camera setting. I will discuss those settings and provide examples in Chapter 4.

You can combine more than one Photo Creativity setting to achieve various effects. For example, if you activate the Partial Color effect using the rightmost block at the bottom of the screen, you can then move the highlight to the Color or Vividness block and change the tint or intensity of the color that you selected for the Partial Color effect. Or, you can decrease the exposure of the image and also decrease the intensity of the colors by using the Brightness and Vividness controls together.

When you have moved a setting's control to the position you want, leave it there and take the picture with the control still on the screen. (Or, as noted above, you can go to another setting and adjust it as well before taking the picture.) Don't press the Menu button, because doing that will cancel the setting you just made.

To reset a setting to its original value, highlight its block and press the Custom/Delete (C) button. For the first 4 blocks, this action will reset the indicator to its default

value (bottom of the scale for Background Defocus; middle of the scale for the other 3). For the Picture Effect setting, this action will turn the selected effect off, leaving no effect active. To reset all 5 blocks at once, turn the Mode dial to another shooting mode (such as Scene or Program) and then back to Intelligent Auto or Superior Auto. To exit from the Photo Creativity screen altogether, press the Menu button.

Photo Creativity is a useful feature, and it is convenient to select one or more of these options while the camera is in this automatic mode, so you don't have to invest too much effort into figuring out what settings to use. However, if you want to exercise more control over the settings, you can use one of the more advanced shooting modes with menu options and controls that let you make more precise adjustments.

Flash

Now I'll go into more detail about using the camera's built-in flash unit, because that is something you may want to use on a regular basis. In Chapter 4 I'll provide details about the Flash Mode and Flash Compensation settings, as well as the prevention of "red-eye" effects. In Appendix A, I'll discuss using external flash units, even though the camera has no flash shoe.

It's important to remember that the flash unit cannot pop up on its own, even if the flash mode is set to Fill-flash, which requires the flash to fire. You have to use the flash pop-up switch on top of the camera to release the flash before it can fire.

For this discussion, I'm assuming the camera is set to Intelligent Auto mode. In some other situations, including some of the Scene mode settings, the Flash menu will not appear; you will see an error message if you press the Right button.

In Intelligent Auto mode, press the Right button once to call up the Flash Mode menu, then press the Up and Down buttons or turn the Control wheel to select a flash mode from that list. Press the Center button to confirm the selection. (You also can summon the Flash Mode menu from the Shooting menu: Flash Mode is the fourth item down on the second screen of the Shooting menu. See Chapter 4 for a discussion of all items on those menu screens.)

The vertical menu at the left of the screen, shown in Figure 2-11, has icons for the 5 flash modes—a lightning bolt with the "no" sign crossing it out, for Flash Off; a lightning bolt with the word "Auto," for Autoflash; a lightning bolt alone, for Fill-flash (meaning the flash will always fire); a lightning bolt with the word "Slow," for Slow Sync; and a lightning bolt with the word "Rear," for Rear Sync. When the camera is in Intelligent Auto mode, the last 2 choices will be dimmed; if you highlight one of them and press the Center button, the camera will display a message saying you cannot make that selection in this shooting mode.

I discussed earlier how to choose Autoflash. If you choose Fill-flash instead, you will see the lightning bolt icon on the screen at all times when the flash is popped up and the detailed display screen is selected. With this setting, the flash will fire regardless of whether the camera's exposure system believes flash is needed. You can use this setting when you are certain you want the flash to fire, such as in a dimly lighted room. This setting also can be of use in some outdoor settings, even when the sun is shining, such as when you need to reduce the shadows on your subject's face. I will provide an illustration of the use of Fill-flash in Chapter 4.

When the camera is set for certain types of shooting, such as using the self-timer with multiple shots, the flash is forced off and cannot be used. If you turn on the flash with burst shooting, the use of flash will limit the shooting speed. Instead of firing a rapid burst, the camera will take multiple images at a very slow rate because the flash needs to recycle between shots. In some cases, such as with the Night Scene setting of Scene mode, you cannot even get the Flash Mode menu to appear; if you press the Flash button, the camera will display a message saying the flash is not available in that shooting mode, as shown in Figure 2-19.

If you set the Mode dial to P, for Program mode, and then press the Flash button to select a flash mode, you will see the same 5 options for Flash Mode on the menu, but this time the Flash Off and Autoflash options will be dimmed because those selections are not available in that shooting mode.

In summary, when using Intelligent Auto mode, if you don't want the flash to fire because you are in a museum or similar location, you can select the Flash Off mode. You also can just leave the flash stored inside the camera, so it cannot pop up and fire.

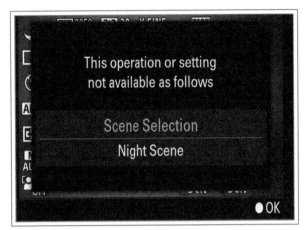

Figure 2-19. Message: Flash Mode Not Available with Night Scene Setting

If you want to let the camera decide whether to fire the flash, you can select Autoflash mode. To make sure that the flash will fire no matter what, you can select Fill-flash mode. In Chapter 4, I'll explain the other flash options, Slow Sync and Rear Sync, and I'll discuss some other flash-related topics. For now, you have the basic information you need to select a flash mode when the camera is set to the Intelligent Auto shooting mode.

Drive Mode: Self-Timer and Continuous Shooting

The Drive Mode menu option includes more adjustments you can make when using Intelligent Auto mode. If you press the Control wheel's Left button, which is marked with a timer dial and an icon that looks like a stack of images, the camera will display a vertical menu for Drive Mode, as shown in Figure 2-20.

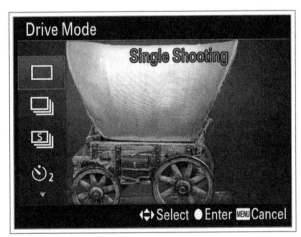

Figure 2-20. Drive Mode Menu

You navigate through the options on this menu by pressing the Up and Down buttons or by turning the Control wheel.

I will discuss the Drive Mode menu options more fully in Chapter 4. For now, you should be aware of a few of the options. (I will skip over some others.) If you select the top option, represented by a single rectangular frame, the camera is set for single shooting mode; when you press the shutter button, a single image is captured. With the second and third options, whose icons look like stacks of images, the camera is set for continuous shooting and takes a rapid burst of images while you hold down the shutter button.

If you choose the fourth option, whose icon is a timer dial with a number beside it, the camera uses the self-timer. Use the Left and Right buttons to choose either 2 or 10 seconds for the timer delay. After the timer has been set, press the shutter button. The shutter will be released after the specified number of seconds. The 10-second delay is useful when you need to place the camera on a tripod and join a group photo; the 2-second delay is useful to make sure the camera is not jiggled by the action of pressing the shutter button. This option helps greatly when you are taking a picture for which focusing is critical, such as an extreme closeup. I will discuss the use of the self-timer and other Drive Mode options in more detail in Chapter 4.

The Drive Mode options also can be reached as the third item on screen 2 of the Shooting menu.

There are other settings that can be made when the camera is set to Intelligent Auto mode, including Image Size, Aspect Ratio, Quality, Focus Mode, Face Detection, and others. I included suggested settings for those items in Table 2-1 earlier in this chapter, and I will discuss the details of those settings in Chapter 4.

Overview of Movie Recording

Now I'll discuss recording a short movie sequence with the RX100 III. With the camera turned on, turn the Mode dial to select the green camera icon, for Intelligent Auto mode. There is a special Movie mode setting marked by the movie-film icon on the Mode dial, but you don't have to use that mode for shooting movies; I'll discuss the use of that option and provide more details about movie-recording options in Chapter 8.

For now, press the Menu button to get access to the menu system, and press the Right or Left button, if necessary, enough times to move the orange cursor

under the number 1 while the camera icon for the Shooting menu is highlighted, as shown in Figure 2-21. With the RX100 III, the major movie-related menu items are located on the Shooting menu; there is no separate Movie menu. On the bottom line of the Shooting menu, highlight File Format and press the Center button to go to the submenu with 3 choices for the format of movie recording.

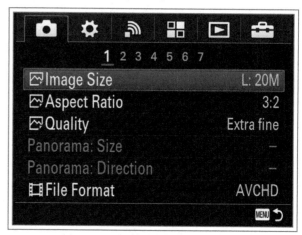

Figure 2-21. Screen 1 of Shooting Menu

For now, be sure the middle option, AVCHD (Advanced Video Coding High Definition), is highlighted; that format provides high quality for your videos without requiring a special memory card. (As discussed in Chapter 1, if you select XAVC S for the movie format, you have to use a 64 GB SDXC card with a speed of Class 10 or greater, or a special Memory Stick card.)

For the rest of the settings, I will provide a table like the one included earlier in this chapter for shooting still images. The settings shown in Table 2-2 are standard ones for shooting high-quality movies.

Table 2-2. **Suggested Shooting Menu Settings for Movies in Intelligent Auto Mode**

File Format	AVCHD
Record Setting	60p 28M (PS)
Dual Video REC	Off
Focus Mode	Single-shot AF
SteadyShot (Movies)	Standard
Auto Slow Shutter	On
Audio Recording	On
Micref Level	Normal
Wind Noise Reduction	Off

There are other settings you can make on the Shooting menu for still images that will affect your movie recording; I will discuss that topic in Chapter 8. For now, if you are going to be shooting a movie that shows people's faces, you may want to go to Screen 5 of the Shooting menu and set the Face Detection item to On. You can leave the other items set as they were for shooting still images, as listed in Table 2-1 for still shooting.

Now you have made all of the necessary settings for recording a movie. Aim the camera at your subject, and when you are ready to start recording, press and release the red Movie button at the upper right corner of the camera's back. (If you see an error message, go to the fourth screen of the Custom menu, marked by a gear icon, and set the Movie Button option to Always.)

The screen will display a red REC icon in the lower left corner of the display, next to a counter showing the elapsed time in the recording, as shown in Figure 2-22.

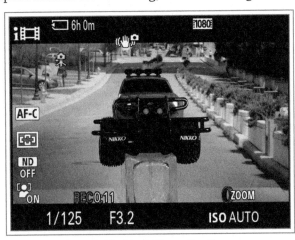

Figure 2-22. Movie Recording Screen

Hold the camera as steady as possible (or use a tripod), and pan (move the camera side to side) slowly if you need to. The camera will keep shooting until it reaches a recording limit, or until you press the Movie button again to stop the recording. (The maximum time for continuous recording of any one scene is about 29 minutes with most recording formats.) Don't be too concerned about the level of the sound that is being recorded, because you do not have much control over the audio volume while recording using the built-in microphone. I will discuss options for audio recording in Chapter 8.

The camera will automatically adjust exposure as lighting conditions change. You can zoom the lens in and out as needed, but you should do so sparingly if at all, to avoid distracting the audience and to avoid putting the sounds of zooming the lens on the sound track. When you are finished, press the Movie button again, and the recording will end.

Those are the basics for recording a video clip with the RX100 III. I'll discuss movie options in more detail in Chapter 8.

Viewing Pictures

Before I talk about more advanced settings for taking still pictures and movies, as well as other topics, I will discuss the basics of viewing your images in the camera.

REVIEWING WHILE IN SHOOTING MODE

Each time you take a still picture, the image will show up on the LCD screen for a short time, if you have the Custom menu's Auto Review option set to turn on this function. I'll discuss the details of that setting in Chapter 7. By default, the image will stay on the screen for 2 seconds after you take a new picture. If you prefer, you can set that display to last for 5 or 10 seconds, or to be off altogether.

REVIEWING IMAGES IN PLAYBACK MODE

To review images taken previously, you enter playback mode by pressing the Playback button—the one with the small triangle icon to the lower left of the Control wheel. To view all still images and movies for a particular date, go to screen 1 of the Playback menu (marked with a triangle icon) and set the View Mode option to Date View. If you prefer, you can set View Mode to show only stills, only MP4 movies, only AVCHD movies, or only XAVC S movies.

Once you choose a viewing option, you can scroll through recorded images and movies by pressing the Left and Right buttons or by turning the Control wheel. Hold down the Left or Right button to move more quickly through the items. You can enlarge the view of any still image by moving the zoom lever on top of the camera toward the T position, and you can scroll around in the enlarged image using the 4 direction buttons.

If you press the zoom lever repeatedly in the other direction, toward the wide-angle setting, the image will return to normal size. If you press the lever once more in that direction, you will see an index screen with a number of thumbnail images (either 9 or 25, depending on a Playback menu option), and a further press brings up a calendar screen for selecting images by date (if you selected Date View). You can view images from the index and calendar screens by pressing the Center button on a highlighted thumbnail image. I'll discuss other playback options in Chapter 6.

PLAYING MOVIES

To play movies in the camera, move through the recorded files by the methods described above until you find the movie you want to play. You should see a triangular playback icon inside a circle, as shown in Figure 2-23.

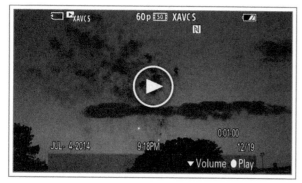

Figure 2-23. Movie Ready to Play in Camera

Press the Center button to start the movie playing. Then, as seen in Figure 2-24, you will see prompts at the bottom of the screen showing the controls you can use, including the Center button to pause. (You may have to press the Display button to show the icons.)

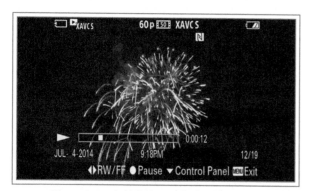

Figure 2-24. Initial Movie Playback Prompts

You also can press the Down button to bring up a more detailed set of controls on the screen, as shown in Figure 2-25. To change the volume, pause the movie and press the Down button to bring up the detailed

controls; then navigate to the speaker icon, next to last at the right of those controls.

Press the Center button to select volume, then use the Control wheel or the Right and Left buttons to adjust the volume. You also can adjust the volume before a movie starts playing, by pressing the Down button to bring up the volume control. To exit from playing the movie, press the Playback button. (I'll discuss other movie playback options in Chapter 8.)

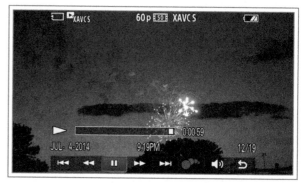

Figure 2-25. Detailed Movie Playback Prompts

If you want to play your movies on a computer or edit them with video-editing software, you can use the PlayMemories Home software that is provided through the Sony web site. You also can use any program that can deal with AVCHD and MP4 video files, such as Adobe Premiere Elements, Adobe Premiere Pro, Final Cut Express, Final Cut Pro, iMovie, or Windows Movie Maker, depending on what type of computer you are using.

Movies recorded by the RX100 III using the newest format, XAVC S, are saved as files with the .mp4 extension, and, in my experience, can be imported and edited with standard software that uses those files, such as iMovie for the Mac and Movie Maker for Windows-based computers.

CHAPTER 3: SHOOTING MODES

Until now, I have discussed the basics of taking quick shots and videos in Intelligent Auto mode. The Sony RX100 III provides many other options and settings, though, especially for taking still images. To explain these features, I will discuss the shooting modes in this chapter and the Shooting menu options in Chapter 4.

To record still images, you need to select one of the available shooting modes: Intelligent Auto, Superior Auto, Program Auto, Aperture Priority, Shutter Priority, Manual exposure, Scene Selection, Sweep Panorama, or Memory Recall. (The only other mode available is for movies.) So far, we have worked primarily with the Intelligent Auto mode. Now I will discuss the others, after some review of the first one.

Intelligent Auto Mode

This is the mode to select for a quick shot when you don't have time to deal with settings such as ISO, white balance, aperture, shutter speed, or metering method. It's a good mode to choose when you hand the camera to someone to take a photo of you and your companions.

To set this mode, turn the Mode dial to the icon of a green camera with the letter "i" (for "intelligent") next to it, as shown in Figure 3-1.

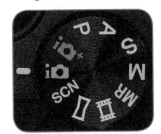

Figure 3-1. Intelligent Auto Mode

In this mode, the camera makes several decisions for you and limits your options in some ways. For example, you can't set the ISO or white balance to any value other than Auto, and you can't choose a metering method or use

exposure bracketing. You can, however, use quite a few features, as discussed in Chapter 2, including the Photo Creativity options, continuous shooting, Flash Mode, Focus Mode, and others. You also can use sophisticated options such as the Raw format, which I will discuss in Chapter 4 along with other Shooting menu options.

In this mode (and in Superior Auto mode, discussed next), the camera uses its programming to try to figure out what subject or scene you are shooting. Some subjects the camera will try to detect are Infant, Portrait, Night Portrait, Night Scene, Landscape, Backlight, Low Light, Spotlight, and Macro. It also will try to detect certain conditions, such as whether a tripod is in use or whether the subject is moving, in bright or dark conditions, and it will display icons for those situations. So, if you see different icons when you aim at various subjects in this shooting mode, that means the camera is evaluating the scene for factors such as brightness, backlighting, the presence of human subjects, and the like, so it can use the best possible settings for the situation.

For Figure 3-2, the camera evaluated a scene with a mannequin's head and appropriately used its Portrait setting. The Portrait scene-recognition icon is seen in the upper left corner of the screen.

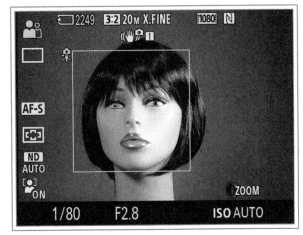

Figure 3-2. Scene Recognition: Portrait Icon

Figure 3-3 shows the use of automatic scene recognition for a small figurine closer to the lens. The camera interpreted the scene as a macro, or closeup shot, and switched automatically into Macro mode, indicated by the flower icon. In addition, the camera correctly detected that it was attached to a tripod, as indicated by the tripod icon to the lower right of the macro symbol.

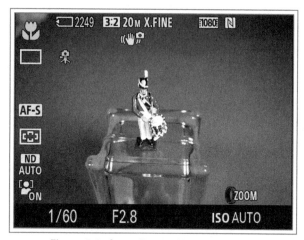

Figure 3-3. Scene Recognition: Macro Icon

Of course, scene recognition depends on the camera's programming, which may not interpret every scene the same way you would. If that becomes a problem, you may want to make individual settings using one of the more advanced shooting modes, such as Program, Aperture Priority, Shutter Priority, or Manual. Or, you can use the SCN setting on the Mode dial and select a Scene mode setting that better fits the current situation.

Superior Auto Mode

With many compact cameras, there is only one largely automatic shooting mode. The RX100 III, however, provides you with 2 choices, both of which provide high degrees of automation but which have one significant difference. The second automatic mode, called Superior Auto, is designated on the Mode dial by the icon of a tan-colored camera with the letter "i" and a plus sign next to it, as shown in Figure 3-4.

Superior Auto mode includes all functions of Intelligent Auto mode, but it adds one extra feature. In Superior Auto mode, as in Intelligent Auto mode, the camera uses its scene recognition capability to determine what subject matter or conditions are present, such as a portrait, a dimly lit scene, and the like.

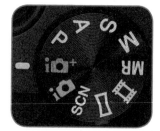

Figure 3-4. Superior Auto Mode

For many of these subjects, the camera operates the same way as in Intelligent Auto mode. However, in a few situations, the camera takes a different approach: It will take a rapid burst of shots and combine them internally into a single image with higher quality than would be possible with a single shot. The higher quality can be achieved because the camera generally has to raise the ISO setting to a fairly high level, which introduces visual "noise" into the image. By taking multiple shots and then merging them, the camera can average out and cancel some of the noise, thereby increasing the quality of the resulting image.

One problem with this system is that you, the photographer, have no control over when the camera decides to use this burst shooting technique. There are only 3 situations in which the camera will do this: when it detects scenes that call for settings called Anti Motion Blur, Hand-held Twilight, or Backlight Correction HDR.

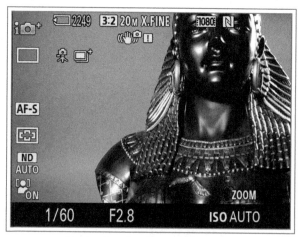

Figure 3-5. Overlay Icon on Screen

When the camera believes the burst method is appropriate, it fires a quick series of shots; you will hear the rapid firing of the shutter. Then, it will take longer than usual for the camera to process the multiple shots into a single image; you will likely see a message saying "Processing" on the screen for several seconds.

When the camera is using this mode, which Sony calls "Overlay," you will see a small white icon in the upper left corner of the display that looks like a stack of frames with a plus sign at its upper right corner, as shown in Figure 3-5, to the right of the tripod icon.

Two of these scenarios—Anti Motion Blur and Hand-held Twilight—are also settings in Scene mode, discussed later in this chapter. The third, Backlight Correction HDR, is available only in Superior Auto mode, and only when the camera decides to use it. None of the 3 multiple-shot settings will function when Quality is set to Raw or Raw & JPEG on the Shooting menu.

I have not found much advantage from using the Superior Auto setting. However, there may be cases when the overlay feature will improve the quality of an image, so it is not a bad idea to set the camera to the Superior Auto mode when you are shooting in low-light or backlit conditions. As a general rule, though, I prefer to use a mode such as Program, discussed below, and set my own values for items such as DRO, HDR, ISO, and metering mode.

Program Auto Mode

Choose this mode by turning the Mode dial to the P setting, as shown in Figure 3-6.

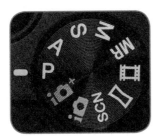

Figure 3-6. Program Mode

Program Auto mode (often called Program mode) lets you control many of the settings available with the camera, apart from shutter speed and aperture, which the camera chooses on its own. You can override the automatic exposure to a fair extent by using exposure compensation, as discussed in Chapter 5, as well as exposure bracketing, discussed in Chapter 4, and Program Shift, discussed later in this section. You don't have to make a lot of decisions if you don't want to, because the camera will make reasonable choices as defaults. However, even though shutter speeds as long as 30 seconds are available in the Shutter Priority and

Manual exposure modes, the camera will never choose a shutter speed longer than one second in Program mode.

The Program Shift function is available only in Program mode; it works as follows. When you aim the camera at your subject, the camera will display its chosen settings for shutter speed and aperture in the lower left corner of the display. At that point, just turn the Control wheel on the back of the camera. The values for shutter speed and aperture will change, if possible under current conditions, to different values for both settings while keeping the same overall exposure of the scene.

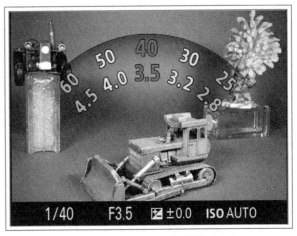

Figure 3-7. Program Shift Display

You also can use the Control ring (the large ring around the lens) to make this setting, if the Control Ring option is set to the Standard setting through the Custom Key Settings item on the Custom menu, as discussed in Chapter 7. If you use the Control ring for Program Shift, you will see 2 circular scales on the display, with shutter speed and aperture values that shift as you turn the ring, as shown in Figure 3-7. (A similar display is visible if you use the Control wheel, but only if the Exposure Settings Guide menu option is turned on through screen 2 of the Custom menu.)

With the Program Shift option, the camera "shifts" the original exposure to any of the matched pairs that appear as you turn the Control wheel. For example, if the original exposure was f/2.0 at 1/30 second, you may see equivalent pairs of f/2.2 at 1/25, f/2.5 at 1/20, and f/2.8 at 1/15, among others. When Program Shift is in effect, the P icon in the upper left corner of the screen will have an asterisk to its right, as shown in Figure 3-8.

To cancel Program Shift, turn the Control wheel until the original settings are back in effect or release the flash by pressing the flash pop-up button. (Program Shift cannot function when the flash is in use.)

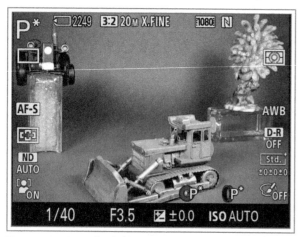

Figure 3-8. Asterisk After P Indicating Program Shift in Effect

Program Shift is useful if, for example, you want to let the camera make the original exposure setting but you want a faster shutter speed to stop action or a wider aperture to blur the background. Of course, if you need to use a particular shutter speed or aperture, you probably should use Aperture Priority mode or Shutter Priority mode. However, Program Shift is a good option when you're taking pictures quickly using Program mode and you need a fast way to tweak the settings somewhat.

One important aspect of Program mode is that it expands the choices available through the Shooting menu, which controls many of the camera's settings. You will be able to make choices involving ISO sensitivity, metering method, DRO/HDR, white balance, Creative Style, and others that are not available in the Auto modes. I won't discuss those settings here; see Chapter 4 for information about all of the different selections that are available.

Aperture Priority Mode

You set the camera to the Aperture Priority shooting mode by turning the Mode dial to the A setting, as shown in Figure 3-9.

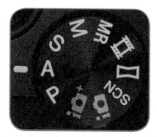

Figure 3-9. Aperture Priority Mode

In this mode, you select the aperture setting and the camera will select a shutter speed that will result in normal exposure.

The main reason to choose this mode is so you can select an aperture to achieve a broad depth of field, with objects in focus at different distances from the lens, or a shallow depth of field, with only one object in sharp focus and other parts of the image blurred to reduce distractions. With a narrow aperture (higher f-stop number) such as f/8.0, the depth of field will be relatively broad; with a wide aperture such as f/1.8, it will be shallow, resulting in the possibility of a blurred background.

In Figure 3-10 and Figure 3-11, I made the same shot with 2 very different aperture settings. I focused on the flower in the foreground in each case. For Figure 3-10, the aperture of the RX100 III was set to f/1.8, the widest possible.

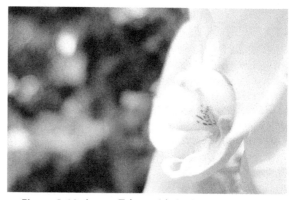

Figure 3-10. Image Taken with Aperture Set to f/1.8

With this setting, because the depth of field at this aperture was shallow, the items in the background are blurry. I took Figure 3-11 with the camera's aperture set to f/11.0, the narrowest possible setting, resulting in a broader depth of field, and consequently bringing the background into sharper focus.

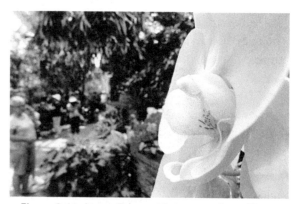

Figure 3-11. Image Taken with Aperture Set to f/11.0

These 2 photos illustrate the effects of varying your aperture by setting it wide (low numbers) when you want to blur the background and narrow (high numbers) when you want to enjoy a broad depth of field and keep subjects at varying distances in sharp focus. The blurred background look, sometimes called "bokeh," can be useful to isolate your subject, as illustrated in Figure 3-10.

Here are the steps to set the aperture. After moving the Mode dial to the A setting, use either the Control ring or the Control wheel to change the aperture. (If the Control ring does not change the aperture, check the setting for the Control Ring in the Custom Key Settings item on the Custom menu, as discussed in Chapter 7; that menu option should be set to Standard or Aperture.)

If you use the Control ring to set the aperture, the camera will display a circular scale showing the changing aperture values, as seen in Figure 3-12, and the selected value will also appear in the bottom center of the screen.

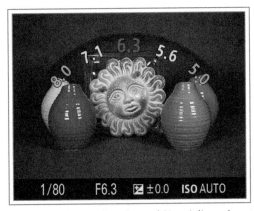

Figure 3-12. Display When Control Ring Adjusts Aperture

If you use the Control wheel instead, the camera will display a circular scale at the bottom of the screen, if the Exposure Settings Guide option on screen 2 of the Custom menu is turned on.

Although, in most cases, the camera will be able to select a corresponding shutter speed that results in a normal exposure, there may be times when this is not possible.

For example, if you are taking pictures in a very bright location with the aperture set to f/1.8, the camera may not be able to set a shutter speed fast enough to yield a normal exposure. In that case, the fastest possible shutter speed (1/2000) will flash on the display to show that a normal exposure cannot be made using the chosen aperture. The camera will let you take the picture, but it may be too bright to be usable. (The neutral density filter may activate to reduce brightness, depending on the ND Filter menu setting, as discussed in Chapter 4, but there still may be times when no shutter speed is available to make a good exposure.)

Similarly, if conditions are too dark for a good exposure at the aperture you have selected, the slowest possible shutter speed (8", meaning 8 seconds) will flash.

In situations where conditions are too bright or dark for a good exposure, the camera's display may become bright or dark, giving you notice of the problem. This will happen if the Live View Display item on screen 2 of the Custom menu is set to Setting Effect On. If that option is set to Setting Effect Off, the display will remain at normal brightness, even if the exposure settings would result in an excessively bright or dark image. I will discuss that menu option in Chapter 7.

One more note on Aperture Priority mode: Not all apertures are available at all times. In particular, the widest aperture, f/1.8, is available only when the lens is zoomed out to its wide-angle setting (zoom lever moved toward the W). At the highest zoom levels, the widest aperture available is f/2.8.

To see an illustration of this point, here is a quick test. Zoom the lens out by moving the zoom lever all the way to the left, toward the W label. Then select Aperture Priority mode and set the aperture to f/1.8. Now zoom the lens in by moving the zoom lever to the right. After the zoom is finished, the aperture will have changed to f/2.8 because that is the limit for the aperture at the full-telephoto zoom level. (The aperture will change back to f/1.8 if you zoom back to the wide-angle setting.) Also, as with Program mode, the full range of the camera's shutter speeds is not available. In Aperture Priority mode, the RX100 III can select shutter speeds from 1/2000 second to 8 seconds.

Shutter Priority Mode

In Shutter Priority mode, you choose the shutter speed you want and the camera will set the corresponding aperture to achieve a proper exposure of the image.

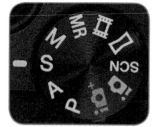

Figure 3-13. Shutter Priority Mode

In this mode, designated by the S position on the Mode dial, as shown in Figure 3-13, you can set the shutter to be open for a time ranging from 30 seconds to 1/2000 of a second. If you are photographing fast action, such as a baseball swing or a hurdles event at a track meet, and you want to stop the motion with a minimum of blur, you should select a fast shutter speed, such as 1/1000 of a second.

To illustrate the effects of different shutter speeds, I photographed a stream of plastic BBs pouring out of a cup. For Figure 3-14, I set the shutter speed to 1/500 second. In that image, you can see the individual BBs as they fall, because the fast shutter speed froze them in mid-air. For Figure 3-15, I used a shutter speed of 1/4 second, which resulted in an image that blends the BBs together into a smooth, steady stream.

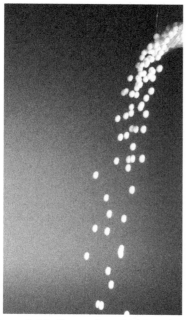

Figure 3-14. Shutter Speed 1/500 second

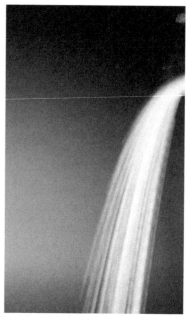

Figure 3-15. Shutter Speed 1/4 Second

Choose this mode by turning the Mode dial to the S position, as seen in Figure 3-13. Select the shutter speed by turning the Control wheel or the Control ring. The Control Ring function must be set to Standard or Shutter Speed using the Custom Key Settings option on the Custom menu for the ring to control shutter speed.

As with Aperture Priority mode, the camera will display a circular scale of shutter speeds as you turn the Control wheel if you have the Exposure Settings Guide option turned on in the Custom menu. It will always display a circular scale when you use the Control ring to make the setting.

Although the Mode dial uses the letter "S" to stand for Shutter Priority, on the detailed display screen, as shown in Figure 3-16, the camera uses the notation Tv in the lower right corner, next to the icons showing that the Control ring or Control wheel can be used to make this setting. Tv stands for time value, a notation often used for this shooting mode.

As you cycle through various shutter speeds, the camera will select the appropriate aperture to achieve a proper exposure, if possible. As I discussed in connection with Aperture Priority mode, if you select a shutter speed for which the camera cannot select an aperture for a normal exposure, the display may (depending on the Live View Display menu option) change appearance to indicate how dark or light the resulting shot will be, and the aperture reading at the bottom of the display will flash. The flashing aperture means that proper exposure at that shutter speed is not possible at any available aperture, according to the camera's calculations.

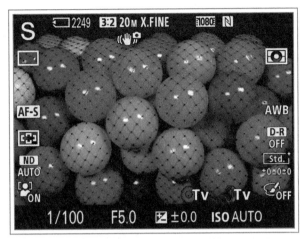

Figure 3-16. Tv Icons Indicating Time Value

For example, if you set the shutter speed to 1/320 second in a fairly dark indoor environment, the aperture number (which will be f/1.8, the widest setting, if the zoom is set to wide angle) may flash, indicating that proper exposure is not possible, and the display may be quite dark. As I discussed for Aperture Priority, you can still take the picture if you want to, though it may not be usable. A similar situation may take place if you select a slow shutter speed (such as 4 seconds) in a relatively bright location.

Manual Exposure Mode

One of the many features of the RX100 III that distinguish it from more ordinary compact cameras is its fully manual exposure mode, a great tool for photographers who want to have full control over exposure decisions.

The technique for using this mode is not too different from what I discussed for the Aperture Priority and Shutter Priority modes. To control exposure manually, set the Mode dial to the M indicator, as shown in Figure 3-17.

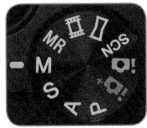

Figure 3-17. Manual Exposure Mode

You now have to control both shutter speed and aperture by setting them yourself. To set the aperture, turn the Control ring around the lens (assuming the Control ring is set for this function through the Custom menu, as discussed in Chapter 7); to set the shutter speed, turn the Control wheel on the back of the camera.

If the Control ring is not set to control aperture, or if you prefer not to use the ring for that purpose, you can use the Control wheel to adjust both aperture and shutter speed. To do that, press the Down button to switch between the 2 selections. When you press that button, either the shutter speed number or the aperture number on the display will turn orange for about 10 seconds to show that that value is currently being controlled by the Control wheel, as seen in Figure 3-18. Also, the label beside the gray icon for the Control wheel in the lower right corner of the display will change between Av (for aperture value) and Tv (for time value) when you press the Down button to switch the wheel's function.

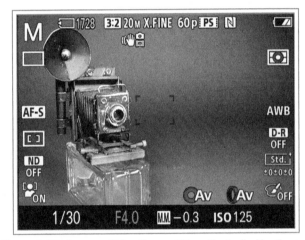

Figure 3-18. Aperture Value Orange When Controlled by Control Wheel

As you adjust shutter speed and aperture, a third value, to the right of the aperture, will also change. That value is a positive, negative, or zero number. The meaning of the number is different depending on the current ISO setting. In Chapter 4, I'll discuss the ISO setting, which controls how sensitive the camera's sensor is to light. With a higher ISO value, the sensor is more sensitive and the image is exposed more quickly, so the shutter speed can be faster or the aperture more narrow, or both.

To set the ISO value, press the Menu button to access the Shooting menu, go to the third screen and highlight the ISO item. Press the Center button to bring up the ISO menu, as shown in Figure 3-19, and scroll through the selections using the Up and Down buttons or by turning the Control wheel.

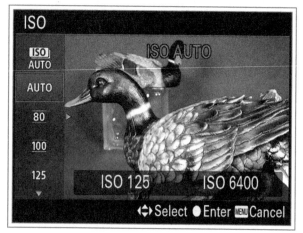

Figure 3-19. ISO Menu at Left of Display

Choose a low number like 125 to maximize image quality when there is plenty of light; use a higher number in dim light. Higher ISO settings are likely to cause visual "noise," or graininess, in your images. Generally speaking, you should try to set ISO no higher than 800 to ensure the highest image quality.

If the ISO value is set to a specific number, such as 125, 200, or 1000, then, in Manual exposure mode, the icon at the bottom center of the display is a box containing the letters "M.M.," which stand for "metered manual," as shown in Figure 3-18.

In this situation, the number next to the M.M. icon represents any deviation from what the camera's metering system considers to be a normal exposure. So, even though you are setting the exposure manually, the camera will still let you know whether the selected aperture and shutter speed will produce a standard exposure.

If the aperture, shutter speed, and ISO values you have selected will result in a darker exposure than normal, the M.M. value will be negative, and vice-versa. This value can vary only by +2.0 or -2.0 EV (exposure value) units; after that, the value will flash, meaning the camera considers the exposure excessively abnormal.

Of course, you can ignore the M.M. indicator; it is there only to give you an idea of how the camera would meter the scene. You very well may want part or all of the scene to be darker or lighter than the metering would indicate to be "correct."

As with Aperture Priority and Shutter Priority modes, the camera's display will become unusually bright or dim to indicate that current settings would result in an abnormal exposure, but only when the Live View Display menu option on screen 2 of the Custom menu is set to Setting Effect On.

If, instead of a specific value, you have set ISO to Auto ISO, the icon at the bottom center of the screen changes. In this situation, the camera displays the exposure compensation icon, which contains a plus and minus sign, as shown in Figure 3-20.

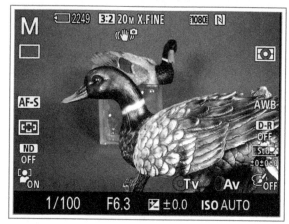

Figure 3-20. Exposure Compensation Icon in Manual Exposure Mode

The reason for this change is that, when you use Auto ISO in Manual exposure mode, the camera can likely produce a normal exposure by adjusting the ISO. There is no need to display the M.M. value, which shows deviation from a normal exposure. Instead, the camera lets you adjust exposure compensation, so you can set the exposure to be darker or brighter than the camera's metering would produce.

To set exposure compensation in Manual mode, you cannot use the ordinary control for that purpose—the Down button—because that button toggles the function of the Control wheel for controlling aperture or shutter speed, as discussed above. To control exposure compensation in Manual mode, you can use the Exposure Compensation item on screen 3 of the Shooting menu, or you can assign exposure compensation to the Control ring or the Custom, Center, Left, or Right button. You make that assignment on the Custom menu, as discussed in Chapter 7.

With Manual exposure mode, the settings for aperture and shutter speed are independent of each other. When you change one, the other one stays unchanged until you adjust it manually. But the effect of this system is different depending on whether you have selected a specific value for ISO as opposed to Auto ISO.

If you select a numerical value for ISO, which can range from 80 to 12800 or even higher when Multi Frame Noise Reduction is selected for the ISO setting, the camera leaves the creative decision about exposure entirely up to you, even if the resulting photograph would be washed out by excessive exposure or underexposed to the point of near-blackness.

However, if you select Auto ISO for the ISO setting, then, as discussed above, the camera will adjust the ISO to achieve a normal exposure if possible. In this case, Manual exposure mode becomes like a different shooting mode altogether. You might call this the "aperture and shutter speed priority mode," because you are able to set both aperture and shutter speed but still have the camera adjust exposure automatically by changing the ISO value.

The ability to use Auto ISO in Manual exposure mode is a very useful option. For example, suppose you are taking photographs of a craftsman using tools in a dimly lighted area. You may want to use a narrow aperture such as f/7.1 to achieve a broad depth of field and keep the tools and other items in focus, but you also may want to use a fast shutter speed, such as 1/100 second, to freeze action. If you use Aperture Priority mode, the camera will choose the shutter speed; with Shutter Priority mode, the camera will choose the aperture, and with Program mode, the camera will choose both values. Only by using Manual exposure mode with Auto ISO can you choose both aperture and shutter speed and still have the camera find a good exposure setting automatically.

Even with the ability to use Auto ISO, though, there may be situations in which the camera cannot produce a normal exposure. This could happen if you have limited the range of the Auto ISO setting by setting a narrow range between the Minimum and Maximum settings for Auto ISO. It also could happen if you have chosen extreme settings for aperture and shutter speed, such as 1/500 second at f/11.0 in dark conditions. In such situations, the ISO Auto label and the exposure compensation value at the bottom of the display will flash, indicating that a normal exposure cannot be achieved with these settings.

The range of apertures you can set in Manual mode is the same as for Aperture Priority mode: f/1.8 to f/11.0. (As in other modes, the widest aperture available is f/2.8 when the lens is zoomed in.)

The range of shutter speeds is the same as for Shutter Priority mode (1/2000 to 30 seconds), with one important addition: In Manual mode, you can set the shutter speed to the BULB setting, just beyond the 30-second mark, as shown in Figure 3-21.

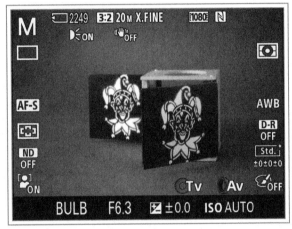

Figure 3-21. BULB Setting Indicator on Screen

With the BULB setting, you have to press and hold the shutter button to keep the shutter open. You can use this setting to take photos in dark conditions by holding the shutter open for a minute or more. One problem is that it is hard to avoid jiggling the camera, causing image blur. In Appendix A, I discuss using a remote control to trigger the camera. After the exposure ends, the camera will process the exposure for the same length of time as the exposure, to reduce noise caused by long exposures. You will not be able to take another shot while this processing continues. (You can disable this setting with the Long Exposure Noise Reduction option on screen 5 of the Shooting menu.)

Another feature available in this mode is Manual Shift, which is similar to Program Shift, discussed earlier. To use Manual Shift, you first have to assign one of the control buttons (Custom, Center, Left, or Right) to the AEL (autoexposure lock) Hold or AEL Toggle function using the Custom Key Settings option on screen 4 of the Custom menu, as discussed in Chapter 7. Then, after making your aperture and shutter speed settings, change the aperture or shutter speed setting while pressing the button assigned to the AEL function.

When you do this, the camera will make new settings with equivalent exposure. For example, if the original settings were f/3.5 at 1/160 second, when you select Manual Shift and change the aperture to f/3.2, the camera will reset the shutter speed to 1/200 second, maintaining the original exposure. In this way, you can tweak your settings to favor a particular shutter speed or aperture without affecting the overall exposure. An asterisk will appear in the lower right corner of the display while you hold down the button that activates AEL. (If you chose the AEL Toggle option rather than AEL Hold, you do not have to hold down the button; just press and release it to activate or deactivate AEL.)

I use Manual exposure mode often, for various purposes. One use is to take images at different exposures to combine into a composite HDR image. I will discuss that technique in Chapter 4. I also use Manual mode when using external flash with the RX100 III, as discussed in Appendix A, because the flash does not interact with the camera's autoexposure system.

Manual mode also is useful for some special types of photography, such as making silhouette images. For example, in Figure 3-22, by adjusting exposure settings manually, I was able to make a silhouette even though I took the image on a sunny day.

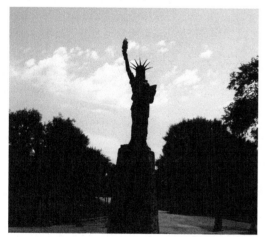

Figure 3-22. Silhouette Taken in Manual Exposure Mode

Scene Mode

Scene mode is designated by the SCN label, shown in Figure 3-23.

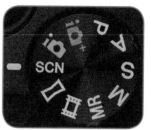

Figure 3-23. Scene Mode

Unlike other modes, Scene mode does not have a single defining feature, such as permitting control over one or more aspects of exposure. Instead, when you select Scene mode and then choose a scene type within that mode, you are telling the camera what sort of environment the picture is being taken in and what type of image you are looking for, and you are letting the camera make the decision as to what settings to use to produce that result.

With most scene types, you cannot select several options that are available in the advanced shooting modes, such as Creative Style, Picture Effect, Metering Mode, White Balance, Focus Area, and ISO. There also are some settings that are available with certain scene types but not others, as discussed later in this chapter.

Although some photographers may feel that Scene mode limits creative decisions, I find it useful. You don't have to use the scene types only for their labeled purposes; some of them may offer settings that are useful for scenarios you regularly encounter. I'll discuss how Scene mode works and you can decide for yourself whether you might take advantage of it on some occasions.

You select Scene mode by turning the Mode dial to the SCN indicator, shown in Figure 3-23. Now, unless you want to use the setting that is already in place, you need to pick one from the fairly impressive list of 13 scene types. There are several ways to do this, depending on current menu settings.

If Mode Dial Guide is turned on in the Setup menu, then, whenever you turn the Mode dial to the SCN setting and press the Center button, the Scene Selection menu in Figure 3-24 appears.

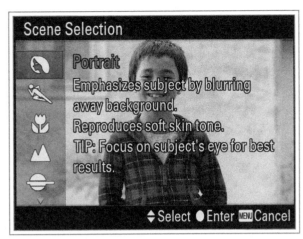
Figure 3-24. Scene Selection Menu

If Mode Dial Guide is not turned on, or if the camera is already in Scene mode, you can use the Shooting menu to call up the Scene Selection screen. Navigate to screen 6 of the Shooting menu and choose the Scene Selection item, as shown in Figure 3-25.

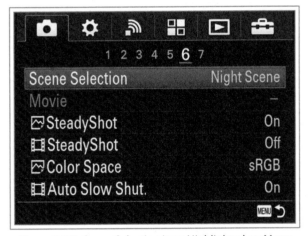
Figure 3-25. Scene Selection Item Highlighted on Menu

Once the Scene Selection menu is displayed, scroll through the 13 selections using the Up and Down buttons or the Control wheel. Press the Center button to select a setting and return to the shooting screen. You will see an icon representing that setting in the upper left corner of the display. (You may need to press the Display button to see the screen that shows the scene setting icon; the icon will disappear after a few seconds on some display screens.) For example, Figure 3-26 shows the display when the Anti Motion Blur setting is selected.

For each scene type the camera displays a screen with a description of the setting's uses as you move the

selector over it, as shown in Figure 3-24, so you are not left to puzzle out what each icon represents.

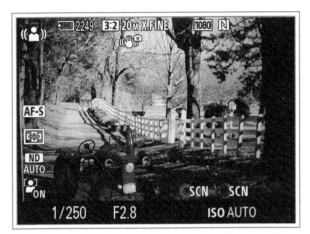
Figure 3-26. Anti Motion Blur Icon in Upper Left Corner of Screen

As you press the Up or Down button or turn the Control wheel to move the selector over the other scene types, when you reach the bottom or top edge of the screen, the selector wraps around to the first or last setting and continues going.

There also are 2 more ways to select a scene type. If the Control ring is set to its Standard setting, then when the camera is in Scene mode, you can just turn the Control ring to cycle through the various scene types. You will see a circular display as the ring turns, as shown in Figure 3-27.

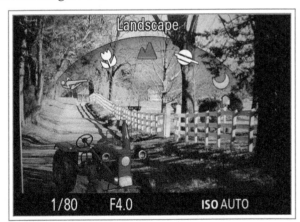
Figure 3-27. Display When Control Ring Selects Scene Type

After you stop turning the ring, the icon for the selected scene type will appear in the upper left corner. (If you are using manual focus or DMF this will not work, because the Control ring will adjust focus and will not be available to display scene types.) Also, you can turn the Control wheel in Scene mode to change scene types, regardless of the function assigned to the Control ring.

That's all you have to do to select a scene type. But you need to know something about each option to decide whether it's one you would want to use. In general, each scene type carries with it a variety of values, including things like focus mode, flash status, range of shutter speeds, sensitivity to various colors, and others.

Note that some settings are designed for certain types of shooting rather than particular environments such as sunset or fireworks. For example, the Anti Motion Blur and High Sensitivity settings are designed for difficult shooting environments, such as dimly lighted areas.

With that introduction, I will discuss each of the 13 choices, with a sample image for each of the settings.

PORTRAIT

The Portrait setting is designed to produce flesh tones with a softening effect, as shown in Figure 3-28.

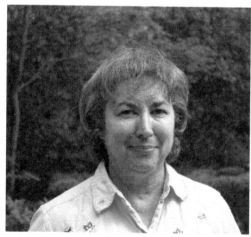

Figure 3-28. Portrait Example Image

You should stand fairly close to the subject and set the zoom to fill the frame. The camera will try to use a wide aperture to blur the background. The flash is initially turned off, but you can use Autoflash or Fill-flash if you want to even out the lighting or reduce shadows on your subject's face. If you want to improve the lighting, consider using off-camera flash with a softbox, as discussed in Appendix A.

If you are shooting a portrait in front of a busy background, such as a house, try to position the subject's head in front of a plain area, such as a light-colored wall, so the head will be seen clearly.

You can use the self-timer, but you cannot use bracketing or continuous shooting. You can use the self-portrait timer feature if it is turned on through screen 3 of the Custom menu. To use that feature, flip the LCD screen up so it is facing in the same direction as the lens, and press the shutter button as you see your face. The shutter will fire after a 3-second on-screen countdown.

SPORTS ACTION

The Sports Action setting is for use when lighting is bright and you need to freeze the action of athletes, children at play, pets, or other objects in motion. The camera may set a high ISO value so it can use a fast shutter speed to stop action. The flash is initially forced off, but you can turn on Fill-flash. The camera sets itself for continuous shooting so you can hold down the shutter button and capture a burst of images. In that way, you increase your chances of capturing the action at a perfect moment. You can switch to the fastest level of continuous shooting if you want, but you cannot set Drive Mode to single shooting or turn on the self-timer. (I'll discuss the Drive Mode options in Chapter 4.) The camera turns on continuous autofocus, so it adjusts focus automatically as the subject moves. You can switch to manual focus or Direct Manual Focus (DMF), which are discussed in Chapter 4. You cannot turn on single autofocus.

For the shot of the skateboarder in Figure 3-29, the camera set itself to f/3.2 with an ISO setting of 125, and used a shutter speed of 1/1600 second to freeze the action.

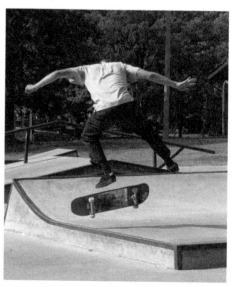

Figure 3-29. Sports Action Example Image

Macro

Although you can focus at close range in other shooting modes, it is convenient to use this setting to call up a group of options that are suited for extreme closeups of flowers, insects, or other small objects.

When you select the Macro option, the camera will let you set the flash to Forced Off, Fill-flash, or Autoflash. You cannot use continuous shooting or bracketing, but you can use the self-timer.

The camera initially uses single autofocus, but you don't have to use autofocus to take macro shots. You can use manual focus to focus on objects very close to the lens. You do, however, lose the benefit of automatic focus, and it can be tricky finding the correct focus manually. If you use the DMF setting, though, you can check focus by pressing the shutter button halfway and having the camera use its autofocus system. You also can take advantage of several aids to manual focusing with the RX100 III: Peaking, MF Assist, and Focus Magnifier, discussed in Chapters 4 and 7.

You don't have to use the Macro setting to shoot extreme closeups with the RX100 III. If you just set the camera to one of its autofocus modes—either Single-shot AF or Continuous AF—it will focus on objects as close as 2 inches (5 cm) when the lens is zoomed out and as close as 12 inches (30 cm) when the lens is zoomed in to its maximum telephoto range.

When shooting extreme closeups, you should use a tripod if possible because the depth of field is very shallow and you need to keep the camera steady to take a usable photograph. It's also a good idea to take advantage of the 2-second self-timer. If you take the picture using the self-timer, you will not be touching the camera when the shutter is activated, so the chance of camera shake is minimized. You also can use Sony's wired remote control, discussed in Appendix A.

If you need artificial illumination, consider using some sort of diffuser over the built-in flash, such as a handkerchief or piece of translucent plastic. Using the flash without some diffusion is likely to result in uneven illumination at such a close range. You might consider using a small lamp that can illuminate the subject without overwhelming it. Another approach is to use off-camera flash triggered by an optical slave system with a softbox to diffuse the light, as discussed in Appendix A.

In Figure 3-30, I took a shot of a butterfly using the Macro setting with autofocus, holding the camera as close as I could.

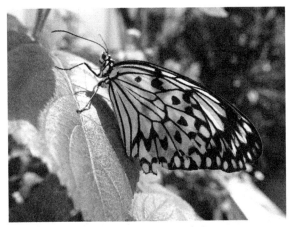

Figure 3-30. Macro Example Image

Landscape

Landscape is a Scene mode setting I use often. It is convenient to turn the Mode dial to the SCN position and pull up the Landscape setting when I'm at a scenic location. The camera lets you use Fill-flash in case you want to shoot an image of a person as part of your composition, and it boosts the brightness and intensity of the colors somewhat. Otherwise, it limits your choices; you cannot use continuous shooting, but you can use the self-timer. Figure 3-31 is an example taken using the Landscape setting for a shot of the Richmond, Virginia, skyline across the James River.

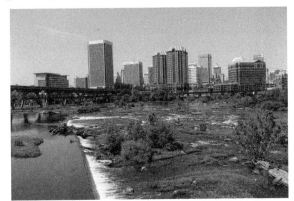

Figure 3-31. Landscape Example Image

Sunset

This setting enhances reddish hues. You can use Fill-flash to take a portrait with the sunset or sunrise in the background. You cannot use continuous shooting, but you can use the self-timer. As I noted earlier, you don't have to limit this, or any Scene mode setting, to the subject its name implies. If you are photographing reddish leaves in autumn, you might want to try the Sunset option to create an enhanced view of the brightly colored foliage.

In Figure 3-32, I used this option to photograph a traditional scene of the setting sun in rural Goochland County, Virginia.

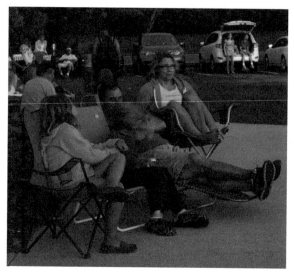

Figure 3-33. Night Scene Example Image

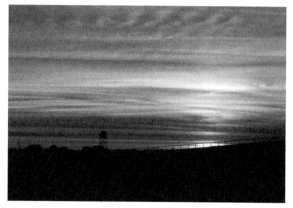

Figure 3-32. Sunset Example Image

NIGHT SCENE

The Night Scene option is designed to preserve the natural look of an evening setting. The camera disables the use of the flash completely; if the scene is quite dark, you should use a tripod to avoid camera motion during the long exposure that may be required. You cannot use continuous shooting, but you can use the self-timer. This setting is good for landscapes and other outdoor scenes after dark when flash would not help. The camera does not raise the ISO or use multiple shots, as it does with other modes used in dim lighting, such as Anti Motion Blur and Hand-held Twilight.

In Figure 3-33, I used the Night Scene setting with the RX100 III on a tripod to photograph some of the spectators at a July 4th fireworks show.

HAND-HELD TWILIGHT

This scene type is meant for taking pictures in low light without flash or tripod. With this special setting, the camera boosts the ISO to a higher level so it can use a fast shutter speed, and takes a rapid burst of 4 shots. The camera combines these shots internally into one composite image to counteract the effects of high ISO, which often causes visible "noise," or grain, in an image.

Although the camera will attempt to select frames with minimal motion blur, the final result with this setting is more likely to show motion blur than a shot made with the Anti Motion Blur setting, discussed later in this section. If the Quality option on the Shooting menu is set to RAW or RAW & JPEG, the camera resets it to Fine while using this setting. However, you can set Quality to Extra Fine, and the camera will use that setting.

Hand-held Twilight is a good option if you are shooting a landscape or other static subject when you cannot use a tripod or flash and the light is dim. If you can use a tripod, you might be better off using the Night Scene setting, discussed above. Or, if you don't mind using flash, you could just use Intelligent Auto, Program, or one of the more ordinary shooting modes. Hand-held Twilight is a useful option when it's needed, but it will not yield the same overall quality as a shot at a lower ISO with the camera on a steady support.

In Figure 3-34, I used this setting to capture an image of an antique chest on display in the local art museum, where flash is not permitted.

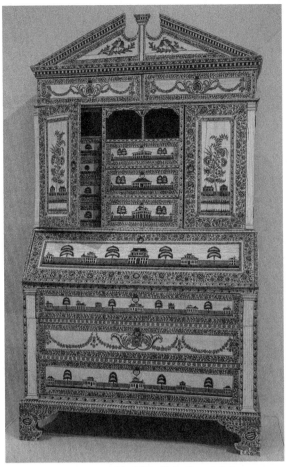

Figure 3-34. Hand-held Twilight Example Image

NIGHT PORTRAIT

This night-oriented setting is for situations when you are taking a portrait and are willing to use the camera's built-in flash. The main differences from the settings discussed above are that with Night Portrait, the camera takes only one shot and it activates the flash, in Slow Sync mode. You cannot set the Flash Mode to Flash Off. (However, you can leave the flash unit retracted, and the camera will let you take the shot without flash.)

I will discuss Slow Sync in more detail in Chapter 4. Basically, with this setting, the camera uses a slow shutter speed, so that as the flash illuminates the portrait subject, there is enough time for natural light to illuminate the background also. You can use the self-timer, but not continuous shooting. You also can use Raw quality if you wish, so this setting is a good choice for a high-quality portrait outdoors at night. Because of the slow shutter speed, you should use a tripod if possible to avoid motion blur.

In Figure 3-35, I used this setting for an indoor portrait.

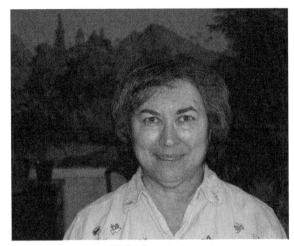

Figure 3-35. Night Portrait Example Image

The mural in the background shows up fairly clearly because the camera used a slow shutter speed of 1/20 second. I used a tripod, which eliminated camera shake, but you also need to advise the subject not to move during the possibly long exposure.

ANTI MOTION BLUR

As noted earlier, this Scene mode setting is not meant for a particular subject, but for a certain type of situation. This option is useful for an area with dim lighting or when the lens is zoomed in to a telephoto setting. In either of those situations, the image is subject to blurring because of camera motion. In dim lighting, blurring can happen when the camera uses a slow shutter speed to expose the image properly, because it is hard to hold the camera steady enough for a sharply focused shot longer than about 1/30 second. In the telephoto case, any camera motion is exaggerated because of the magnification of the image.

To counter the effects of this blurring, with Anti Motion Blur the camera raises the ISO to a higher-than-normal level so the camera can use a fast shutter speed and still let in enough light to expose the image properly. Because higher ISO settings result in increased visual noise, the camera takes a rapid burst of 4 shots and combines them internally into a single image with reduced noise. The camera also counteracts blur from motion of the subject to a fair extent, by analyzing the shots and rejecting those with motion blur as much as possible.

Anti Motion Blur is useful as the light is fading if you don't want to use flash. It is similar to the Hand-held Twilight setting, discussed above, but the camera is likely to use a higher ISO value with this option, which may result in more noise in the image. For Figure 3-36, taken in the art museum, the camera used a high ISO setting of 4000 along with its multiple-shot processing.

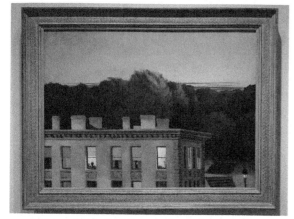

Figure 3-36. Anti Motion Blur Example Image

You should not expect good results if you use this setting with fast-moving subjects, because the camera will not be able to eliminate motion blur. With slower-moving subjects, though, the RX100 III can do a good job of reducing or avoiding blur. With this setting, you cannot set the Drive Mode or the Flash Mode options. As with the Hand-held Twilight setting, if Quality is set to RAW or RAW & JPEG, the camera resets it to Fine while using this setting, though you can set Quality to Extra Fine if you want.

PET

The Pet setting is for taking photos of cats, dogs, and other animals. It is similar to Sports Action in that the flash is off by default but can be set to Fill-flash. The Pet setting, though, lets you use the Soft Skin Effect setting on the Shooting menu, and does not let you use continuous shooting. I would recommend that you use this setting when you are shooting a relatively posed or calm shot of your dog, cat, or other pet; if the animal is running around, you might be better off with the Sports Action selection.

I used this setting for Figure 3-37, a shot of a Canadian goose that had wandered away from its companions momentarily.

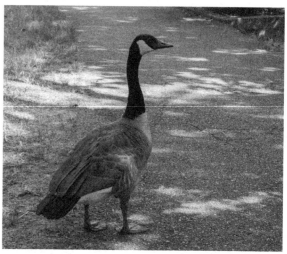

Figure 3-37. Pet Example Image

GOURMET

The Gourmet setting, according to Sony, is meant to let you shoot food so that it looks "delicious." In terms of settings, the RX100 III raises the brightness and vividness of colors to enhance the appearance of food. This setting is useful for people who write food blogs, or who just like to record their meals for posterity. The camera lets you have the flash either forced off or set to Fill-flash. Continuous shooting is not available, but you can use the self-timer. In Figure 3-38, the color and brightness enhancements of this setting gave the image a bit of a boost, making a plate of dried peaches look more colorful and appetizing than it would with the normal appearance of Program mode.

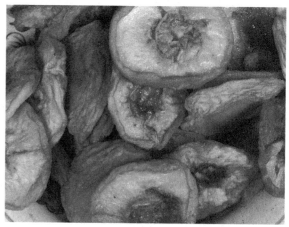

Figure 3-38. Gourmet Example Image

FIREWORKS

This scene type is designed to capture vivid images of fireworks bursts. It sets the camera to a 2-second shutter speed and intensifies colors. If you can, you should set the camera on a tripod or other sturdy support and turn off the SteadyShot image stabilization option on the Shooting menu. The camera disables the flash and continuous shooting.

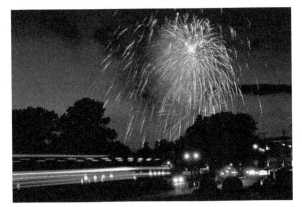

Figure 3-39. Fireworks Example Image

On Independence Day, I took the shot in Figure 3-39 using a tripod. We were viewing the show from a spot next to the highway, and a car happened to drive by during the 2-second exposure, adding a stream of taillights to the fireworks display.

This setting is one you can also use as an alternative to the Night Scene setting when you are using a tripod after dark. You might want to try this approach to take advantage of the different color processing that the camera uses with this option.

High Sensitivity

This final Scene mode setting is another option for low-light shooting. The camera disables the flash and continuous shooting, but it allows use of the self-timer. The camera is likely to use an ISO of 3200 or higher, all the way to the maximum of 25600 if the light is dim enough to require it. However, unlike the case with Hand-held Twilight and Anti Motion Blur, the camera takes only a single shot. As a result, there is no special processing of multiple images to reduce visual noise, so the image may be rather grainy.

If you need to shoot in dim light without a tripod and produce an image that is smooth and as noise-free as possible, you probably should use Hand-held Twilight or Anti Motion Blur instead of High Sensitivity. However, there might be occasions when you don't mind the grainy, noisy appearance that a high ISO can bring. It's good to have various choices available when you are confronted with a dimly lit location.

Note that you cannot set the ISO to 25600 with the ISO setting on the Shooting menu; as discussed in Chapter 4, the highest setting on that menu is 12800. To get the camera to use the 25600 value for ISO, you have to use the Multi Frame Noise Reduction setting on the ISO menu or this High Sensitivity setting of Scene mode.

In Figure 3-40, I used the High Sensitivity setting to photograph another group of spectators at the fireworks show. Because of the darkness, the camera set the ISO to 25600 and exposed the image for 1/8 second at an aperture of f/2.8.

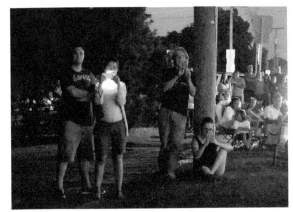

Figure 3-40. High Sensitivity Example Image - ISO 25600

Sweep Panorama Mode

The next setting on the Mode dial is designed for the shooting of panoramic images. The RX100 III, like many other Sony cameras, has an excellent capability for automating the capture of panoramas. If you follow the fairly simple steps involved, the camera will stitch together a series of images internally to create a wide (or tall) view of a scenic vista or other subject that lends itself to panoramic depiction.

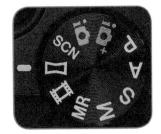

Figure 3-41. Sweep Panorama Mode

Just turn the Mode dial to select the icon that looks like a long, squeezed rectangle, as shown in Figure 3-41. You will see a message telling you to press the shutter button and move the camera in the direction of the arrow that appears on the screen, as shown in Figure 3-42.

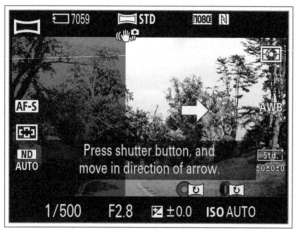

Figure 3-42. Message for Taking Panorama Image

At that point, you can follow the directions and likely get excellent results. However, the camera also lets you make several choices for your panoramic images using the Shooting menu. Just press the Menu button, and you will go to the menu screen that is currently being displayed.

Navigate to the Shooting menu, which limits you to fewer choices than in most other shooting modes because several options are not appropriate for panoramas. For example, the Image Size, Aspect Ratio, and Quality settings are dimmed and unavailable. Also, options such as Drive Mode, Flash Mode, and Focus Area are of no use in this situation and cannot be selected. In addition, you will not be able to zoom the lens in; it will be fixed at its wide-angle position. (If the lens was zoomed in previously, it will zoom back out automatically when you switch the Mode dial to the Sweep Panorama selection.)

You will, however, see 2 options on the first screen of the Shooting menu that are not available for selection in any other shooting mode: Panorama Size and Panorama Direction, as shown in Figure 3-43.

If you select Panorama Size, you will see 2 options, Standard and Wide. With Standard, a horizontal panorama will have a size of 8192 by 1856 pixels, which is a resolution of about 15 megapixels (MP). If you choose Wide, a horizontal panorama will have a size of 12416 by 1856 pixels, resulting in a resolution of about 23 MP. (This figure is larger than the camera's maximum resolution of 20 MP because with the panorama

settings, the camera is taking multiple images and stitching them together.)

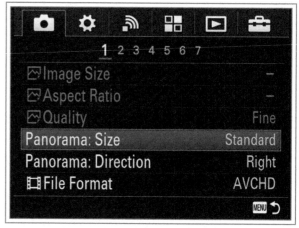

Figure 3-43. Panorama Size and Direction Menu Options

A vertical panorama at the Standard setting is 3872 by 2160 pixels, or about 8.3 MP; a vertical panorama at the Wide setting is 5536 by 2160 pixels, or about 12 MP.

The Panorama Direction option lets you choose Right, Left, Up, or Down for the direction in which you will sweep the camera. If you have the Control ring set to the Standard option through the Custom Key Settings item on the Custom menu and you are not using manual focus or DMF, you can turn the Control ring, and the camera will cycle through the 4 arrows for the 4 panorama directions, so you will not have to use the Shooting menu for that purpose. You also can turn the Control wheel to change the direction, regardless of the setting for the Control ring.

Also, you can use the Direction settings with different orientations of the camera to get different results than usual. For example, if you set the direction to Up and then hold the camera sideways while you sweep it to the right, you will create a horizontal panorama that has 2160 pixels in its vertical dimension rather than the standard 1856.

Those are the main settings for most panoramas. There are a few other options you can select for panoramas on the Shooting menu, including Focus Mode, Metering Mode, White Balance, Creative Style, and SteadyShot. I will discuss all of these menu options in Chapter 4. My preferred settings for shooting panoramas are the ones shown in Table 3-1, at least as a starting point.

Table 3-1. **Suggested Settings for Panoramas**

Focus Mode	Single-shot AF
Metering Mode	Multi
White Balance	Auto White Balance
Creative Style	Standard
SteadyShot	On (unless using a tripod)

One other setting you can make when shooting panoramas is exposure compensation, which is set using the Down button on the Control wheel. I will discuss that function in Chapter 5. In the context of shooting panoramas, this feature can be useful because the camera will not change the exposure if the camera is pointed at areas with varying brightness. So, for example, if you start sweeping from a dark area on the left, the camera will set the exposure for that area. If you then sweep the camera to the right over a bright area, that part of the panorama will be overexposed and possibly washed out in excessive brightness. To correct for this effect, you can reduce the exposure using exposure compensation. In this way, the initial dark area will be underexposed, but the brighter area should be properly exposed. Of course, you have to decide what part of the panorama is the most important one for having proper exposure.

Another way to deal with this issue is to point the camera at the bright area before starting the shot and press the shutter button halfway to lock the exposure, and then go back to the dark area at the left and start sweeping the camera. In that way, the exposure will be locked at the proper level for the bright area.

Once you have made the settings you want, follow the directions on the screen. Press and release the shutter button and start moving the camera at a steady rate in the direction you have chosen. I tend to shoot my panoramas moving the camera from left to right, but you may have a different preference. You will hear a steady clicking as the camera takes multiple shots during the sweep of the panorama. A white box and arrow will proceed across the screen; your task is to finish the camera's sweep at the same moment that the box and arrow finish their travel across the scene. If you move the camera either too quickly or too slowly, the panorama will not succeed; if that happens, just try again.

Generally speaking, panoramas work best when the scene does not contain moving objects such as cars or pedestrians because when items are in motion, the multiple shots are likely to capture images of the same object more than once in different positions.

It is advisable to use a tripod if possible so you can keep the camera steady in a single plane as it moves. If you don't have a tripod available, you might try using the electronic level that Sony provides with the RX100 III. You have to activate the level with the Display Button option on screen 2 of the Custom menu, as discussed in Chapter 7. Then press the Display button until the screen with the electronic level appears. Make sure the outer tips of the level stay green as much as possible, and the resulting panorama should benefit from the level shooting.

In addition to exposure, as discussed above, focus and white balance are fixed as soon as the first image is taken for the panorama.

When a panoramic shot is played back in the camera, it is initially displayed at a small size so the whole image can fit on the display screen. You can press the Center button to make the panorama scroll across the display at a larger size, using the full height of the screen.

Figure 3-44 and Figure 3-45 are sample panoramas, both shot from left to right using the Standard setting for Panorama Size. For Figure 3-44 I used a tripod; I took Figure 3-45 with the camera hand-held.

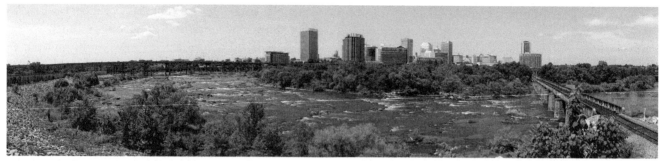

Figure 3-44. Panorama: Skyline of Richmond, Virginia, Across the James River

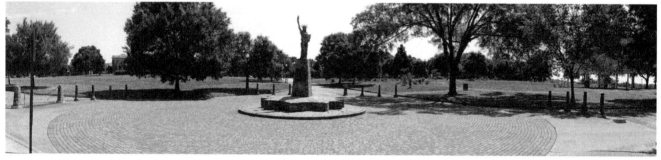

Figure 3-45. Panorama: Miniature Statue of Liberty, Chimborazo Park, Richmond, Virginia

Memory Recall Mode

There is one more shooting mode to discuss (apart from Movie mode, which I will discuss in Chapter 8). This last mode, called Memory Recall, is a powerful tool that gives you expanded options for your photography.

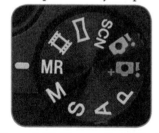

Figure 3-46. Memory Recall Mode

When you turn the Mode dial to the MR position (shown in Figure 3-46) and then select one of the 3 groups of settings that can be stored there, you are, in effect, selecting a custom-made shooting mode with your own favorite settings. You can set up the camera just as you want it—with stored values for items such as shooting mode, shutter speed, aperture, zoom amount, white balance, ISO, and other settings—and then recall all of those values instantly just by turning the Mode dial to the MR position and selecting option 1, 2, or 3 on the Memory Recall screen. With the RX100 III, unlike some other camera models, you can store settings for any shooting mode, including the Auto and Scene modes.

To use this feature, set up the camera with all of the settings you want to be able to recall. For example, suppose you are going to do street photography. You may want to use a fast shutter speed, say 1/250 second, in black and white, at ISO 400, using continuous shooting with autofocus, Large and Extra Fine JPEG images, shooting in the 4:3 aspect ratio.

The first step is to make all of these settings. Set the Mode dial to Shutter Priority and use the Control wheel to set a shutter speed of 1/250 second. Then press the Menu button to call up the Shooting menu and, on the first screen, select L for Image Size, 4:3 for Aspect Ratio, and Extra Fine for Quality. Then move to the second screen and choose Continuous Shooting for Drive Mode. On the third screen, set Continuous AF for Focus Mode and set ISO to 400. On the fourth screen, set White Balance to Daylight, then scroll down 2 more positions to the Creative Style option and select the B/W setting for black and white. You also may want to push the zoom lever all the way to the left for wide-angle shooting. You can set any other available menu options as you wish, but the ones listed above are the ones I will consider for now.

Once these settings are made, press the Menu button (if the menu isn't still on the screen) to call up the Shooting menu, and navigate to the Memory item, shown in Figure 3-47, which is the final item on the last screen of the Shooting menu.

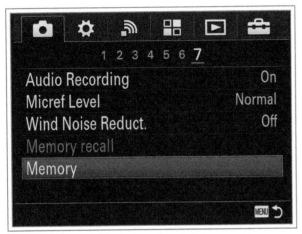

Figure 3-47. Memory Item Highlighted on Menu

After you press the Center button, you will see a screen like the one in Figure 3-48, showing icons and values for all of the settings currently in effect and the numbers 1, 2, and 3 at the upper right corner of the display. The message "Select Register" appears at the upper left of the screen, indicating that you can now assign the group of settings shown on the display to register number 1, 2, or 3 of the Memory Recall mode. In the example shown here, the number 1 is highlighted. Now press the Center button, and you will have selected register 1 to store all of the settings you just made.

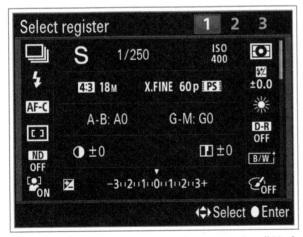

Figure 3-48. Select Register Screen for Memory Recall Mode

Note the short gray bar at the right side of the Memory screen shown in Figure 3-48. That bar indicates that you can scroll down through other screens to see additional settings that are in effect, such as ISO Auto Maximum and Minimum, Panorama Direction, AF Illuminator, SteadyShot, and several others. Use the Up and Down buttons to scroll through those screens if you want to see the settings that are in effect.

Next, to check how this worked, try making some very different settings, such as setting the camera for Manual exposure with a shutter speed of one second, Creative Style set to Vivid, continuous shooting turned off, the zoom lever moved all the way to the right for telephoto, and Quality set to Raw. Then turn the Mode dial back to the MR position, make sure the number 1 for Register 1 is highlighted, and press the Center button to return to the shooting display. You will see that all of the custom settings you made have instantly returned, including the zoom position, shutter speed, and everything else.

This is a wonderful feature, and it is more powerful than similar options on some other cameras, which can save menu settings but not values such as shutter speed and zoom position, or can save settings only for the less-automatic shooting modes, but not the Scene and Auto modes. What is also quite amazing is that if you now switch back to Manual exposure mode, the camera will restore the settings that you had in that mode before you turned to the MR mode. (The position of the zoom lens will not revert to where it was, though.)

Memory Recall mode lets you store settings for any shooting mode, including Program, Aperture Priority, Shutter Priority, Manual exposure, and even the Scene, Auto, Sweep Panorama, and Movie modes. You can store settings from the Shooting menu as well as the aperture, shutter speed, exposure compensation, and optical zoom settings. So, for example, you could set up one of the 3 memory registers to recall Scene mode set to the Macro setting, with the lens zoomed back to its wide-angle position. In that way, you could be ready for closeup shooting on a moment's notice.

The Memory Recall feature is especially useful with a camera as small as the RX100 III because there are not many physical controls and it can be cumbersome to change settings when you have to dig into the menu system to make settings for ISO, white balance, focus mode, and other basic items. With one twist of the Mode dial and the press of a button, you can call up a complete group of settings tailored for a particular type of shooting. It is worth your while to experiment with this feature and develop 3 groups of settings that work well for your shooting needs.

CHAPTER 4: SHOOTING MENU

Much of the power of the Sony RX100 III comes from options on the Shooting menu, which gives you many ways to control the appearance of images and how you capture them. Depending on your preferences, you may not have to use this menu too much. You may prefer to use the camera's physical controls, with which you can make many settings, or you may use the Scene or Auto mode settings, which choose many options for you. However, it's nice to have this degree of control if you want it, and it is useful to understand the settings you can make. In addition, with the RX100 III, more than with many other cameras, you can control a fair number of settings on the Shooting menu even when the camera is in a Scene or Auto mode. Therefore, it is well worth exploring this powerful menu.

The Shooting menu is easy to use once you have played with it a bit. The available options can change depending on the setting of the Mode dial. For example, if the camera is set to Intelligent Auto mode, the Shooting menu options are limited because that mode is for a user who wants the camera to make many decisions without input. If the camera is in Sweep Panorama mode, the Shooting menu options are limited because of the specialized nature of that mode. For this discussion, I'm assuming you have the camera set to Program mode, because with that mode you have access to most of the options on the Shooting menu.

Turn the Mode dial on top of the camera to P, which represents Program mode, as shown in Figure 4-1. Enter the menu system by pressing the Menu button and move through the numbered screens of the menu system by pressing the Right button on the Control wheel. With each press of that button, the small orange line (cursor) at the top of the screen moves underneath a number that represents a menu screen.

When the menu system first appears, the cursor should sit beneath the number 1 while the camera icon, which

represents the Shooting menu, is highlighted in the group of icons at the top of the screen, as shown in Figure 4-2.

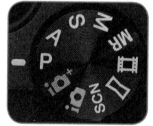

Figure 4-1. Program Mode

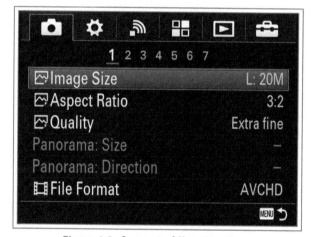

Figure 4-2. Screen 1 of Shooting Menu

As you keep pressing the Right button, the cursor will move through all 7 screens of the Shooting menu.

As you continue to move the cursor through the menu screens with the RX100 III set to shooting mode, after the Shooting menu comes the Custom menu, marked by a gear icon, followed by the Wi-Fi menu, headed by a wireless network icon. The last 3 menus are the Application menu, designated by a set of black and white blocks; the Playback menu, marked by a triangle icon; and, finally, the Setup menu, marked by a toolbox icon.

To navigate quickly through the 6 menu systems, you can press the Up button to move the orange highlight block into the line of menu icons at the top of the screen. When one of those icons is highlighted, you can use the Left and Right buttons to navigate directly from one menu system to another without going through the various screens of each menu.

For example, in Figure 4-3, the Wi-Fi menu icon is highlighted.

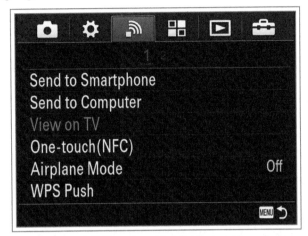

Figure 4-3. Wi-Fi Menu Icon Highlighted on Menu Screen

From there, you can press the Left button twice to move the highlight to the camera icon for the Shooting menu at the far left, as shown in Figure 4-4. Then you can press the Down button to move the highlight into the list of items on screen 1 of the Shooting menu, as shown in Figure 4-2.

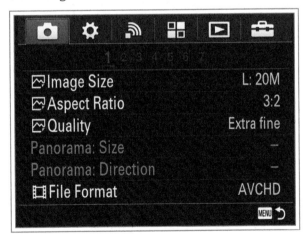

Figure 4-4. Shooting Menu Icon Highlighted on Menu Screen

In this chapter, I am going to discuss only the Shooting menu; I will discuss the other menus in Chapter 6 (Playback), Chapter 7 (Custom and Setup), and Chapter 9 (Wi-Fi and Application).

The Shooting menu contains numerous options divided into 7 numbered screens. In most cases, each option (such as Image Size) occupies one line, with its name on the left and its current setting (such as L: 20M) on the right. In

other cases (such as Scene Selection, Movie, and Memory), there may be only a small dash on the right side of the screen, meaning the selection is not currently applicable. For example, if the camera is set to Program mode, the Scene Selection item on screen 6 of the Shooting menu will be followed by a dash because a scene type cannot be selected when the camera is in Program mode.

You also will see that some items on the menu screens are dimmed, as the Scene Selection, Movie, and Auto Slow Shutter options are in Figure 4-5, for example.

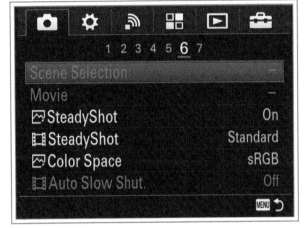

Figure 4-5. Three Items Dimmed on Shooting Menu

This means those options are not available for selection in the current context. In this case, the camera was set to Program mode; the Scene Selection option is available only when the Mode dial is set to Scene mode, the Movie option is available only in Movie mode, and the Auto Slow Shutter option is available only with certain settings for Record Setting.

To follow the discussion below of the options on the Shooting menu, leave the shooting mode set to Program, which gives you access to all but a few options on that menu. (I'll also discuss the options that are available in other modes as I come to them.) I'll start at the top of screen 1 and discuss each option on the way down the list for each of the 7 screens.

Image Size

This first option on the Shooting menu lets you select the resolution, or pixel count, of your still images. The Image Size setting is related to the next 2 entries on the menu, Aspect Ratio and Quality, to control the overall appearance and "quality" of your images, in a broad sense.

The Image Size setting controls the size in pixels of a still image recorded by the camera. The Sony RX100 III has an unusually large digital sensor for a camera of its size, and that sensor has a high maximum resolution, or pixel count. The sensor is capable of recording a still image with 5472 pixels, or individual points of light, in the horizontal direction and 3648 pixels vertically. When you multiply those 2 numbers together, the result is about 20 million pixels, often referred to as megapixels, MP, or M.

The resolution of still images is important mainly when it comes time to enlarge or print your images. If you need to produce large prints (say, 8 by 10 inches or 20 by 25 cm), then you should select a high-resolution setting for Image Size. You also should choose the largest Image Size setting if you may need to crop out a small portion of the image and enlarge it for closer viewing. For example, if you are shooting photos of wildlife and the animal or bird you are interested in is in the distance, you may need to enlarge the image digitally to see that subject in detail. In that case, also, you should choose the highest setting for Image Size.

The available settings for Image Size with the RX100 III are L, M, S, and VGA, for Large, Medium, Small, and VGA, as shown in Figure 4-6.

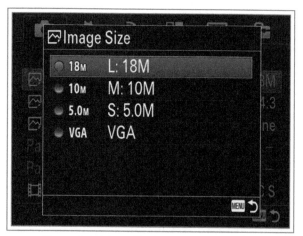

Figure 4-6. Image Size Menu Options Screen

When you select one of the first 3 options, the camera displays a setting such as L: 20M, meaning Large: 20 megapixels. The number of megapixels changes depending on the Aspect Ratio setting, discussed below. This is because when the shape of the image changes, the number of horizontal pixels or the number of vertical pixels changes also to form the new shape. For example, if the Aspect Ratio setting is 3:2, the maximum number of pixels is used because 3:2 is the aspect ratio of the

camera's sensor. However, if you set Aspect Ratio to 16:9, the number of horizontal pixels (5472) stays the same, but the number of vertical pixels is reduced from 3648 to 3080 to form the 16:9 ratio of horizontal to vertical pixels. When you multiply those two numbers (5472 and 3080) together, the result is about 17 million pixels, which the camera states as 17M, as in Figure 4-7.

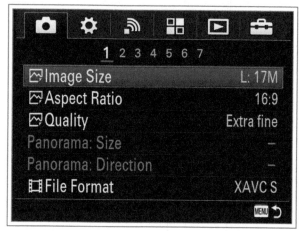

Figure 4-7. Image Size L:17M Highlighted on Menu

The VGA option, the smallest size possible, is available only if Aspect Ratio is set to 4:3. Otherwise, this choice does not even appear on the menu option for Image Size. VGA stands for video graphics array, the designation used for older-style computer screens, which have a 4:3 aspect ratio. The pixel count for this setting is very low—just 640 by 480 pixels, yielding a resolution of 0.3 M, much less than one megapixel. This very small size is suitable if you need to send images by e-mail or need to store a great many images on a memory card.

One of the few reasons to choose an Image Size smaller than L is if you are running out of space on your memory card and need to keep taking pictures in an important situation. Table 4-1 shows approximately how many images can be stored on an 8 GB memory card for various settings.

Table 4-1. **Number of Images That Fit on an 8 GB Card (Image Size vs. Quality at 3:2 Aspect Ratio)**

	Large	Medium	Small
Raw & JPEG	246	287	312
Raw	371	-----	-----
Extra Fine	539	850	1,282
Fine	727	1,286	1,954
Standard	1,249	1,986	2,818

As you can see, if you are using an 8 GB memory card, which is a fairly small size nowadays, you can fit about 246 images on the card even at the maximum settings of 3:2 for Aspect Ratio, Large for Image Size, and Raw & JPEG for Quality. If you limit the image quality to Fine, with no Raw images, you can fit about 727 images on the card. If you reduce the Image Size setting to Small, you can store 1,954 images. I am unlikely ever to need more than about 200 or 300 images in any one session. And, of course, I can use a larger memory card or multiple memory cards.

If space on your memory card is not a consideration, then I recommend you use the L setting at all times. You never know when you might need the larger-sized image, so you might as well use the L setting and be safe. Your situation might be different, of course. If you were taking photos purely for a business purpose, such as making photo identification cards, you might want to use the Small setting to store the maximum number of images on a memory card and reduce expense. For general photography, though, I rarely use any setting other than L for Image Size. (One exception could be when I want to increase the range of the optical zoom lens without losing image quality; see the discussion of Clear Image Zoom and related topics in Chapter 7.)

When Quality, discussed later in this chapter, is set to Raw, the Image Size option is dimmed and unavailable for selection because you cannot select an image size for Raw images; they are always at the maximum size, as is shown above on the table showing the numbers of images that can fit on a memory card.

Aspect Ratio

This second option on the Shooting menu lets you choose the shape of your still images. The choices are the default of 3:2, as well as 4:3, 16:9, and 1:1, as shown in Figure 4-8. These numbers represent the ratio of the units of width to the units of height. For example, with the 16:9 setting, the image is 16 units wide for every 9 units of height. The aspect ratio that uses all pixels on the image sensor is 3:2; with any other aspect ratio, some of the pixels are cropped out. So, if you want to record every possible pixel, you should use the 3:2 setting. If you shoot using the 3:2 aspect ratio, you can always alter the aspect ratio of the image later in editing software such as Photoshop by cropping away parts of

the image. However, if you want to have your images in a certain shape and don't plan to do post-processing in software, the aspect ratio settings of this menu item may be just what you want. It's helpful to set the aspect ratio if you know what shape you want the final image to be in, so you can compose your image in the camera using the appropriate aspect ratio on the display.

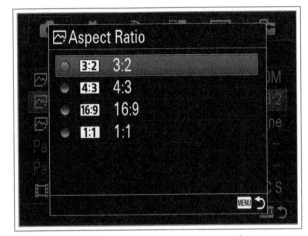

Figure 4-8. Aspect Ratio Menu Options Screen

The RX100 III provides more options in this area than many other cameras do. After each of the aspect ratios discussed below, I am including an image I took using that setting in the same location at the same time, to give a general idea of what the different aspect ratios look like.

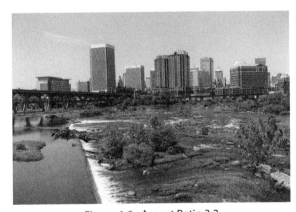

Figure 4-9. Aspect Ratio 3:2

The default 3:2 setting, used for Figure 4-9, includes the maximum number of pixels, and is the ratio used by traditional 35mm film. This aspect ratio can be used without cropping to make prints in the common U.S. size of 6 inches by 4 inches (15 cm by 10 cm).

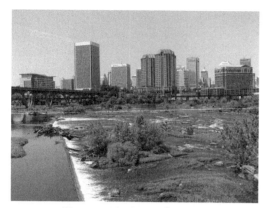

Figure 4-10. Aspect Ratio 4:3

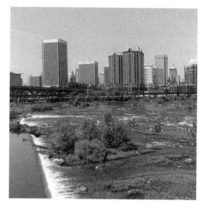

Figure 4-12. Aspect Ratio 1:1

The 4:3 setting, shown in Figure 4-10, is in the shape of a traditional (non-widescreen) computer screen, so if you want to view your images on that sort of display, this may be your preferred setting. As I noted earlier in connection with Image Size, if you want to use the VGA setting for Image Size, the camera must be set to the 4:3 aspect ratio. With this setting, some pixels are lost at the left and right sides of the image.

The Aspect Ratio setting is available in all shooting modes except Sweep Panorama. However, although you can set Aspect Ratio when the camera is in Movie mode (Mode dial turned to movie-film icon), that setting will have no effect until you switch to a mode for taking still images, such as Program mode. This is because when the Mode dial is set to the Movie position, you cannot take still images. The aspect ratio of a movie is determined by the File Format and Record Settings menu options, not by the Aspect Ratio option.

Quality

The Quality setting, below Aspect Ratio, is one of the most important Shooting menu options. The choices are Raw, Raw & JPEG, Extra Fine, Fine, and Standard, as shown in Figure 4-13.

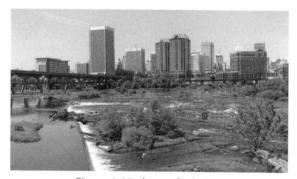

Figure 4-11. Aspect Ratio 16:9

The 16:9 setting, illustrated in Figure 4-11, is the "widescreen" option, like that found on many modern HD television sets. You might use this setting when you plan to show your images on an HDTV set. Or, it might be suitable for a particular composition in which the subject matter is stretched out in a horizontal arrangement. With this setting, some pixels are cropped out at the top and bottom, though none are lost at the left or right.

The 1:1 ratio, illustrated in Figure 4-12, produces a square shape, which some photographers prefer because of its symmetry and because the neutrality of the shape leaves open many possibilities for composition. With the 1:1 setting, the camera crops pixels from the left and right sides of the image.

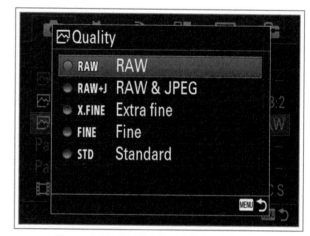

Figure 4-13. Quality Menu Options Screen

The term "quality" in this context concerns the way in which digital images are processed. In particular, JPEG (non-Raw) images are digitally "compressed" to reduce their size without losing too much information or detail from the picture. However, the more an image is compressed, the greater the loss of detail and clarity in the image. Raw files, which are in a class by themselves, are the least compressed of all and have the greatest level of quality, though they come with some complications, as discussed below. All other (non-Raw) formats used by the RX100 III (as with most similar cameras) are classified as JPEG, which is an acronym for Joint Photographic Experts Group, an industry group that created the JPEG standard. The JPEG files, in turn, come in 3 varieties on the RX100 III: Extra Fine, Fine, and Standard. The Extra Fine setting provides the least compression; images captured with the Fine or Standard setting undergo increasingly more compression, resulting in smaller files with somewhat reduced quality.

Here are some guidelines for using these settings. First, you need to choose between Raw and JPEG images. Raw files are larger than other files, so they take up more space on your memory card, and on your computer, than JPEG files. But Raw files offer advantages over JPEG files. When you shoot in the Raw format, the camera records as much information as it can about the image and preserves that information in the file it saves to the memory card. When you open the Raw file later on your computer, your software can process that information in various ways. For example, you can change the exposure or white balance of the image when you edit it on the computer, just as if you had changed your settings while shooting. In effect, the Raw format gives you what almost amounts to a chance to travel back in time to improve some of the settings that you didn't get quite right when you pressed the shutter button.

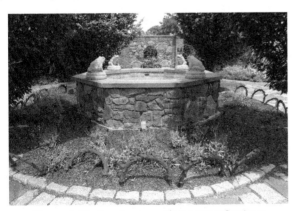

Figure 4-14. Raw Image with Incorrect Settings

For example, Figure 4-14 is an image I took with the RX100 III using the Raw format, with the exposure purposely set too dark and the white balance set to Incandescent, even though I took the picture outdoors on a sunny day.

Figure 4-15 shows the same image after I opened it up in Adobe Camera Raw software and adjusted the settings to correct the exposure and white balance. The result was an image that looked just as it would have if I had used the correct settings when I shot it.

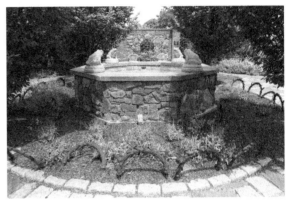

Figure 4-15. Raw Image with Settings Adjusted in Software

Raw is not a cure-all; you cannot fix bad focus or excessive exposure problems. But you can improve some exposure-related issues and white balance with Raw-processing software. You can use Sony's Image Data Converter software to view or edit Raw files, and you also can use other programs, such as Adobe Camera Raw, that have been updated to handle Raw files from this camera.

Using Raw can have disadvantages, also. The files take up a lot of storage space; Raw images taken with the RX100 III are about 20 MB in size, while Large JPEG images I have taken are between about 2 and 12 MB, depending on the settings used. Also, Raw files have to be processed on a computer; you can't take a Raw image and immediately send it by e-mail or print it; you first have to use software to convert it to JPEG, TIFF, or some other standard format for manipulating digital photographs. If you are pressed for time, you may not want to take that extra step. Finally, some features of the RX100 III are not available when you are using the Raw format, such as the Auto HDR, Picture Effect, and Digital Zoom menu options.

If you're undecided as to whether to use Raw or JPEG, you have the option of selecting Raw & JPEG, the second choice for the Quality menu item. With that setting, the camera records both a Raw and a JPEG image when you press the shutter button.

The advantage with that approach is that you have a Raw image with maximum quality and the ability to do extensive post-processing, and you also have a JPEG image that you can use for viewing, e-mailing, printing, and the like. Of course, this setting consumes storage space more quickly than saving your images in just Raw or JPEG format, and it can take the camera longer to store the images, so there may be a slowdown in the rate of continuous shooting, if you are using that option. You also cannot use some menu options that conflict with the Raw setting.

When you choose Raw & JPEG, you can select an Image Size setting that will apply only to the JPEG image; the Raw image, as noted earlier, is always at the maximum size. You cannot select a Quality setting for the JPEG image with the Raw & JPEG selection; the JPEG image will be fixed at the Fine setting.

The best bet for preserving the quality of your images and your options for post-processing and fixing exposure mistakes later is to choose Raw files. However, if you want to use features such as Sweep Panorama mode, some Scene mode types such as Anti Motion Blur, the Picture Effect menu option, and others, which are not available with Raw files, then choose JPEG. If you do choose JPEG, I strongly recommend that you choose the Large size and Extra Fine quality, unless you have an urgent need to conserve storage space on your memory card or on your computer. If you want Raw quality and are not concerned about storage space or speed of shooting, choose Raw & JPEG. However, you will still not be able to use Picture Effect and some other options.

Panorama Size and Panorama Direction

The next 2 commands on the Shooting menu are available only when the Mode dial is set to Sweep Panorama mode. I discussed these settings in Chapter 3, in connection with the discussion of that shooting mode. Note that when the Control ring is set to its Standard setting through the Custom menu, you can set the panorama direction by turning that ring (unless you are using manual focus or DMF, which take over the use of the ring). You also can change the direction by turning the Control wheel, regardless of the setting for the Control ring.

File Format

This final option on screen 1 of the Shooting menu is preceded by a movie-film icon, meaning it applies only for movies. I will discuss this option in Chapter 8. For now, you should know that XAVC S gives the highest quality but is available only if you are using a high-speed SD card with a size of 64 GB or larger or an equivalent Memory Stick card. The AVCHD option yields very high quality and MP4 gives somewhat lower quality but can be easier to work with for editing. I recommend that you choose AVCHD for most purposes, unless you have a reason to do otherwise.

Next, I will discuss the options on screen 2 of the Shooting menu, shown in Figure 4-16.

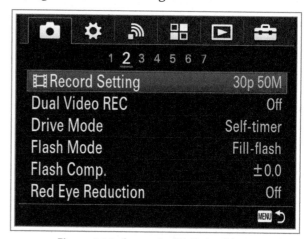

Figure 4-16. Screen 2 of Shooting Menu

Record Setting

This first option on screen 2 of the Shooting menu is related to the File Format option, discussed above. I will discuss the details of this option in Chapter 8. For now, if you want the highest quality for AVCHD video, choose the third option, 60p 28M (PS). (These options will be different if you choose XAVC S or MP4 for File Format. They also will be different if you have a 50i version of the camera, as sold in Europe and some other locations.)

Dual Video Recording

This next option is somewhat like a video version of the RAW & JPEG setting. When it is turned on, the camera records a video simultaneously in 2 formats: either XAVC S and MP4, or AVCHD and MP4. I recommend leaving this option turned off unless you have a specific reason to need it. I will discuss it further in Chapter 8. There are some limitations on this setting, which I will also discuss in Chapter 8.

Drive Mode

This next option on screen 2 of the Shooting menu gives you access to the continuous-shooting and related features of the RX100 III, a powerful set of capabilities for shooting bursts of images, bracketing exposures, and using the self-timer. You can also get access to this menu option by pressing the Drive Mode button (Left button), as discussed in Chapter 5.

When you highlight this option and press the Center button, a menu appears at the left of the screen as shown in Figure 4-17, with 9 choices represented by icons: Single Shooting, Continuous Shooting, Speed Priority Continuous Shooting, Self-timer, Self-timer (Continuous), Continuous Exposure Bracketing, Single Exposure Bracketing, White Balance Bracketing, and DRO Bracketing. (You have to scroll down to see the last 5 choices.)

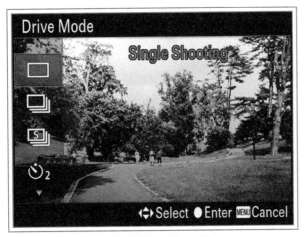

Figure 4-17. Drive Mode Menu

Details for each of these Drive Mode settings are discussed below.

SINGLE SHOOTING

This is the normal mode for shooting still images. Select this top choice on the Drive Mode menu to turn off all continuous shooting. In some cases, having one of the continuous-shooting options selected will make it impossible to make other settings, such as Soft Skin Effect or Long Exposure Noise Reduction. If you find you cannot make a certain setting, try selecting single

shooting to see if that removes the conflict and fixes the problem.

As noted earlier, this option is not available with the Sports Action setting of Scene mode.

CONTINUOUS SHOOTING

Continuous shooting, sometimes called burst shooting, is useful in many contexts, from shooting an action sequence at a sporting event to taking a series of shots of a portrait subject to capture changing facial expressions. I often use this setting for street photography to increase my chances of catching an interesting scene.

The Continuous Shooting option is the first of 2 types of burst shooting available with the RX100 III. With this setting, whose icon is highlighted in Figure 4-18, the camera shoots continuously when you hold down the shutter button.

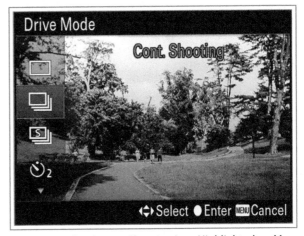

Figure 4-18. Continuous Shooting Icon Highlighted on Menu

If you have Focus Mode set to single autofocus, the camera will not adjust its focus during the burst of shots. But, if you set the focus mode to AF-C for continuous autofocus, the camera will adjust focus for each shot. As you can imagine, this focusing may not be exact because of motion by the subject, the camera, or both, but the camera will try to re-focus while the burst continues.

If you want the camera to adjust its exposure during the series of continuous shots, you need to go to screen 3 of the Custom menu and check the setting of the AEL w/ Shutter menu item. If that item is set to On, the camera will lock exposure when you press the shutter button, and exposure will be locked throughout the burst as it was set for the first image, even if lighting changes dramatically. However, if you set AEL w/Shutter to Off, then the camera will adjust its exposure as needed during the burst of shots. If you set AEL w/Shutter to Auto, then the camera will adjust exposure during continuous shooting if Focus Mode is set to continuous autofocus. If it is set to single autofocus, then the camera will keep the exposure locked.

Depending on conditions such as image size and quality, lighting, settings for autofocus and autoexposure lock, and the speed of the memory card, the rate of burst shooting can vary considerably. With optimal conditions, the camera can shoot at between 2.5 and 3.5 frames per second (fps) using this setting until the memory buffer fills up. Then the rate slows to about 1.5 fps. When shooting with Quality set to Raw & JPEG, I found that the shooting speed slowed down after about 35 shots. When shooting with lower Quality settings, the camera was able to take substantially more shots before slowing down. For example, with Quality set to Extra Fine, the camera fired off almost 100 shots before slowing down.

Although you can turn on the flash when the Continuous Shooting option is selected, and the camera will actually take a series of shots with flash as you hold down the shutter button, the time between shots may be several seconds because the flash cannot recycle quickly enough to take a rapid series of shots.

The speed of this first continuous-shooting mode is not very great compared to that of the Speed Priority option, discussed below. However, being able to take a stream of shots with focus adjusted for each one can be worth the reduction in speed when your subject is moving or when you need to focus on moving subjects or subjects at varying distances.

SPEED PRIORITY CONTINUOUS SHOOTING

To shoot a series of images at the fastest rate possible, choose the Speed Priority Continuous Shooting option, highlighted in Figure 4-19. With this setting, the camera captures images at a rate up to about 10 fps. The trade-off for speed is that the camera will not adjust focus between shots, even if you set the focus mode to continuous autofocus.

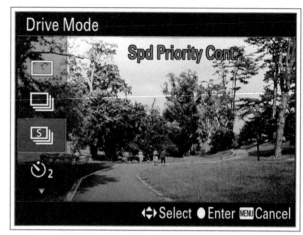

Figure 4-19. Speed Priority Continuous Shooting Icon Highlighted

As with the standard Continuous Shooting setting, with Speed Priority the camera will adjust exposure for each shot if the AEL w/Shutter menu option is set to Off; if that menu option is set to On, the camera will lock the exposure with the first shot and will not adjust it for the remaining shots. With the Auto setting, it will adjust exposure if continuous AF is turned on, though, as noted, the camera will not adjust focus between shots.

As with normal continuous shooting, various factors including the Quality setting affect the shooting rate of the Speed Priority setting. When I used my fastest memory card and set the camera to take either Raw & JPEG or just Raw shots, the continuous shooting slowed to a pace of less than 1 fps after an initial high-speed burst of about 25 shots. As with the standard Continuous Shooting option, using the flash slows down the shooting drastically. Also, using slower memory cards has a noticeable impact on the speed of continuous shooting.

After taking a burst of shots, it can take the camera a while to save them to the memory card. You can't use the menu system or play back existing shots until the data has been saved, although you can take additional shots. There is an access lamp that lights up in red while the camera is writing to the card, but you cannot readily see it. It is inside the battery compartment near the edge of the camera, as shown in Figure 2-8. While that light is illuminated, be sure not to remove the battery or the memory card.

Figure 4-20 includes a series of images I took using continuous shooting, to illustrate how rapidly the camera can fire its shutter with the burst settings. The camera captured several clear images of a blue jay as it adjusted its position on a railing.

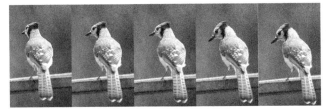

Figure 4-20. Composite Image with Burst of Continuous Shots

SELF-TIMER

The next icon down on the menu of Drive Mode options represents the self-timer, as shown in Figure 4-21.

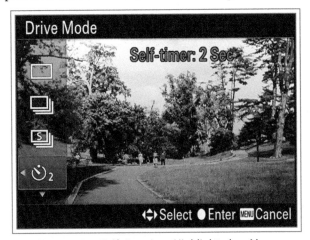

Figure 4-21. Self-timer Icon Highlighted on Menu

The self-timer is useful when you need to be the photographer and also appear in a group photograph. You can place the RX100 III on a tripod, set the timer for 10 seconds, and insert yourself into the group before the shutter clicks. The self-timer also is helpful when you don't want to cause blur by jiggling the camera as you press the shutter button. For example, when you're taking a macro shot very close to the subject, focusing can be critical, and any bump to the camera could cause motion blur. Using the self-timer gives the camera a chance to settle down after the shutter button is pressed, before the image is recorded.

Once you select the self-timer option, you are presented with 2 choices: 10 seconds and 2 seconds. When the self-timer option is highlighted, press the Left or Right button on the Control wheel to choose between these options. After you make this selection, the self-timer icon will appear in the upper left corner of the display with the chosen number of seconds (10 or 2) displayed next to the icon, as shown in Figure 4-22. (If you don't

see the icon, press the Display button until the screen with the various shooting icons appears.)

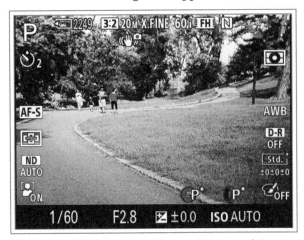

Figure 4-22. Self-timer Icon in Upper Left Corner of Shooting Screen

Once the self-timer is set, when you press the shutter button to take a picture, the timer will count down for the specified number of seconds and then take the picture. The reddish lamp on the front of the camera will blink, and the camera will beep during the countdown.

SELF-TIMER (CONTINUOUS)

The next item down on the Drive Mode menu, shown in Figure 4-23, gives you another variation on the self-timer.

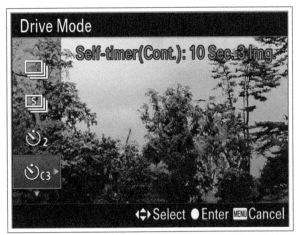

Figure 4-23. Self-timer Continuous Icon Highlighted on Menu

In this case, the menu option lets you set the timer to take multiple shots after the timer counts down. The delay for this timer is set at 10 seconds and cannot be changed. Using the Left and Right buttons, you can set the camera to take either 3 or 5 shots after the delay. This option can be useful when you are taking a group photo; when a series of shots is taken, you increase your chances of getting at least one shot in which everyone is looking at the camera and smiling. You can choose any settings you want for Image Size and Quality, including Raw & JPEG, and you will still get 3 or 5 rapidly fired shots, though the speed of the shooting will decrease slightly at the highest Quality settings. You cannot use the Continuous AF setting for Focus Mode with this option.

CONTINUOUS EXPOSURE BRACKETING

This next option on the Drive Mode menu, shown in Figure 4-24, sets the camera to take 3 or 5 images with one press of the shutter button but with a different exposure level for each image, giving you a greater chance of having one image that is properly exposed.

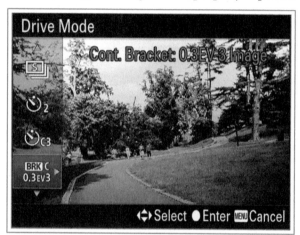

Figure 4-24. Exposure Bracket Icon Highlighted

When you highlight this option, you will see a horizontal triangle indicating that, using the Left and Right buttons, you can select one of 10 combinations of the difference in exposure value and the number of images in the bracket. These choices include exposure value (EV) intervals of 0.3, 0.7, 1.0, 2.0, or 3.0 EV, each with a bracket of either 3 or 5 exposures. The decimal numbers represent the difference in EV among the multiple (3 or 5) exposures that the camera will take.

For example, if you select 0.7 EV as the interval for 3 exposures, the camera will take 3 shots—one at the metered exposure level; one at a level 0.7 EV (or stop) below that, resulting in a darker image; and one at a level 0.7 EV above that, resulting in a brighter image. If you want the maximum exposure difference among the shots, select 3.0 EV as the interval for the 3 or 5 shots.

Once you have set this option as you want it and composed your scene, press and hold the shutter button and the camera will take the 3 or 5 shots in rapid succession while you hold down the button.

If you set this option for 3 exposures, the first one will be at the metered value, the second one underexposed by the selected interval, and the third one overexposed to the same extent. If you set it for 5 exposures, the first 3 shots will have the values noted above, the fourth will have the most negative EV, and the fifth will have the most positive EV. (You can change this order using the Bracket Order menu option, discussed in Chapter 7.)

If you pop up the flash and set it to fire, using the Fill-flash setting for example, the flash will fire for each of the bracketed shots and the exposure will be varied, but you have to press the shutter button for each shot, after the flash has recycled. (The orange dot to the right of the flash icon on the screen shows when the flash is ready to fire again.)

You can use exposure compensation, in which case the camera will use the image with exposure compensation as the base level, and then take exposures that deviate under and over the exposure of the image with exposure compensation.

When ISO is set to Auto, the camera adjusts the ISO setting to achieve the different exposure levels for the multiple images. If ISO is set to a specific value, the camera varies the shutter speeds for the multiple shots.

SINGLE EXPOSURE BRACKETING

The next option is similar to the previous one, except that, with this selection, you have to press the shutter button for each shot; the camera will not take multiple shots while you hold down the shutter button. You have the same 10 choices for combinations of EV intervals and numbers of exposures. You might want to choose this option when you need to pause between shots for some reason, such as if you are using a model who needs to have some costume or makeup adjustments for each exposure. It also could be useful if you want to look at the resulting image after each shot to see if you need to make further adjustments to your settings.

Apart from requiring individual shutter presses, this option works the same as continuous exposure bracketing. For example, you can use flash and you can change the order of the exposures using the Bracket Order menu option.

None of the bracketing options—exposure, white balance, or DRO—is available in the Intelligent Auto, Superior Auto, Scene, Sweep Panorama, or Movie shooting mode.

WHITE BALANCE BRACKETING

The next option on the Drive Mode menu, White Balance Bracket, whose icon is highlighted in Figure 4-25, works the same way as Exposure Bracket, except that only 3 images can be taken and the value that is varied for the 3 shots is white balance rather than exposure.

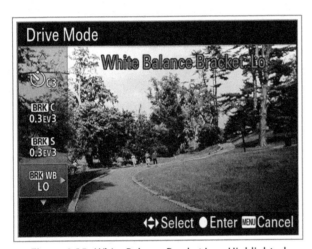

Figure 4-25. White Balance Bracket Icon Highlighted

Using the Left and Right buttons, select either Lo or Hi for the amount of deviation from the normal white balance setting. Then, when you press the shutter button (you don't have to hold it down), the camera will take a series of 3 shots—one at the normal setting; the next one with a lower color temperature, resulting in a "cooler," more-bluish image; and the last one with a higher color temperature, resulting in a "warmer," more-reddish image. When you use this form of bracketing, unlike exposure bracketing, you will hear only one shutter sound because the camera takes just one image, with one quick shutter press, and then electronically creates the other 2 exposures with the different white balance values.

You can change the order of the exposures using the Bracket Order option on screen 3 of the Custom menu.

DRO BRACKETING

This final option on the Drive Mode menu, whose icon is shown in Figure 4-26, sets the RX100 III to take a series of 3 shots at different settings of the DRO (dynamic range optimizer) option.

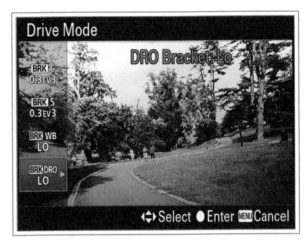

Figure 4-26. DRO Bracket Icon Highlighted

I'll discuss DRO later in this chapter. Essentially, DRO alters the RX100 III's image processing to even out the contrast between shadowed and bright areas. It can be difficult to decide how much DRO processing to use, and this option gives you a way to experiment with several different settings before you decide on the amount of DRO for your final image.

As with White Balance Bracket, you can select between Hi and Lo for the DRO interval. Also, as with White Balance Bracket, you only need to press the shutter button once, briefly; the camera will record the 3 different exposures electronically. The order of these exposures is not affected by the Bracket Order menu option.

Flash Mode

In Chapter 2, I discussed the use of the RX100 III's built-in flash, which is controlled with the Flash Mode menu option. As I discussed earlier, that option can be reached by pressing the Flash button, which is the Right button on the Control wheel. Flash Mode also is the fourth option on screen 2 of the Shooting menu.

There are 5 options on the Flash Mode menu—Flash Off, Autoflash, Fill-flash, Slow Sync, and Rear Sync—the first 4 of which are shown in Figure 4-27.

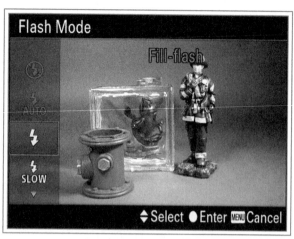

Figure 4-27. Flash Mode Menu

There is no shooting mode in which all 5 options are available. Here is a brief summary of the options I discussed in Chapter 2, followed by a discussion of the ones I did not discuss there.

FLASH OFF

To make sure the flash will not fire, choose Flash Off. This is a good choice when you are in a museum or other place where it would be inappropriate for the flash to fire, or when you know you will not be using flash. It also can be helpful to avoid depleting a battery that is running low. This option is available in the Intelligent Auto and Superior Auto modes and with the Portrait, Sports Action, Macro, Landscape, Sunset, Pet, and Gourmet settings of Scene mode. Of course, with the RX100 III you also have the option of just not popping up the flash with the flash release switch, which will have the same effect as using this Flash Mode option.

AUTOFLASH

When you select Autoflash, you are leaving it up to the camera to decide whether to fire the flash. The camera will analyze the lighting and other aspects of the scene and decide whether to use the flash without any further input from you. This selection is available only in the Intelligent Auto and Superior Auto modes, and with the Portrait and Macro settings of Scene mode.

FILL-FLASH

With Fill-flash, you are making a decision to use flash no matter what the lighting conditions are. If you choose this option, the flash will fire every time you press the shutter button, if the flash is popped up. This is the setting to use when the sun is shining and you

need to soften shadows on a subject's face, or when you need to correct the lighting when a subject is backlit.

For example, for Figure 4-28, I took 2 shots of a mannequin outdoors: one using Flash Off (left image) and one using Fill-flash (right image). Although the differences between the images are not that dramatic, you probably can see that the image on the right, for which flash was used, has additional highlights on the mannequin's hair and lips, and that the skin tone is slightly altered.

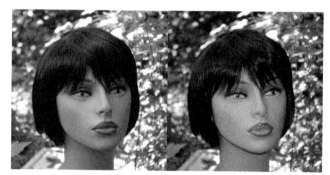

Figure 4-28. Left: No Flash, Right: Fill-flash

With this option, the camera uses what could be called "Front Sync," as opposed to Rear Sync, the final option on the Flash Mode menu, discussed later in this section. Fill-flash is available in all shooting modes except Movie and Sweep Panorama, and the following Scene mode settings: Night Scene, Hand-held Twilight, Night Portrait, Anti Motion Blur, Fireworks, and High Sensitivity.

SLOW SYNC

Slow Sync is one of the settings I did not discuss in detail in Chapter 2. This option is designed for use when you are taking a flash photograph of a subject at night or in dim lighting. With this setting, the camera uses a relatively slow shutter speed so the ambient (natural) lighting will have time to register on the image. In other words, if you're in a fairly dark environment and fire the flash normally, it will likely light up the subject (such as a person), but because the exposure time is short, the surrounding scene may be black. If you use the Slow Sync setting, the slower shutter speed allows the surrounding scene to be visible also.

I took the 2 images in Figure 4-29 with identical room lighting and camera settings, except that I took the top image with the flash set to Fill-flash and exposure set to f/7.1 at 1/30 second, and I took the bottom image with the flash set to Slow Sync, resulting in an exposure at f/7.1 for 1.3 second.

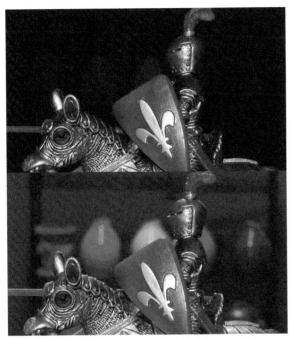

Figure 4-29. Top: Fill-flash, 1/30 sec., Bottom: Slow Sync, 1.3 sec.

In the top image, the flash illuminated the knight figure in the foreground, but the background is dark. In the bottom image, the objects behind the knight are illuminated by ambient light because of the much slower shutter speed.

When you use the Slow Sync setting, you should plan to use a tripod because the camera may choose a very slow shutter speed, in the range of 3 seconds or even longer. Also, note that you can choose Slow Sync even when the camera is set to Shutter Priority mode. If you do so, you should select a slow shutter speed because the whole point of this setting is to use a slow shutter speed to light the background with ambient light. If you set the camera to Shutter Priority mode, you can decide precisely which shutter speed to use, but it would not make sense to select a relatively fast speed, such as, say, 1/30 second. The same considerations apply for Manual exposure mode; the camera also will let you select Slow Sync for the Flash Mode setting in that shooting mode.

The Slow Sync setting is available only in the Program, Aperture Priority, Shutter Priority, and Manual exposure modes. With the Night Portrait setting of Scene mode, Slow Sync is set by the camera and cannot be changed.

REAR SYNC

The last setting on the Flash Mode menu is Rear Sync. You should not need this option unless you encounter the particular situation it is designed for. If you don't activate this setting (that is, if you select any other flash mode in which the flash fires), the camera uses the unnamed default setting, which could be called "Front Sync." In that case, the flash fires very soon after the shutter opens to expose the image. If you choose the Rear Sync setting instead, the flash fires later—just before the shutter closes.

The reason for using Rear Sync is to help avoid a strange-looking result in some situations. This issue arises, for example, with a relatively long exposure, say one-half second, of a subject with lights, such as a car or motorcycle at night, moving across your field of view. With normal (Front) sync, the flash will fire early in the process, freezing the vehicle in a clear image. However, as the shutter remains open while the vehicle keeps going, the camera will capture the moving lights in a stream extending in front of the vehicle. If, instead, you use Rear Sync, the initial part of the exposure will capture the lights in a trail that appears behind the vehicle, while the vehicle itself is not frozen by the flash until later in the exposure. With Rear Sync in this particular situation, if the lights in question are taillights that look more natural behind the vehicle, the final image is likely to look more natural than with the Front Sync (default) setting.

The images in Figure 4-30 illustrate this concept using a remote-controlled model truck with a taillight. I took both pictures using the built-in flash, using an exposure of 0.5 second. In the top image, using the normal (Fill-flash) setting, the flash fired quickly, and the light beam continued on during the long exposure to make the streaks of bright light appear in front of the truck.

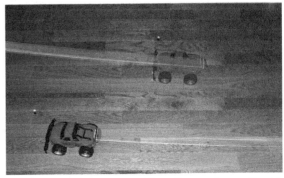

Figure 4-30. Top Image: Normal Sync, Bottom Image: Rear Sync

In the bottom image, using Rear Sync, the flash did not fire until the truck had traveled to the left, overtaking the place where the lights had made their streaks visible. If you are trying to convey a sense of natural motion, the Rear Sync setting, as seen here, is likely to give you better results than the default setting.

A good general rule is to use Rear Sync only when you have a definite need for it. Using this option makes it harder to compose and set up the shot because you have to anticipate where the main subject will be when the flash finally fires late in the exposure process. But, in the relatively rare situations when it is useful, Rear Sync can make a dramatic difference. Rear Sync is available in the more advanced shooting modes: Program, Aperture Priority, Shutter Priority, and Manual exposure.

Flash Compensation

This menu item lets you control the output of the camera's built-in flash unit. This function works similarly to exposure compensation, which is available by pressing the Down button in the more advanced shooting modes. (Exposure compensation is discussed in Chapter 5.) The difference between the 2 options is that flash compensation varies only the brightness of the light emitted by the flash, while exposure compensation varies the overall exposure of a given shot, whether or not flash is used.

Flash compensation is useful when you want to use flash but don't want the subject overwhelmed with light. I often use this setting when I am shooting a portrait outdoors with the Fill-flash setting to reduce shadows on the subject. With a bit of negative flash compensation, I can keep the flash from overexposing the image.

To use this option, highlight it on the menu screen and press the Center button, then, on the next screen, shown in Figure 4-31, press the Left and Right buttons or turn the Control wheel to set the amount of positive or negative compensation you want. Whenever the flash unit is popped up, an icon will appear in the upper right corner of the display showing the amount of flash compensation in effect, even if it is zero, as shown in Figure 4-32.

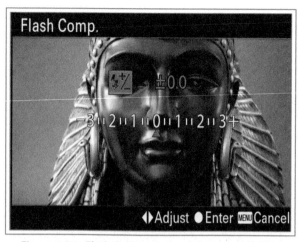

Figure 4-31. Flash Compensation Adjustment Screen

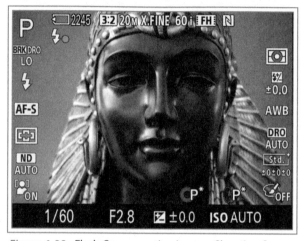

Figure 4-32. Flash Compensation Icon on Shooting Screen

Be careful to set the value back to zero when you are done with the setting, because any setting you make will stay in place even after the camera has been powered off and back on again. Note, also, that the Flash Compensation option is not available on the menu in the Auto, Scene, or Sweep Panorama modes.

Red Eye Reduction

This final option on screen 2 of the Shooting menu lets you set up the RX100 III's flash to combat "red-eye"— the eerie red glow in human eyes that appears in images when on-camera flash lights up the blood vessels on the retinas. This menu item can be set to either On or Off. If it is turned on, then, whenever the flash is used, it fires a few times before the actual flash that illuminates the image. The pre-flashes cause the subject's pupils to narrow, reducing the ability of the later, full flash to bounce off the retinas and produce the unwanted red glow in the eyes.

I prefer to leave this option turned off and deal with any red-eye effects using editing software. However, if you will be taking flash photos at a party, you may want to use this menu option to minimize the occurrence of red-eye effects in the first place.

Figure 4-33 shows the options on screen 3 of the Shooting menu.

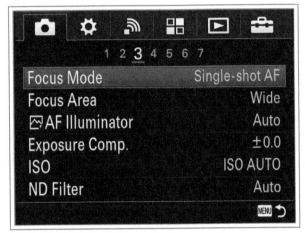

Figure 4-33. Screen 3 of Shooting Menu

Focus Mode

The Focus Mode option gives you 4 choices for the method the camera uses for focusing. This is one of the more important choices you can make for your photography. Following are details about each of the 4 selections, which are shown in Figure 4-34.

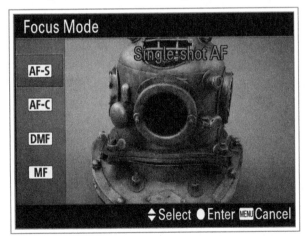

Figure 4-34. Focus Mode Menu Options Screen

SINGLE-SHOT AF

The first option on the Focus Mode menu is Single-shot AF, indicated by the AF-S icon. With this option, the camera tries to focus on the scene the camera is

aimed at, using the focus area that is selected using the Focus Area menu option, discussed below. If the Pre-AF option on screen 2 of the Custom menu is turned on, the camera will continuously adjust focus, even before you press the shutter button halfway down. When you do press the button halfway down, the camera will lock in the focus and keep it locked as long as you keep the button pressed halfway.

If the Pre-AF menu option is not turned on, then the camera will not make any attempt to adjust focus until you press the shutter button halfway down.

Once you press the shutter button halfway down, you will see one or more green focus brackets on the screen indicating the point or points where the camera achieved sharp focus, as shown in Figure 4-35, and you will hear a beep. In addition, a green disc in the lower left corner of the display will light up steadily indicating that focus is confirmed. If focus cannot be achieved, the green disc will blink and no focus brackets will appear on the screen.

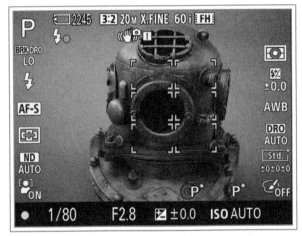

Figure 4-35. Green Focus Brackets on Display

Once you have pressed the shutter button halfway to lock focus, you can use the locked focus on a different subject that is at the same distance as the one the camera originally locked its focus on. For example, if you have focused on a person at a distance of 15 feet (4.6 m), and then you decide you want to include another person or object in the scene, once you have locked the focus on the first person by pressing the shutter button halfway down, you can move the camera to include the other person or object in the scene as long as you keep the camera at about the same distance from the subject. The focus will remain locked at that distance until you press the shutter button the rest of the way down to take the picture.

Continuous AF

The next option for Focus Mode, Continuous AF, is designated by the AF-C icon on the menu. With this option, as with Single-shot AF, the RX100 III focuses continuously before you press the shutter button if the Pre-AF menu option is turned on. If that option is turned off, the camera does not adjust focus until you press the shutter button halfway.

The difference with this mode is that the camera does not lock in the focus when you press the shutter button halfway. Instead, the focus will continue to be adjusted if the subject moves or the distance to the subject changes through camera motion. You will not hear a beep or see any focus brackets to confirm focus. Instead, the green disc in the lower left corner of the display will change its appearance to show the focus status.

If the green disc is surrounded by curved lines, as shown in Figure 4-36, that means focus is currently sharp but is subject to adjustment if needed.

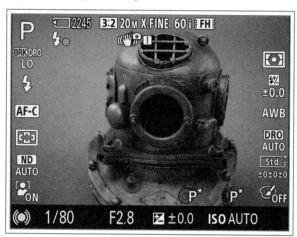

Figure 4-36. Green Focus Disc with Curves

If only the curved lines appear, as shown in Figure 4-37, that means the camera is still trying to achieve focus. If the green disc flashes, that means the camera is having trouble focusing. This focusing mode can be useful when you are shooting a moving subject. With this option, you can get the RX100 III to fix its focus on the subject, but you won't have to let up the shutter button to refocus; instead, you can hold the button down halfway until the instant when you take the picture. In this way, you may save some time, rather than having to keep starting the focus and exposure process over by pressing the shutter button halfway again.

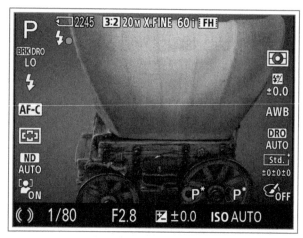

Figure 4-37. Green Curves Showing Focus Being Adjusted

DMF

The third option for Focus Mode is DMF, which stands for direct manual focus. This feature lets you use a combination of autofocus and manual focus. One area in which DMF can be helpful is when you are shooting an extreme closeup of a small object, when focus can be critical and hard to achieve. You can choose the DMF feature, and start the focusing process by pressing the shutter button halfway down. The camera will make its best attempt to focus sharply using the autofocus mechanism. Then you can use the camera's manual focusing mechanism (turning the Control ring, as discussed below in this section) to fine-tune the focus, concentrating on the parts of the subject that you want to be most sharply focused.

Another time DMF can be useful is when you are shooting a scene with objects at varying distances and you want to focus on one of the more distant ones. In this case, you can start out using manual focus, adjusting it for the most important object to let the camera know which item to focus on. Then you can press the shutter button halfway to let the camera take over and use autofocus to improve the sharpness of the focus.

When DMF is activated, you can turn on the Peaking Level feature on the Custom menu, as discussed below, and it will function for autofocus as well as for manual focus. In addition, you can use the MF Assist feature with DMF. That feature is discussed below in connection with manual focus. If you use MF Assist with DMF, you have to hold the shutter button halfway down while turning the Control ring to focus.

MANUAL FOCUS

The final selection on the Focus Mode menu, Manual Focus, is another important option. As I indicated above in the discussion of DMF, there are various situations in which you may achieve sharper focus by adjusting it according to your own judgment rather than by relying on the camera's autofocus system. Those situations include shooting extreme closeups; shooting a group of objects at differing distances; or shooting through a barrier such as a wire fence.

Also, manual focus gives you the freedom to use a soft focus effect purposely. As I will discuss later in this chapter, the RX100 III includes a setting on the Picture Effect menu called "Soft Focus," which imparts a pleasing softness to your image. If you would rather achieve this sort of effect on your own by controlling the focusing directly, you can set the camera for manual focus and defocus all or part of the subject in precisely the way you want.

Using manual focus with the RX100 III is a pleasure because of the way the controls are set up. All you have to do is turn the Control ring—the large ring around the lens, next to the camera's body. This action is quite intuitive, and it is similar to the way most lenses were focused in the days before autofocus existed.

In addition, there are several functions available to assist with your manual focusing. I will discuss those menu options in Chapter 7, but I will briefly describe these focus aids here because you may need them when focusing manually.

The first option, MF Assist, is turned on or off through the second option on screen 1 of the Custom menu. When MF Assist is turned on, then, whenever you start turning the Control ring to adjust focus in manual focus mode, the image on the display is magnified 8.6 times, as shown in Figure 4-38, so you can more clearly check the focus.

Once the magnified image is displayed, if you press the Center button, the image is magnified further to 17.1 times normal. Press the Center button again to return to the 8.6-times view and press the shutter button halfway to return the display to normal size. You can adjust how long the magnified display stays on the screen using the Focus Magnifier Time option, which is directly below MF Assist on the Custom menu. I prefer

to set the time to No Limit, so the magnification does not disappear just as I am getting the focus adjusted as I want it. With the No Limit setting, the magnification remains on the screen until you dismiss it by pressing the shutter button halfway.

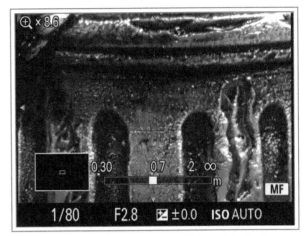

Figure 4-38. Enlarged Screen with MF Assist Option

If you don't want the camera to enlarge the image as soon as you start focusing, you can use the Focus Magnifier option instead of MF Assist. You can activate Focus Magnifier through screen 4 of the Shooting menu or you can assign it to a control button using the Custom Key Settings option on screen 4 of the Custom menu. You can set the Custom, Center, Left, or Right button to activate the Focus Magnifier option.

Once the Focus Magnifier option is activated, an orange frame appears on the screen, as seen in Figure 4-39.

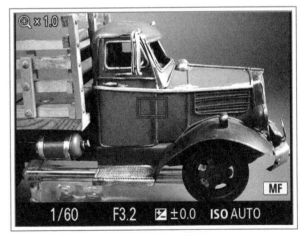

Figure 4-39. Orange Focus Magnifier Frame on Screen

You can move that frame around the screen using the Control wheel or the direction buttons. The frame represents the area of the scene that will be magnified when you press the Center button. By pressing the

Center button, you can switch magnification to various levels.

You can use both MF Assist and Focus Magnifier, though I see no need to do so. My preference is to use only the MF Assist option, which is sufficient for my needs. I prefer not to go through the steps to turn on the Focus Magnifier option, which does not add that much to the focusing options. However, when I am faced with a challenging task such as shooting in dim lighting, I sometimes use the Focus Magnifier option because it is easier to deal with that situation by being able to see the subject clearly at its normal size before using magnification.

The RX100 III provides one more aid to manual focusing, called Peaking Level, the second item on screen 2 of the Custom menu. That option can be turned off, or it can be set to Low, Mid, or High. When Peaking Level is turned on, then, when you are using manual focus, the camera places bright lines around the areas of the image that it judges to be in focus, as shown in Figure 4-40 (without Peaking) and Figure 4-41 (with Peaking set to Mid).

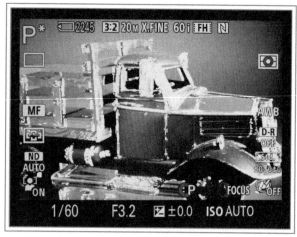
Figure 4-41. Peaking Example: Peaking Level Mid

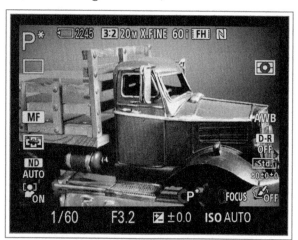
Figure 4-40. Peaking Example: Peaking Level Off

Besides setting the intensity of this display, you can set its color—white, red, or yellow—using the Peaking Color option on the Custom menu. I initially did not find much benefit from using Peaking, but as I have worked with it more, I have found it especially useful in dark conditions because the Peaking effect contrasts with the dark display. Also, as noted above, Peaking works with both the autofocus and manual focus aspects of the DMF option. I will discuss Peaking further in Chapter 7.

Finally, there is another way to customize the use of manual focus with the RX100 III. On screen 4 of the Custom menu, as noted above, you can assign the Custom, Center, Left, or Right button to control any one of a long list of functions. One of those functions, called AF/MF Control Toggle, is useful if you need to switch back and forth between autofocus and manual focus on frequent occasions. When this function is assigned to a button, you can press the button to switch instantly between these 2 focus modes. This is so much more convenient than going back to the Shooting menu and using the Focus Mode menu option, that it may be worthwhile giving up a button to this use.

Focus Area

The second option on this menu screen, Focus Area, lets you choose what area the camera focuses on when using autofocus. This option is applicable when the camera uses single autofocus, continuous autofocus, or direct manual focus.

The choices for Focus Area, as shown in Figure 4-42, are, from top to bottom, Wide, Center, Flexible Spot, and Lock-on AF. The ways these selections operate vary somewhat depending on whether you select single autofocus or continuous autofocus for the Focus Mode option. If you select direct manual focus, you can use autofocus in the same way as with single autofocus, so DMF is the same as single autofocus with respect to Focus Area.

I will discuss the following options assuming at first that you are using single autofocus or direct manual focus as your focus mode.

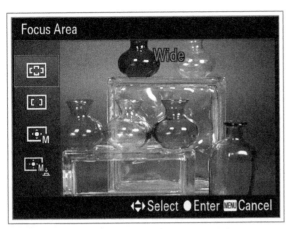

Figure 4-42. Focus Area Menu Options Screen

WIDE

With Wide, the RX100 III uses 25 focus zones and tries to detect one or more items within the scene to focus on based on their locations. When it has achieved sharp focus on one or more items, the camera displays a green frame indicating the focus point. You may see one or several green frames, depending on how many objects are at the same distance. An example with multiple objects is shown in Figure 4-43.

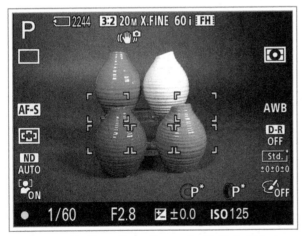

Figure 4-43. Green Focus Frames for Multiple Objects

If the camera has difficulty picking out a subject to focus on, it will display a larg, broken green frame around the whole image, as shown in Figure 4-44. When you are using single autofocus, the Wide option is excellent for general shots of landscapes, buildings, and the like.

In continuous autofocus mode, the RX100 III does not display any focus frame with the Wide setting. The camera tries to keep its focus on the subjects that appear to be the main ones. I don't recommend using Wide

for Focus Area with continuous autofocus unless you are focusing on a single, clearly defined subject, so the camera will be able to maintain focus on the proper area.

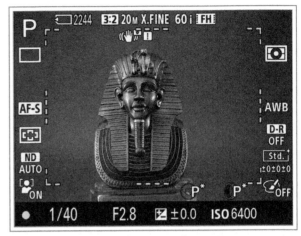

Figure 4-44. Large Dotted Focus Frame

CENTER

If you select Center for the Focus Area setting, the camera places a black focus frame in the center of the display, as shown in Figure 4-45, and focuses on whatever it finds within that frame.

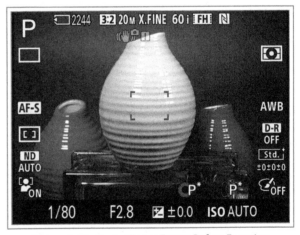

Figure 4-45. Center Focus Frame Before Focusing

When you press the shutter halfway, if the camera can focus it will beep and the frame will turn green, as shown in Figure 4-46. This option is useful for an object in the center of the scene. Even if you need to focus on an off-center object, though, you can use this setting. To focus on an object at the right, center that object in the focus frame and press the shutter button halfway to lock focus. Keeping the button pressed halfway, move the camera so the object is on the right, and press the button to take the picture.

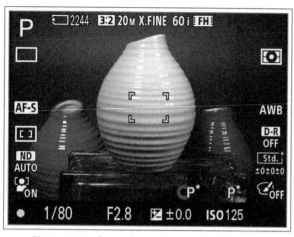

Figure 4-46. Center Focus Frame After Focusing

If you turn on continuous autofocus with the Center setting, the camera still will display a black focus frame. When you press the shutter button halfway, the frame will turn green when focus is sharp. As the camera or subject moves, the camera will continue to re-focus as you hold the shutter button halfway. You can use this technique to carry out your own focus tracking, by moving the camera to keep the center frame targeted on a moving subject.

FLEXIBLE SPOT

The Flexible Spot option gives you the most control over the focus area, with a frame you can move around the screen and re-size. When you highlight this option on the Shooting menu, the camera displays the menu shown in Figure 4-47.

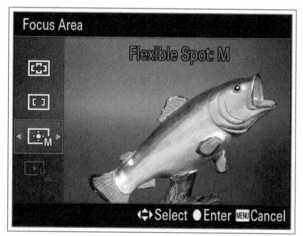

Figure 4-47. Flexible Spot Icon Highlighted

On this screen, press the Right or Left button to select the size of the Flexible Spot focus frame: L, M, or S, for Large, Medium, or Small. After choosing a size, press the Center button and you will see a screen like that

in Figure 4-48, with an orange focus frame of that size with white arrows pointing to the 4 edges of the display.

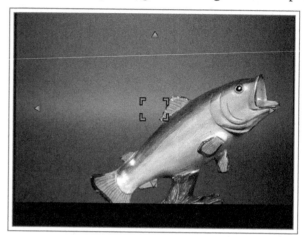

Figure 4-48. Flexible Spot Frame Ready to Move

Use the 4 direction buttons to move the frame around the display, and turn the Control wheel to change the frame's size. When the frame is located and sized as you want it, press the Center button to fix it in place. The camera will display a black frame of the chosen size in the chosen location. When you press the shutter button halfway to focus, the focus frame will turn green when focus is sharp, as shown in Figure 4-49.

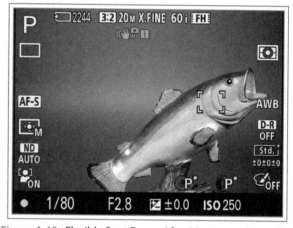

Figure 4-49. Flexible Spot Frame After Moving and Focusing

This frame operates the same way as the frame for the Center option, except for the ability to change the location and size. To return the frame quickly to the center of the screen, press the Custom (Delete) button while the frame is activated for moving, and it will move back to the center of the display.

This option is useful for focusing on a particular point, such as an object at the far right, without having to move the camera to place a focus frame over that object. This might be the situation if you are using a tripod, for example, and need to set up the shot with precision, focusing on an off-center subject. If the subject is small, using the smallest focus frame can make the process even easier.

If you use continuous autofocus, the Flexible Spot option works the same way as the Center option, discussed above, but with the added ability to change the size and location of the frame.

One problem with the Flexible Spot menu option is that it can be cumbersome to move the frame again once you have fixed it in place. One way to do this is to select the Focus Area menu option and repeat all of the steps discussed above. There are a couple of quicker ways to move the frame, though.

The easiest way to do this is to go to screen 4 of the Custom menu and select the Custom Key Settings option. On the next screen, select Center Button, and assign the Standard setting to that button. Then, whenever Flexible Spot is in effect, just press the Center button on the shooting screen, and the screen for moving the focus frame will appear. You can quickly use the direction buttons to move the frame where you want it, or you can press the Custom (Delete) button to center it. You also can turn the Control wheel to change the size of the focus frame.

If you want to use the Center button for some other operation, you can assign Focus Area to the Custom, Left, or Right button using the Custom Key Settings menu option. Then, when you press the assigned button, the camera will display the menu for choosing the size of the Flexible Spot frame. Or, you can assign Focus Area to the Function menu, which is called up by pressing the Function button. I will discuss that menu in Chapter 7.

My preference is to assign the Standard setting to the Center button. Then, to move the focus frame, I just press that button and it is an easy matter to adjust the frame's location and size. I will discuss the Custom Key Settings options further in Chapter 7.

LOCK-ON AF

The final option for Focus Area is Lock-on AF, which sets up the camera to track a moving object. This option is available for selection only when Focus Mode is set to Continuous AF. When you highlight this option on the menu, as shown in Figure 4-50, the camera gives you

5 choices for the Lock-on focus frame: Wide, Center, Flexible Spot Small, Flexible Spot Medium, or Flexible Spot Large. These frames correspond to the other choices for Focus Area, discussed above, and they also include the Lock-on frame's ability to "lock on" to a subject and track it as it moves.

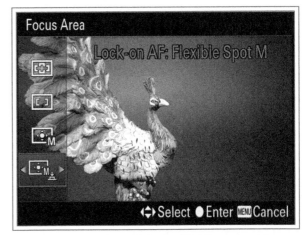

Figure 4-50. Lock-on AF Option Highlighted on Menu

After choosing one of these 5 frames, aim the camera at the subject, place the focus frame over it, and press the shutter button halfway. The camera will make an attempt to keep the subject within a double-bordered green frame as the subject moves. When you are ready to take the picture, press the shutter button all the way. If the autofocus system worked as expected, the image should be in focus. Of course, this process will not give good results if the subject moves too rapidly or erratically, or moves completely out of the frame. But, for subjects that are moving moderately in stable patterns, the Lock-on AF system is worth trying.

AF Illuminator

The AF Illuminator menu item gives you the option of disabling the use of the reddish lamp on the front of the camera for autofocusing. By default, this option is set to Auto, which means that when you are shooting in a dim area, the camera will turn on the lamp briefly if needed to light up the subject and assist the autofocus mechanism in gauging the distance to the subject. If you would rather make sure the light never comes on for that purpose—to avoid causing distractions in a museum or other sensitive area, or to avoid alerting a subject of candid photography—you can set this option to Off. In that case, the lamp will never light up for focusing assistance, though it will still illuminate if the self-timer is activated.

Exposure Compensation

This next option on the Shooting menu gives you a second way to adjust exposure compensation. As I discuss in Chapters 2 and 5, the primary way to adjust this option is by pressing the Down button, which has the exposure compensation icon, with its plus and minus signs, below it. However, when the camera is set to Manual exposure mode, the Down button is used to toggle the function of the Control wheel between adjusting aperture and adjusting shutter speed. Therefore, the Down button is not available for setting exposure compensation, and this menu option can be used for that purpose. (Another option is to assign exposure compensation to the Control ring or a control button using the Custom Key Settings menu option, as discussed in Chapter 7.)

When you use this menu option, there is no difference from the procedure when you press the Down button. Once the exposure compensation scale appears on the display, use the Left and Right buttons or the Control wheel to set the amount of positive or negative compensation, to make the image brighter or darker than it would be otherwise.

ISO

ISO is a measure of the sensor's sensitivity to light. When ISO is set to higher values, the camera's sensor needs less light to capture an image and the camera can use faster shutter speeds and narrower apertures. The problem with using higher values is that their use produces visual "noise" that can reduce the clarity and detail in your images, adding a grainy, textured appearance.

In practical terms, you should shoot with low ISO settings (around 125) when possible; shoot with high ISO settings (800 or higher) when necessary to allow a fast shutter speed to stop action and avoid motion blur, or when desired to achieve a creative effect with graininess.

With that background, here is how to set ISO on this camera. As is discussed in Chapters 5 and 7, with the RX100 III you can get quick access to certain important settings, such as ISO, using the Function menu, or, if you want, using the Custom, Center, Left, or Right button or the Control ring. However, you can also set

ISO from the Shooting menu, and you can get access to some additional ISO settings only from this menu. So, it's important to know how to use this menu item.

ISO is the fifth item on screen 3 of the Shooting menu. After you highlight it, press the Center button to bring up the vertical ISO menu at the left of the screen, as seen in Figure 4-51.

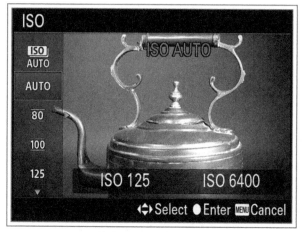

Figure 4-51. ISO Menu

Scroll through the options by turning the Control wheel or by pressing the Up and Down buttons to select a value ranging from one of the top 2 options— Multi Frame Noise Reduction and Auto ISO—through 80, 100, 125, 160, 200, and other specific values, to a maximum of 12800 at the bottom of the scale. (If you want to use an ISO value higher than 12800, you need to use the Multi Frame Noise Reduction feature, discussed below, or the High Sensitivity setting of Scene mode, discussed in Chapter 3.)

If you choose Auto ISO (the second option on the menu, highlighted in Figure 4-51), the camera will select a numerical value automatically depending on the lighting conditions. One helpful feature of the RX100 III is that you can select both the minimum and maximum levels for Auto ISO. In other words, you can set the camera to choose the ISO value automatically within a defined range such as, say, ISO 200 to ISO 1600. In that way, you can be assured that the camera will not select a value outside that range, but you will still leave some flexibility for the setting.

To set minimum and maximum values, while the orange highlight is on the Auto ISO option, press the Right button to move the highlight to the right side of the screen, where there are 2 rectangles that are labeled (when highlighted) ISO Auto Minimum and ISO Auto Maximum, as shown in Figure 4-52.

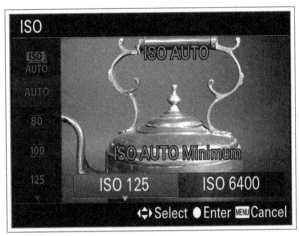

Figure 4-52. ISO Minimum Value Highlighted

Move the highlight to each of these blocks in turn using the Right button and change the value as you wish, pressing the Up and Down buttons or turning the Control wheel. You can set both the minimum and the maximum to values from 125 to 12800. When both values have been set, press the Center button to move to the shooting screen.

Once those values are set, the camera will keep the ISO level within the range you have specified whenever you select Auto ISO or the Auto setting for Multi Frame Noise Reduction, discussed below. Of course, you can always set a specific ISO value at any other level by selecting it from the ISO menu.

MULTI FRAME NOISE REDUCTION

Finally, I will discuss the top item on the ISO menu, whose icon includes the ISO label and a stack of frames, shown in Figure 4-53. If you highlight that icon with the orange selection block, you will see that the name of this option is Multi Frame Noise Reduction (MFNR).

This setting lets you set an ISO value as high as 25600, twice as high as the maximum value on the standard ISO menu. When you use MFNR, the camera takes multiple shots in a rapid burst and creates a composite image with reduced noise. The camera also attempts to select frames with minimal motion blur.

After you have selected MFNR, use the Right button to move the highlight to the right side of the screen, on the selection block for the ISO setting to be used, as shown in Figure 4-54.

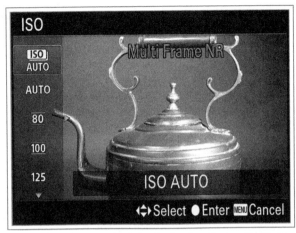

Figure 4-53. Multi Frame Noise Reduction Option Highlighted

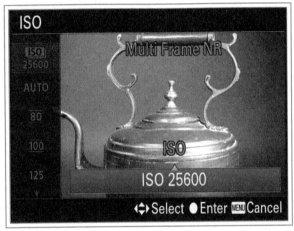

Figure 4-54. Multi Frame Noise Reduction Value Selection Block Highlighted

Use the Up and Down buttons or turn the Control wheel to select a value, which can be Auto or a specific value from 200 all the way up to 25600. If you choose Auto, the camera will select an ISO within the limits set for ISO Auto Minimum and Maximum, and it will take multiple shots using that value. You cannot use the flash when MFNR is in effect. Also, you cannot use Raw quality or continuous shooting with this setting.

Using the MFNR setting is the only way to set the RX100 III to an ISO level above 12800. (You can, however, use the High Sensitivity setting of Scene mode, in which case the camera may use that high setting if it finds it necessary.) If you are faced with the prospect of taking pictures in an unusually dark environment, consider using this specialized setting, which really is more akin to a shooting mode than to an ISO setting.

In Figure 4-55, I used the Auto setting of MFNR to capture a view of Civil War-era medicine bottles in a dimly lighted museum. The RX100 III set the ISO to

6400, enabling the camera to use a shutter speed of 1/25 second despite the dark conditions. The result was a final image with good detail and no motion blur.

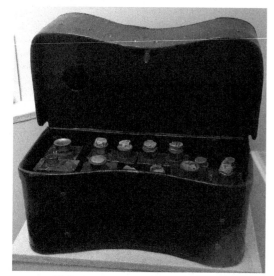

Figure 4-55. Multi Frame Noise Reduction Sample Image - ISO 6400

Here are some more notes on ISO. As I discussed in Chapter 3, with the RX100 III, unlike many other cameras, you can select Auto ISO in Manual exposure mode. In that way, you can set both the shutter speed and aperture, and still have the camera set the exposure automatically by varying the ISO level. In the Auto shooting modes, Scene mode, and Sweep Panorama mode, Auto ISO is automatically set, and you cannot adjust the ISO setting. The available ISO settings for movie recording are different from those for stills; I will discuss that point in Chapter 8.

Also, note that the settings for ISO 80 and 100 are surrounded by lines on the menu, as shown in Figure 4-53. The lines indicate that those 2 settings are not "native" to the RX100 III's sensor, whose base ISO is 125. So, although using the 2 lower settings reduces the sensor's sensitivity to light and darkens the exposure, it does not improve dynamic range or reduce noise in your images significantly.

ND Filter

The last item on screen 3 of the Shooting menu is the ND Filter setting. With this option, you can use a built-in neutral density filter to reduce the amount of light entering the lens, so you will have more flexibility in setting shutter speed and aperture.

The main use for this feature is when the light is bright and you need to use a slow shutter speed or wide aperture. You may need a slow shutter speed to blur the appearance of a waterfall or a wide aperture to blur the background for a portrait. If conditions are bright, it may not be possible to make the setting you need.

For example, I took the photo in Figure 4-56 on a bright day when I needed to use a slow shutter speed to smooth out the water spraying from a fountain in a pond. For this image, I set the camera to Shutter Priority mode and set the shutter speed to 1/10 second. I set the ISO to its lowest native value, 125. As you can see, the image was overexposed and unusable.

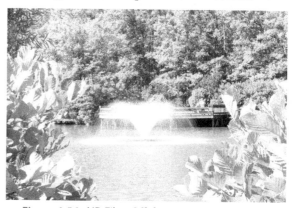

Figure 4-56. ND Filter Off: f/11.0, 1/10 Sec., ISO 125

For Figure 4-57, I turned on the ND Filter option, which reduced the exposure setting by 3 EV. With this option enabled, I was able to use a shutter speed of 1/6 second at ISO 125. With these settings, the image was exposed normally, and the water in the fountain was smoothed out as I wanted.

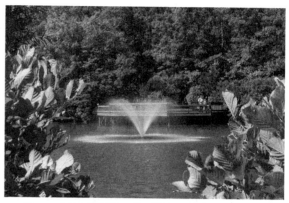

Figure 4-57. ND Filter On: f/11.0, 1/6 Sec., ISO 125

This menu option has 3 possible settings, as shown in Figure 4-58: Auto, On, and Off.

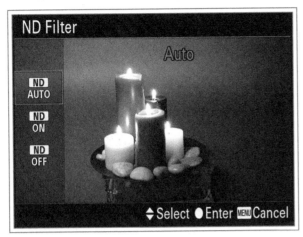

Figure 4-58. ND Filter Menu Options Screen

The second 2 are self-explanatory: The ND Filter is either used or not used. With Auto, the camera will activate the ND Filter if it detects a need to reduce the light. I prefer not to use that setting, because I like to make my own decisions about settings. In the Auto, Scene, and Sweep Panorama modes, you can't adjust this setting; the camera automatically uses the Auto option. In Manual exposure mode, you can't select the Auto option for ND Filter.

If you're using one of the advanced shooting modes (Program, Aperture Priority, or Shutter Priority) and taking casual shots, you might want to set ND Filter to Auto to give you more leeway in the settings you use for aperture and shutter speed without having to dig through the menu to turn on that feature. However, it might be a better idea to assign ND Filter to one of the camera's control buttons, as discussed in Chapter 7; if you do that, then it's an easy matter to press that button to call up the ND Filter menu screen and turn the filter on or off whenever you need to.

The next menu items to discuss are on screen 4 of the Shooting menu, shown in Figure 4-59.

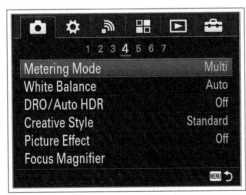

Figure 4-59. Screen 4 of Shooting Menu

Metering Mode

This option lets you choose among the 3 patterns of exposure metering offered by the RX100 III—Multi, Center, and Spot—as shown in Figure 4-60.

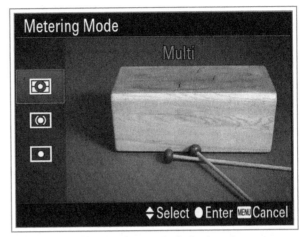

Figure 4-60. Metering Mode Options Screen

This choice tells the camera's automatic exposure system what part of the scene to consider when setting the exposure. With Multi, the camera uses the entire scene that is visible on the display. With Center, the camera still measures all of the light from the scene, but it gives additional weight to the center portion of the image on the theory that your main subject is in or near the center. Finally, with Spot, the camera evaluates only the light that is found within the spot metering zone.

In Spot mode, the camera places a small circle in the center of the screen indicating the metered area, as seen in Figure 4-61.

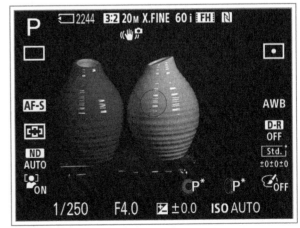

Figure 4-61. Spot Meter Circle on Screen

With this setting, you can see the effects of the exposure system clearly by selecting the Program exposure mode and aiming the small circle at various points, some bright and some dark, and seeing how sharply the brightness of the scene on the camera's display changes. If you try the same experiment using Multi or Center mode, you will see more subtle and gradual changes.

If you choose Spot metering, the circle you will see is different from the rectangular frames the camera uses to indicate the Center or Flexible Spot Focus Area mode settings. If you make either of those Focus Area settings at the same time as the Spot metering setting, you will see both a spot-metering circle and an autofocus frame in the center of the LCD screen, as in Figure 4-62, which shows the screen with the Spot metering and Center Focus Area settings in effect.

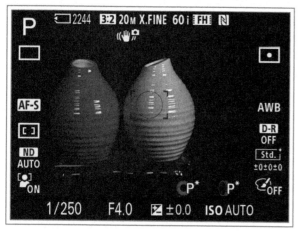

Figure 4-62. Spot Meter and Center Focus Frames on Screen

Be aware which one of these settings is in effect, if a circle or a frame is visible in the center of the screen. Remember that the circle is for spot metering, and the rectangular bracket is for Center or Flexible Spot autofocus (or an equivalent Lock-on AF setting).

In the 2 Auto modes and all varieties of Scene mode, the only metering method available is Multi. That method also is the only one available when Clear Image Zoom or Digital Zoom is in use. (The conflict arises only when the lens is actually zoomed beyond the limit of optical zoom; at that point, the camera will change the metering method to Multi, and will change it back when the lens is zoomed back within the optical zoom limit.)

The Multi setting is best used for scenes with relatively even contrast, such as landscapes, and for action shots, in which the location of the main subject may move

through different parts of the frame. The Center setting is useful for sunrise and sunset scenes, and for other situations in which there is a large, central subject that exhibits considerable contrast with the rest of the scene. The Spot setting is good for portraits, macro shots, and other images in which there is a relatively small part of the scene whose exposure is critical. Spot metering also is useful when lighting is intense in one portion of a scene, such as when a concert performer is lit by a spotlight.

White Balance

The White Balance menu option is needed because cameras record the colors of objects differently according to the color temperature of the light source that illuminates those objects. Color temperature is a value expressed in Kelvin (K) units. A light source with a lower K rating produces a "warmer," or more reddish light. A source with a higher rating produces a "cooler," or more bluish light. Candlelight is rated about 1,800 K, indoor tungsten light (ordinary light bulb) is rated about 3,000 K, outdoor sunlight and electronic flash are rated about 5,500 K, and outdoor shade is rated about 7,000 K. If the camera is using a white balance setting that is not designed for the light source that illuminates the scene, the colors of the recorded image are likely to be inaccurate.

The RX100 III, like most cameras, has an Auto White Balance setting that chooses the proper color correction for any given light source. The Auto White Balance setting works well, and it will produce good results in many situations, especially if you are taking snapshots whose colors are not critical.

If you need more precision in the white balance of your shots, the RX100 III has settings for common light sources, as well as options for setting white balance by color temperature and for setting a custom white balance based on the existing light source.

Once you have highlighted this menu option, press the Center button to bring up the vertical menu at the left of the screen, shown in Figure 4-63. Press the Up and Down buttons or turn the Control wheel to scroll through the choices on the first screen: Auto White Balance (AWB), Daylight (sun icon), Shade (house icon), Cloudy (cloud icon), and Incandescent (round light bulb icon).

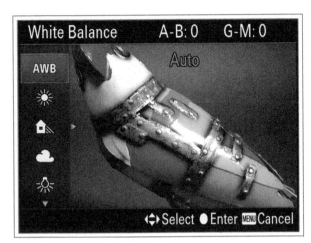

Figure 4-63. White Balance Menu Screen 1

The second screen, seen in Figure 4-64, includes Fluorescent Warm White (bulb icon with -1), Fluorescent Cool White (same, with 0), Fluorescent Day White (same, with +1), Fluorescent Daylight (same, with +2), and Flash (WB with lightning icon).

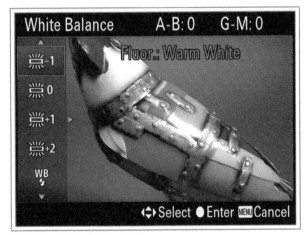

Figure 4-64. White Balance Menu Screen 2

The choices on the third screen, shown in Figure 4-65, are Color Temperature/Filter (K and filter icon) and 3 numbered Custom choices. Below the 3 Custom icons is an icon with the word "SET," which represents the option for setting a Custom value.

To select a setting, highlight it and press the Center button. Most of the settings describe a light source in common use. There are 4 settings for fluorescent bulbs, so you should be able to find a good setting for any fluorescent light, though you may need to experiment to find the best setting for a given bulb. For settings such as Daylight, Shade, Cloudy, and Incandescent, select the setting that matches the dominant light in your location. If you are indoors and using only incandescent lights, this decision will be easy. If you

have a variety of lights turned on and sunlight coming in the windows, you may want to use either the Color Temperature/Filter setting or the Custom option.

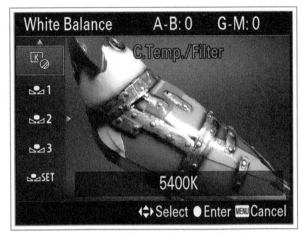

Figure 4-65. White Balance Menu Screen 3

The Color Temperature/Filter option lets you set the camera's white balance according to the color temperature of the light source. One way to determine that value is with a device like the Sekonic Prodigi Color meter shown in Figure 4-66.

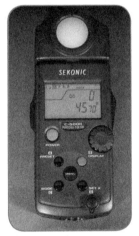

Figure 4-66. Prodigi Color Meter

That meter works well when I need extra accuracy in my white balance settings. If you don't want to purchase a meter, you can still use the Color Temperature/Filter option, but you will have to do some guesswork or use your own sense of color. For example, if you are shooting under lighting that is largely incandescent, you can use the value of 3,000 K as a starting point, because, as noted earlier in this discussion, that is an approximate value for the color temperature of that light source. Then you can try setting the color temperature figure higher or lower, and watch the camera's display to see how natural the colors look. As you lower the color temperature setting, the image will become more "cool," or bluish; as you raise it, the image will appear more "warm," or reddish. Once you have found the best setting, leave it in place and take your shots. (The Live View Display option on screen 2 of the Custom menu must be set to Setting Effect On for these changes to appear on the display, as discussed in Chapter 7.)

To make this setting, after you highlight the icon for Color Temperature/Filter, press the Right button to move the orange highlight to the right side of the camera's screen, so that it highlights the color temperature value, as shown in Figure 4-67.

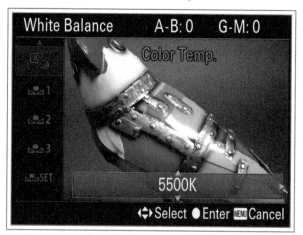

Figure 4-67. Color Temperature Value Selection Block

Then raise or lower that number by pressing the Up and Down buttons or by turning the Control wheel.

If you don't want to work with color temperatures, you can set a Custom White Balance. This process can be confusing, because the Custom setting has several icons on the White Balance menu. The first 3 Custom icons, just below the Color Temperature/Filter icon, are used to set the camera to one of 3 currently stored Custom White Balance settings. The fourth icon, with the word "SET", is the one to use to get a new reading for a Custom setting using the camera's procedure for setting that value. Before you can use any of the 3 upper Custom icons, you need to use the lowest Custom icon to set the Custom White Balance value.

To set and store a Custom White Balance, highlight the Custom SET icon at the bottom of the White Balance menu. Press the Center button to select this option, and the camera will display a message saying "Press the [Center] button to capture data of central area of screen," as shown in Figure 4-68.

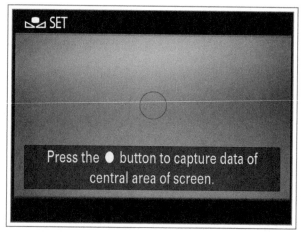

Figure 4-68. Message to Press Center Button to Set Custom White Balance

Aim the camera at a gray or white surface, lit by the light source you are measuring, that fills the circle on the screen. Press the Center button, and the camera will set the white balance. The lower area of the screen will show the measured color temperature along with letters and numbers indicating variations along 2 color axes. If there is some variation, you will see an indication such as G-M: G1, meaning 1 unit of variation toward green along the green-magenta axis, as shown in Figure 4-69.

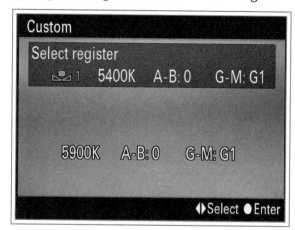

Figure 4-69. Results Screen for Setting Custom White Balance

Press the Right and Left buttons or turn the Control wheel to select Register 1, 2, or 3. Press the Center button to store the new setting to that register, replacing the existing setting.

Whenever you want to use the Custom White Balance setting you saved, select the number 1, 2, or 3 Custom icon on the White Balance menu, depending on which slot you used to save the setting. You can change any of the Custom settings whenever you want to, if you are shooting under different lighting conditions.

There is one more way to adjust the white balance setting by taking advantage of the 2 color axes discussed above. If you want to tweak the white balance setting to the nth degree, when you have highlighted your desired setting (whether a preset or the Custom setting), press the Right button, and you will see a screen for fine adjustments, as shown in Figure 4-70.

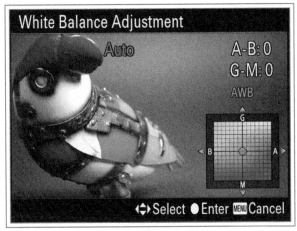

Figure 4-70. White Balance Adjustment Axes

You will see a pair of axes that intersect at a zero point marked by an orange dot. The 4 axes are labeled G, B, M, and A for green, blue, magenta, and amber. You can now use all 4 direction buttons to move the orange dot away from the center along any of the axes to adjust these 4 values until you have the color balance exactly how you want it. If you prefer, you can turn the Control wheel to adjust the G-M axis, but you still need to press the Left and Right buttons to adjust the B-A axis. Be careful to undo any adjustments using these axes when they are no longer needed; otherwise, the adjustments will alter the colors of all of your images that are shot in a shooting mode for which white balance can be adjusted, even after the camera has been powered off and then back on.

Some final notes about white balance: First, if you shoot using Raw quality, you can always correct the white balance after the fact in your Raw software. So, if you are using Raw, you don't have to worry so much about what setting you are using for white balance. Still, it's a good idea always to check the setting before shooting to avoid getting caught with incorrect white balance when you are not using the Raw format.

Second, before you decide to use the "correct" white balance in every situation, consider whether that is the best course of action to get the results you ultimately want. For example, I know of one photographer who

generally keeps his camera set for Daylight white balance even when shooting indoors because he likes the "warmer" appearance that comes from using that setting. It's not a bad idea to give some thought to straying from a strict approach to white balance, at least on occasion.

Also note that the White Balance menu setting is fixed to Auto White Balance in the Auto and Scene modes.

The chart in Figure 4-71 shows how white balance settings affect images taken by the RX100 III. The images in this chart were taken under daylight-balanced light with the camera set for each white balance option, as indicated on the chart. Most of the results are acceptable. The only ones that clearly look incorrect for this light source are the Incandescent, Fluorescent Warm White, and Fluorescent Cool White settings.

White Balance Chart for Sony RX100 III

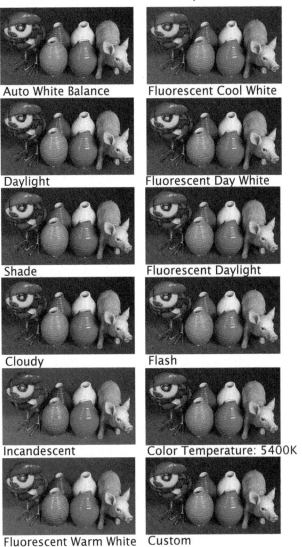

Figure 4-71. White Balance Settings Comparison Chart

DRO/Auto HDR

The next option on the Shooting menu lets you control the dynamic range of your shots using the DRO/HDR processing of the RX100 III. These settings can help avoid problems with excessive contrast in your images. Such issues arise because digital cameras cannot easily process a wide range of dark and light areas in the same image—that is, their "dynamic range" is limited. So, if you are taking a picture in an area that is partly lit by bright sunlight and partly in deep shade, the resulting image is likely to have some dark areas in which details are lost in the shadows, or some areas in which highlights, or bright areas, are excessively bright, or "blown out," so, again, the details of the image are lost.

One way to deal with this situation is to use high dynamic range, or HDR techniques, in which multiple photographs of the same scene with different exposures are combined into a composite image that has clearly visible details throughout the entire scene. The RX100 III can take HDR shots on its own, or you can take separate exposures yourself and combine them in software on your computer into a composite HDR image. I will discuss the details of those HDR techniques later in this chapter.

The RX100 III's DRO (dynamic range optimizer) setting gives you another way to deal with the problem of uneven lighting, with special processing in the camera that can boost details in dark areas and reduce overexposure in bright areas at the same time, resulting in a single image with better-balanced exposure than would be possible otherwise. To do this, the DRO setting uses digital processing to reduce highlight blowout and pull details out of the shadows.

To use the DRO feature, press the Menu button and highlight this option, then press the Center button to bring the DRO/Auto HDR menu up on the camera's display, as shown in Figure 4-72. Scroll through the options on that menu using the Up and Down buttons or by turning the Control wheel.

With D-R Off, no special processing is used. With the second choice, press the Right and Left buttons to move through the DRO choices: Auto, or Level 1 through Level 5. With the Auto setting, the camera analyzes the scene to pick an appropriate amount of DRO processing. Otherwise, you can pick the level; the

higher the number, the greater the processing to even out contrast between light and dark areas. Figures 4-73 through 4-75 are examples of the various levels of DRO processing, ranging from Off to Level 5.

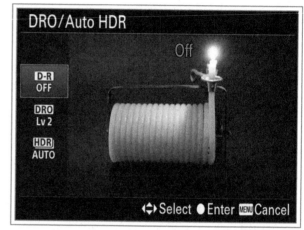

Figure 4-72. DRO/Auto HDR Menu Options Screen

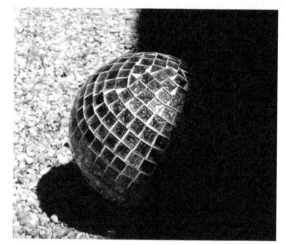

Figure 4-73. DRO Off

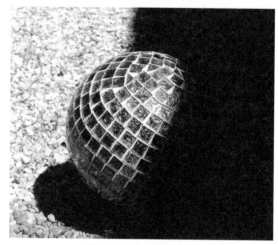

Figure 4-74. DRO LV3

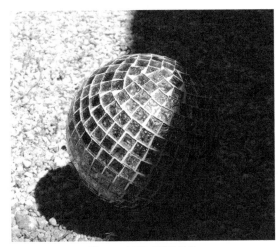

Figure 4-75. DRO LV5

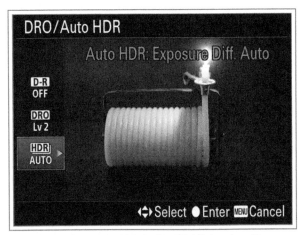

Figure 4-76. Auto HDR Option Highlighted on Menu

As you can see, the greater the level of DRO used, the more evenly the RX100 III processed the lighting in the scene, primarily by selectively enhancing details in the shadowy area. There is some risk of increasing visual noise in the dark areas with this sort of processing, but the RX100 III does not seem to do badly in this respect; I have not seen increased noise levels in images processed with the DRO feature.

The final option for this item, HDR, involves in-camera HDR processing. With traditional HDR processing, the photographer takes 2 or more shots of a scene with contrasting lighting, some shots underexposed and others overexposed, and merges them in Photoshop or HDR software to blend differently exposed portions from the images. The end result is a composite HDR image with clear details through all parts of the image.

Because of the popularity of HDR, many makers have incorporated some degree of DR processing into their cameras in an attempt to help the cameras even out areas of excessive brightness and darkness to preserve details. With the RX100 III, as with many modern cameras, Sony has provided an automatic method for taking multiple shots that the camera combines internally to achieve one HDR composite image. To use this feature, highlight the bottom option on the DRO/Auto HDR menu, as shown in Figure 4-76.

Press the Right and Left buttons to scroll through the various options for the HDR setting until you have highlighted the one you want, then press the Center button to select that option and exit to the shooting screen. The available options are Auto HDR and HDR with EV settings from 1.0 through 6.0.

If you select Auto HDR, the camera will analyze the scene and the lighting conditions and select a level of exposure difference on its own. If you select a specific level from 1.0 to 6.0, the camera will use that level as the overall difference among the 3 shots it takes.

For example, if you select 1.0 EV for the exposure difference, the camera will take 3 shots, each 0.5 EV level (f-stop) different in exposure from the next—one shot at the metered EV level, one shot at 0.5 EV lower, and one shot at 0.5 EV higher. If you choose the maximum exposure difference of 6.0 EV, then the shots will be 3.0 EV apart in their brightness levels.

When you press the shutter button, the camera will take 3 shots in a quick burst; you should either use a tripod or hold the camera very steady. When it has finished processing the shots, the camera will save the composite image as well as the single image that was taken at the metered exposure.

For Figure 4-77 through Figure 4-79, I took additional shots of the same subject I used for the DRO series, above, to illustrate the HDR settings. For Figure 4-77, HDR was at Level 3; for Figure 4-78, HDR was set to its highest value, Level 6. The image using HDR at Level 6 gave the best results in terms of pulling details out of the shadows.

For comparison, I took several shots of the subject using a range of exposure levels in Manual exposure mode. I merged those images together in Photomatix Pro software and tweaked the result until I got what seemed to be the optimal dynamic range.

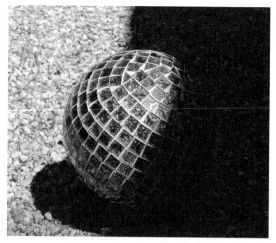

Figure 4-77. Auto HDR 3.0EV

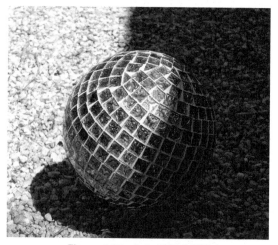

Figure 4-78. Auto HDR 6.0EV

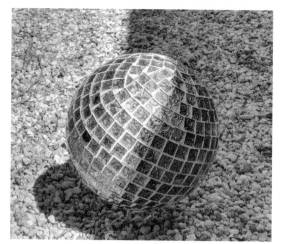

Figure 4-79. Composite HDR Image from Photomatix Pro

inclination to take multiple pictures and combine them later with HDR software into a composite image.

My recommendation is to leave the DRO Auto setting turned on for general shooting, especially if you don't plan to do post-processing. If the contrast in lighting for a given scene is extreme, then try at least some shots using the Auto HDR feature.

If you are planning to do post-processing, you may want to use the Raw quality setting so you can work with the shots later using software to achieve evenly exposed final images. You also could use Manual exposure mode or exposure bracketing to take shots at different exposures and merge them with Photoshop, Photomatix, or other HDR software. The RX100 III provides high levels of dynamic range in its Raw files, particularly if you shoot with low ISO settings. Therefore, you very well may be able to bring details out of the shadows and reduce overexposure in highlighted areas using your Raw processing software.

Note that the Auto HDR setting cannot be used if you are using Raw quality for your images. The other DRO settings do work with Raw images, but they will have no effect on the Raw images unless you process them with Sony's Image Data Converter software.

You cannot adjust DRO and Auto HDR settings in the Auto, Scene, and Sweep Panorama modes. With the Sunset, Night Scene, Night Portrait, Hand-held Twilight, Anti Motion Blur, and Fireworks settings, DRO/Auto HDR is turned off. With other scene types, DRO is turned on. You can use flash with these settings, but it will fire only for the first HDR shot, and it defeats the purpose of the settings to use flash, so you probably should not do so.

In my opinion, the HDR image done in software, shown in Figure 4-79, does a better job of evening out the contrast than the Auto HDR images processed in the camera. However, these images were taken under fairly extreme conditions. The in-camera HDR option is an excellent option for subjects that are partly shaded and partly in sunlight, when you don't have the time or

Creative Style

The Creative Style setting provides options for altering the appearance of your images with in-camera adjustments to their contrast, saturation (color intensity), and sharpness. Using these settings, you can add or subtract intensity of color or make subtle changes to the look of your images, as well as shooting in monochrome.

Of course, if you plan to edit your images on a computer using software such as Photoshop, you can duplicate these effects readily at that stage. But, if you don't want to spend time processing your images in that way, having the ability to alter the look of your shots using this menu option can add a good deal to the enjoyment of your photos.

Using this feature is straightforward. Highlight Creative Style, the fourth item on screen 4 of the Shooting menu, and press the Center button to go to the next screen, as shown in Figure 4-80.

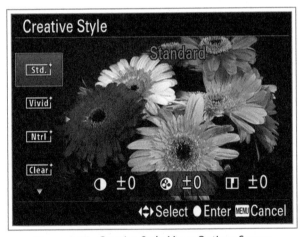

Figure 4-80. Creative Style Menu Options Screen

Using the Up and Down buttons or turning the Control wheel, scroll through the 13 main settings: Standard, Vivid, Neutral, Clear, Deep, Light, Portrait, Landscape, Sunset, Night Scene, Autumn Leaves, Black and White, and Sepia. If you want to choose one of these settings with no further adjustment, just press the Center button when your chosen option is highlighted.

If you select an option other than Standard, you may see a change on the camera's display in shooting mode. For example, if you choose Sepia or Black and White, the screen will have that coloration. This effect will be visible, though, only if the Live View Display option on

screen 2 of the Custom menu is set to Setting Effect On. If that menu option is set to Setting Effect Off, the display will not show any change from the Creative Style setting. You will still see an icon showing which setting is in effect, in the lower right of the screen. For example, Figure 4-81 shows the display when the Sepia setting is active but Setting Effect is off.

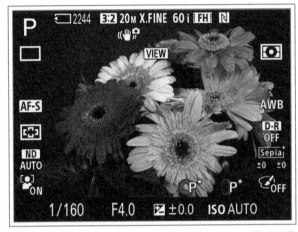

Figure 4-81. Sepia Setting Selected with Setting Effect Off

ADJUSTING CONTRAST, SATURATION, AND SHARPNESS

To fine-tune the contrast, saturation, and sharpness for one of the Creative Style settings, move the orange highlight bar to the desired setting, such as Vivid or Portrait, and press the Right button to move a second highlight bar into the right side of the screen.

You will see a label above a line of 3 icons accompanied by numbers at the bottom of the screen, as shown in Figure 4-82.

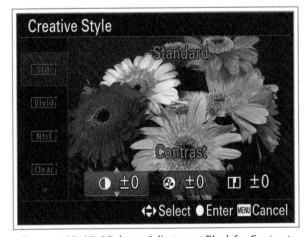

Figure 4-82. Highlight on Adjustment Block for Contrast

As you move the highlight over each icon with the Left and Right buttons, the label will change to show which value is active and ready to be adjusted. When the chosen value (contrast, saturation, or sharpness) is highlighted, use the Up and Down buttons or turn the Control wheel to adjust the value upward or downward by up to 3 units. When the Black and White or Sepia setting is active, there are only 2 adjustments available—contrast and sharpness. Saturation is not available because it adjusts the intensity of colors and there are no colors to adjust for those 2 settings.

By varying the amounts of these 3 parameters, you can achieve a considerable range of different appearances for your images. For example, by increasing saturation, you can add punch and make colors stand out. By adding contrast and/or sharpness, you can impose a "harder" appearance on your images, making them look grittier and more realistic.

Figure 4-83 is a composite image in which the top shot was taken with the Standard setting with all 3 parameters adjusted to their minimums, and the bottom shot was taken with the same setting, but with the contrast, sharpness, and saturation all adjusted to their maximum levels of +3 units.

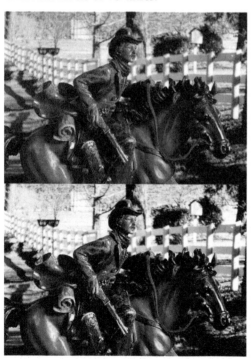

Figure 4-83. Top: Creative Style Minimum Adjustments: Bottom: Maximum Adjustments

As you can see, the bottom image is noticeably darker, with a grittier look than the top one.

If you want to save your adjusted settings for future use, you can create and save 6 different custom versions, using any of the 13 basic settings with whatever adjustments you want. To do this, scroll down on the Creative Style menu to the numbered items, starting just below the Sepia item, as shown in Figure 4-84.

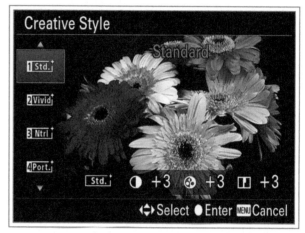

Figure 4-84. Numbered Icons for Saving Custom Creative Style Settings

There are 6 numbered icons, of which 4 are visible on this screen. They all work the same. Highlight an icon, then, using the Right button, move the highlight to the right side of the screen, on the name of the setting (Vivid, Neutral, Deep, etc.). Use the Control wheel or the Up and Down buttons to select any one of the 13 settings. Then, scroll to the right and adjust contrast, saturation, and sharpness as you want them.

When all the adjustments are made, press the Center button to accept them. Then, whenever you want to recall that setting for use, call up the Creative Style menu and scroll to the numbered icon for the style you adjusted.

The Creative Style option works with all shooting modes except the 2 Auto modes and Scene mode. You can use it with the Raw format, but the results will vary depending on the Raw-conversion software you use. For example, I just shot a Raw image in Program mode using the Black and White setting. The image showed up in black and white on the camera's screen.

However, when I opened the image in Adobe Camera Raw and then in Photoshop, the image was in color; the Adobe software ignored the information in the image's data about the Creative Style setting. When I opened the image using Sony's Image Data Converter software, though, the image appeared in black and white because Sony's software recognized the Creative Style information. So, if you want to use this menu option with Raw files, be aware that not all software will use that information when processing the images. Creative Style cannot be used when Picture Effect is being used.

Figures 4-85 and 4-86 include comparison photos showing each setting as applied to the same scene under the same lighting conditions to illustrate the different effects you can achieve with each variation. General descriptions of these effects are provided after the comparison charts.

Creative Styles Chart - Part 1

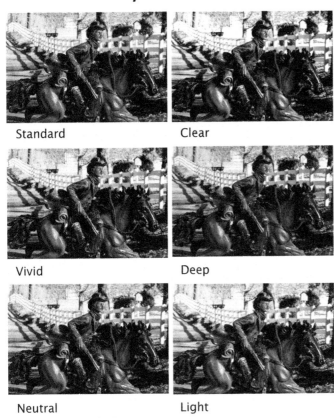

Figure 4-85. Creative Style Settings Comparison Chart - Part 1

Creative Styles Chart - Part 2

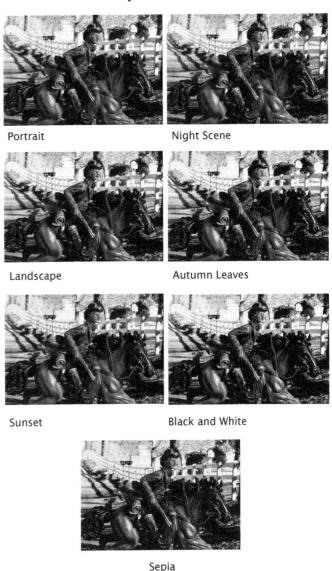

Figure 4-86. Creative Style Settings Comparison Chart - Part 2

STANDARD

The Standard setting is equivalent to having the Creative Style feature turned off; no special processing is applied to your images.

VIVID

The Vivid setting increases the saturation, or intensity, of all colors in the image. As you can see from the samples, it calls attention to the scene, though it does not produce very dramatic effects. The Vivid setting might work well if you want to emphasize the colors in images taken at a birthday party or at a carnival.

NEUTRAL

With the Neutral setting, the RX100 III leaves images with reduced saturation and sharpness, so you can process them to your own taste using software.

CLEAR

Clear, according to Sony, emphasizes the highlighted areas in the image, giving them added intensity. Some users feel this setting yields images with more intensity than the Vivid setting.

DEEP

Sony says that this setting is intended to show the "solid presence" of the subject. In effect, it emphasizes the shadow tones and lowers the overall brightness of the image.

LIGHT

This setting is the opposite of Deep; it emphasizes the highlight tones and results in a brighter, lighter appearance.

PORTRAIT

The main feature of the Portrait setting is a reduction in the saturation and sharpness of colors to soften the appearance of skin tones. You might want to use this setting to take portraits that are flattering rather than harsh and realistic. Because this setting provides midrange values for the colors and contrast, some photographers find this to be their favored Creative Style setting for general photography.

LANDSCAPE

With the Landscape setting, the RX100 III increases all 3 values—contrast, saturation, and sharpness—to make the features of a landscape, such as trees and mountains, stand out with clear, sharp outlines. It is similar to Portrait in its processing of colors, but the sharper outlines and contrast might be too strong for portraits.

SUNSET

With the Sunset option, the camera increases the saturation to emphasize the red hues of the sunset. In my opinion, this setting produces more changes in color images than any of the others.

NIGHT SCENE

Night Scene lowers contrast in an attempt to soften the harsh effect that may result from shots taken in dark surroundings, without affecting the saturation or hues of the colors.

AUTUMN LEAVES

This setting, designed for enhancing shots of fall foliage, increases the intensity of existing red and yellow tones in the image, but does not alter the color balance or introduce new reddish shades, as the Sunset setting does.

B/W

This setting removes all color, converting the scene to black and white. Some photographers use this setting to achieve a realistic look for their street photography.

SEPIA

This second monochrome setting also removes the color from the image, but adds a sepia tone that gives an old-fashioned appearance to the shot.

The RX100 III also has settings for Portrait, Landscape, and Sunset in Scene mode, discussed in Chapter 3. However, the similar settings of the Creative Style option are available in the more advanced shooting modes, including Program, Aperture Priority, Shutter Priority, and Manual exposure, so you have access to settings such as ISO, Metering Mode, and others. And, as noted above, you can tweak Creative Style settings by fine-tuning contrast, saturation, and sharpness.

I don't often use the Creative Style settings, because I prefer to shoot with the Raw format and process my images in software such as Photoshop. I occasionally use the Sunset setting to enhance an evening view. The Creative Style settings are of value to a photographer who needs to take numerous photographs with a certain appearance and process them quickly. For example, a wedding or sports photographer may not have time to process images in software; he or she may need to capture hundreds of images in a particular visual style and have them ready for a client or a publication without delay. For this type of application, the Creative Style settings are invaluable. The settings also are useful for any photographer who wants to maintain a consistent appearance of his or her images and is not satisfied with how the JPEG files look when captured with the factory-standard settings.

Picture Effect

The Picture Effect menu option includes a rich array of settings for shooting images with in-camera special effects. The Sony RX100 III gives you a variety of ways to add creative touches to your shots, and the Picture Effect settings are probably my favorites.

The Picture Effect settings do not work with Raw images. If you set a Picture Effect option and then select Raw (or Raw & JPEG) quality, the Picture Effect setting will be canceled. However, you still have control over many of the most important settings on the camera, including Image Size, White Balance, ISO, and even, in most cases, Drive Mode. So, unlike the situation with the Scene mode settings, when you select a Picture Effect option, you are still free to control the means of taking your images as well as other aspects of their appearance.

To use these effects, select the Picture Effect menu option as seen in Figure 4-87, and scroll through the choices at the left.

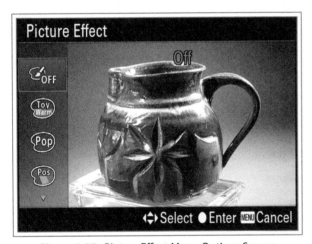

Figure 4-87. Picture Effect Menu Options Screen

Some selections have no other options, and some have settings that you can make by pressing the Left and Right buttons.

I will discuss each option in turn. In Figures 4-88 and 4-89, I provide charts with one example image taken with each effect, all taken of the same scene. Despite the fact that some settings are intended for other types of scenes, I believe the chart is useful to show how the

various settings affect the same scene. After the charts, I will discuss each of the settings and provide a more individualized example image for each one.

Picture Effect Chart - Part 1

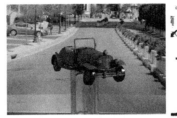
Off

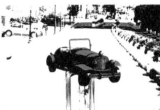
Posterization

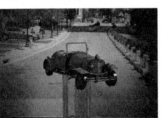
Toy Camera - Warm

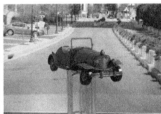
Retro Photo

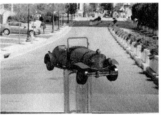
Pop Color

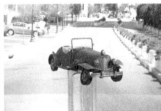
Soft High-key

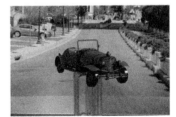
Partial Color - Red

Figure 4-88. Picture Effect Settings Comparison Chart - Part 1

Picture Effect Chart - Part 2

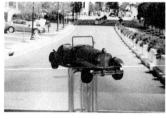

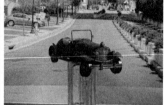

High Contrast Monochrome   **Rich-tone Monochrome**

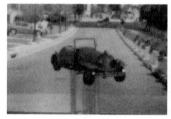

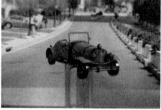

Soft Focus - Mid   **Miniature - Horizontal**

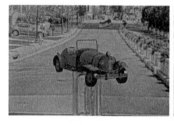

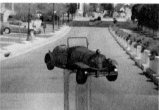

HDR Painting - Mid   **Watercolor**

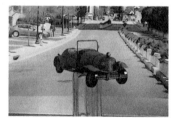

Illustration - Mid

Figure 4-89. Picture Effect Settings Comparison Chart - Part 2

Following are details about each of the settings.

OFF

The top setting on the Picture Effect menu is used to cancel all Picture Effect settings. When you are engaged in ordinary picture-taking, you should make sure the Off setting is selected so that no unwanted special effects interfere with your images.

TOY CAMERA

The Toy Camera option is an alternative to using one of the "toy" film cameras such as the Holga, Diana, or Lomo, which are popular with hobbyists and artists who use them to take photos with grainy, low-resolution appearances. With all of the Toy Camera settings, the RX100 III processes the image so it looks as if it were taken by a camera with a cheap lens: The image is dark at the corners and somewhat blurry.

The several sub-settings for Toy Camera, reached by pressing the Right and Left buttons, act as follows:

Normal: No additional processing.

Cool: Adjusts color to the "cool" side, resulting in a bluish tint.

Warm: Uses a "warm" white balance, giving a reddish hue.

Green: Adds a green tint, similar to dialing in an adjustment on the green axis for white balance.

Magenta: Similar to the Green setting, but adjustment is along the magenta axis.

Figure 4-90 was taken with the Toy Camera feature using its Warm setting. This setting seemed to give an antique aura to this bust of Cleopatra.

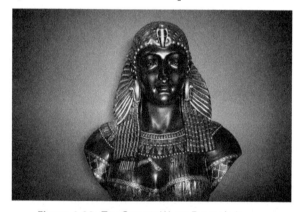

Figure 4-90. Toy Camera Warm Example Image

POP COLOR

This next setting, according to Sony, is intended to give a "pop art" feel to your images through emphasis on bright colors. I don't have much background in art history, but I'm not sure that pop art is distinguished primarily by bright colors; I thought it had more to do with the subject matter, including images that originated from advertising and comic strips.

Be that as it may, as you can see in Figure 4-91, which shows some colorful flowers in an indoor display, what you get with this setting is another way to add "punch" and intensity, along with added brightness, to your color images.

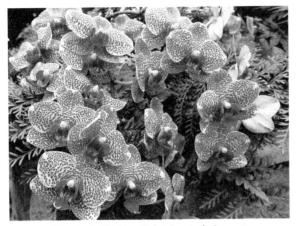

Figure 4-91. Pop Color Example Image

POSTERIZATION

The Posterization setting is a fairly dramatic effect. Using the Right and Left buttons, you can choose to apply this effect in color or in black and white. In either case, with this setting the camera applies processing with heightened emphasis on colors (or dark and light areas if you select black and white) and uses a high-contrast, pastel-like look. It is somewhat like an exotic type of HDR processing. The number of different colors (or shades of gray) used in the image is decreased to make it look as if the image were created from just a few poster paints; the result has an unrealistic but dramatic effect, as you can see in Figure 4-92.

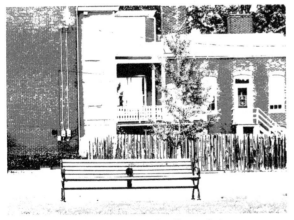

Figure 4-92. Posterization Example Image

Remember that with all of the Picture Effect settings, you can also adjust other settings, including white balance, exposure compensation, and others. With Posterization, you might try using positive or negative exposure compensation, which can change the

appearance of this effect dramatically. I have found the results with this setting often are improved by using negative exposure compensation to reduce the excessive brightness of the image. I recommend using Posterization to achieve a striking effect, perhaps for a distinctive-looking poster or greeting card.

RETRO PHOTO

With the Retro Photo setting, the RX100 III uses sepia coloring and reduced contrast to mimic the appearance of an aging photo. This effect is not as pronounced as the sepia effects I have seen on other cameras; with the RX100 III, a good deal of the image's original color still shows up, but there is a subtle softening of the image with the sepia coloration.

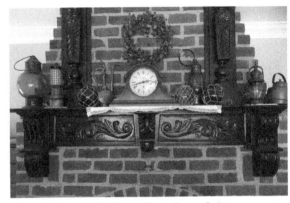

Figure 4-93. Retro Photo Example Image

In Figure 4-93 I used this effect for a shot of an old-fashioned mantelpiece on a brick fireplace.

SOFT HIGH-KEY

"High key" is a technique that uses bright lighting throughout a scene for an overall look with light colors and few shadows. This technique often is used in fashion and advertising photography. With the RX100 III, Sony has added softness to give the image a light appearance without the harshness that might otherwise result from the unusually bright exposure. Image 4-94 illustrates the use of this setting for an outdoor scene.

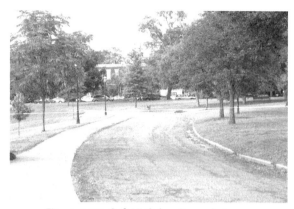

Figure 4-94. Soft High-key Example Image

PARTIAL COLOR

The Partial Color effect lets you choose a single color to retain in an image; the camera reduces the saturation of all other colors to monochrome, so that only objects of that single color remain in color in the image. I really enjoy this setting, which can be used to isolate a particular object with dramatic effect. In Figure 4-95, I used this setting to emphasize the blue sky over the city skyline.

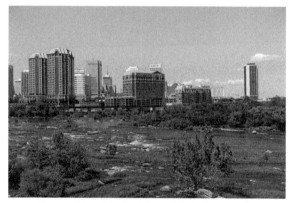

Figure 4-95. Picture Effect Partial Color - Blue

The choices for the color to be retained are red, green, blue, and yellow; use the Left and Right buttons to select one of those colors. When you aim the camera at your subject, you will see on the display what objects will show up in color, if the Live View Display menu option is set to Setting Effect On. There is no direct way to adjust the color tolerance of this setting, so you cannot, for example, set the camera to accept a broad range of reds to be retained in the image. However, if you change the white balance setting, the camera will perceive colors differently. So, if there is a particular object that you want to depict in color, but the camera does not "see" it as red, green, blue, or yellow, you can try selecting a different white balance setting and see

if the color will be retained. You also can fine-tune the white balance using the color axes to add or subtract these hues if you want to bring a particular object within the range of the color that will be retained. Also, by choosing a color that does not appear in the scene at all, you can take a straight monochrome photograph.

HIGH CONTRAST MONOCHROME

This setting lets you take black and white photographs with a stark, high-contrast appearance. You might want to consider this setting for street photography or any other situation in which you are not looking for a soft or flattering appearance.

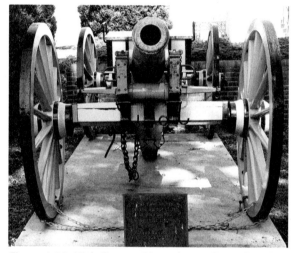

Figure 4-96. High Contrast Monochrome Example Image

I used this setting for Figure 4-96, an image of a cannon from the Civil War era, to emphasize the shape and shadows of the subject.

SOFT FOCUS

The Soft Focus effect is another setting that is variable; you can select either Low, Mid, or High by pressing the Right and Left buttons to scroll through those options. This effect is quite straightforward; the camera blurs the focus to achieve a dreamlike aura. Note that this is the first of several Picture Effect settings that cannot be previewed on the screen; you have to take the picture and then play it back to see the results of the Soft Focus setting. As I noted earlier in this chapter, you also have the option of selecting manual focus and defocusing the image to your own taste to achieve a similar effect.

For Figure 4-97, I used this effect for an image of a pathway through a wooded area to try to lend an air of mystery.

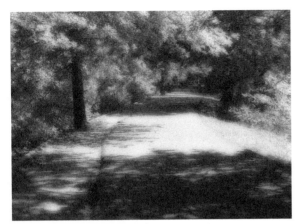

Figure 4-97. Soft Focus Mid Example Image

HDR PAINTING

The HDR Painting setting is similar to the HDR setting of the DRO/Auto HDR menu option. With this option, the camera takes a burst of 3 shots at different exposure settings and combines them internally into a single image to achieve even exposure over a wide range of areas. Unlike the more standard HDR setting, this one does not let you select the specific exposure differential for the 3 shots, but it lets you choose Low, Mid, or High for the intensity of the effect. Also, it adds stylized processing to give the final image a painterly appearance. I have often found the best results with this setting are achieved when I shoot from an indoor area through a window on a sunny day, especially when there is a variety of colorful items outside, as in Figure 4-98.

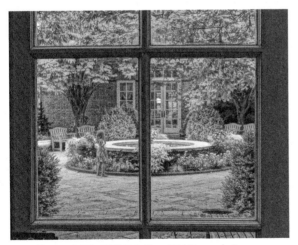

Figure 4-98. HDR Painting Mid Example Image

Because the camera takes multiple images with this effect, you can't preview the results on the screen before taking the picture. Using a tripod is advisable to avoid blur from camera motion while the 3 shots are being taken.

RICH-TONE MONOCHROME

The Rich-tone Monochrome setting can be considered as a black and white version of the HDR Painting setting. With this option, like that one, the RX100 III takes a triple burst of shots at different exposures and combines them digitally into a single composite photo with a broader dynamic range than would otherwise be possible. Unlike the color setting, though, this one does not let you select the intensity of the effect. I used it in Figure 4-99 for a shot of an old wooden door surrounded by weathered brick walls.

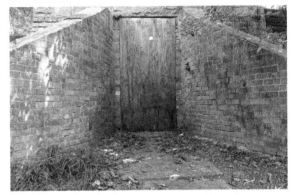

Figure 4-99. Rich-tone Monochrome Example Image

MINIATURE EFFECT

With the Miniature Effect option, the camera adds blurring at one or more sides or the top or bottom of an image to simulate the look of a photograph of a tabletop model or miniature. Such images often appear hazy in one or more areas, either because of the narrow depth of field of these closeup photos, or because of the use of a tilt-and-shift lens, which causes blurring at the edges.

For this feature to work well, you need an appropriate subject. I have found that this effect looks interesting when applied to something like a street scene or a train, which might actually be reproduced in a tabletop model. For example, if you are able to get a high vantage point above a road intersection or a railroad, you may be able to use this processing to make it look as if you had photographed a high-quality tabletop display.

After highlighting this option on the Shooting menu, press the Right and Left buttons to choose either Top, Middle (Horizontal), Bottom, Right, Middle (Vertical), Left, or Auto for the configuration of the effect. If you choose a specific area, that area will remain sharp. For example, if you choose Top, then, after you take the picture, the top area (roughly one-third) will remain sharp, and the rest of the image below that area will appear blurred. If you choose Auto, then the camera will select the area to remain sharp based on the area that was focused on by the autofocus system and by the camera's sensing how you are holding the camera.

You will not see how the effect will alter your image while viewing the scene, although the camera will place gray areas on the parts of the image that will ultimately be blurred to give you a general idea of how the final product will look. I used the RX100 III for an image of this sort in Figure 4-100, with the Miniature effect set to Middle (Vertical) for a view from a hill overlooking a road leading to the downtown area.

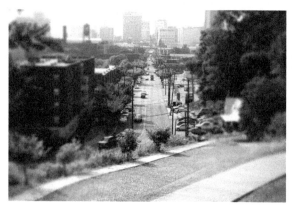

Figure 4-100. Miniature Effect Example Image

This effect can provide a lot of fun if you experiment with it; it can take some work to find the right subject and the best arrangement of sharp and blurry areas to achieve a satisfying result.

WATERCOLOR

The Watercolor effect blurs the colors of an image to make it look as if it were painted with watercolors that are bleeding together. You need to choose a subject that lends itself to this sort of distortion. For example, I have found that the faces of dolls and other figures can be pleasantly altered to have an impressionistic appearance; larger objects may not be affected significantly by this somewhat subtle effect. I have also had some pleasing results with plants and trees. In Figure 4-101, I thought this effect worked well for an indoor arrangement of flowers and bushes.

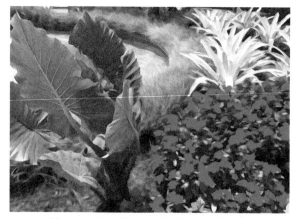

Figure 4-101. Watercolor Example Image

ILLUSTRATION

The final option for the Picture Effect setting, Illustration, is one of my favorites. This effect finds edges of objects within the scene and adds contrast to them, making it appear as if they are outlined with dark ink as in a pen-and-ink illustration that has been colored in. You can set the intensity of the effect to Low, Mid, or High using the Right and Left buttons. If you choose a subject that has a fair number of edges that can be outlined and has a repeating pattern, you can achieve a very pleasing appearance. This is another one of the effects whose final result you cannot judge while viewing the live scene; you need to see the recorded image to know what the actual effect will look like.

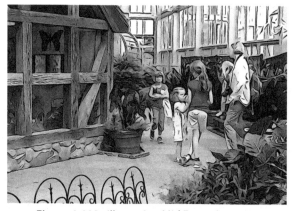

Figure 4-102. Illustration Mid Example Image

As you can see in Figure 4-102, taken with Illustration set to Mid level, this effect can transform an ordinary view into a stylized image while leaving the scene recognizable. The images produced with this effect may be more suited as decorative items than as depictions of actual objects or locations, but their appearance can be very striking and unusual. I have found that this setting often produces good results when people are included in the scene, especially if they are wearing clothes with bright colors.

Here are some more notes about the Picture Effect settings. First, several of the options are not available for shooting movies. Those settings are Soft Focus, HDR Painting, Rich-tone Monochrome, Miniature Effect, Watercolor, and Illustration. If one of those effects is turned on when you press the Movie button, the camera will turn off the effect while the movie is being recorded, and turn it back on after the recording has ended. You also cannot use Drive Mode with any of those 6 effects. Note that you can activate several of the Picture Effects settings with the Photo Creativity feature in the Auto shooting modes, as discussed in Chapter 2.

Finally, as I will discuss in Chapter 9, with the RX100 III, Sony has provided in-camera apps, or applications, some of which come with the camera and others of which can be downloaded from a Sony website. As of this writing, one of those apps is Picture Effect+, which provides enhanced versions of some of the effects discussed above.

Focus Magnifier

The Focus Magnifier menu option is available for shooting still images only when the focus mode is set to manual focus or direct manual focus (DMF). (It works differently for movies, as discussed below.) This option gives you a way to enlarge a small portion of the display so you can check the focus of that area as you turn the Control ring.

When you select this menu option, the camera places an orange frame on the display, as seen in Figure 4-103. You can move that frame to any position on the display using the direction buttons or the Control wheel. When the frame is located over the area where you want to check focus, press the Center button. The camera will then enlarge the area within the frame to 8.6 times normal, as shown in Figure 4-104. (The enlargement factor is different when shooting movies; see discussion below.) An inset square will show the position of the Focus Magnifier frame. You can move the frame around the display while the display is enlarged. Press the Center button again, and the focus area will be magnified to 17.1 times normal.

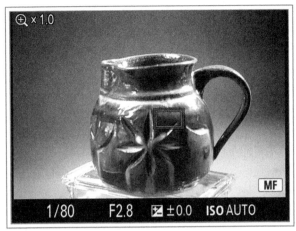

Figure 4-103. Focus Magnifier Frame at Normal Size

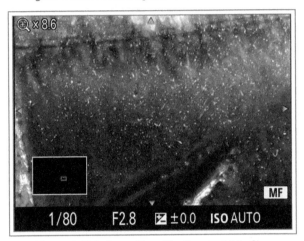

Figure 4-104. Focus Magnifier Frame at 8.6x Size

A final press will restore the display to normal size. Once you press the shutter button halfway, the magnifier frame will disappear. You can then call it up again using this menu option if you want to.

This option can be a bit confusing because it acts in a similar way to another option that is activated from screen 1 of the Custom menu, called MF Assist. As I discussed earlier in this chapter and will discuss in Chapter 7, when you turn on MF Assist with manual focus in effect, the focus area is enlarged to 8.6 times normal as soon as you start turning the Control ring to adjust the focus. Then, once the focus area is enlarged with that option, pressing the Center button will magnify the focus area to 17.1 times normal. You can toggle between the 8.6 and 17.1 magnifications using the Center button, and exit to the shooting screen by half-pressing the shutter button.

In other words, if the MF Assist menu option is active, the Center button always acts to magnify the focus area once you have started to adjust focus in manual focus mode. If you select the Focus Magnifier menu option, the difference is that pressing the Center button will magnify the display before you start focusing.

The advantage of using the Focus Magnifier menu option is that you can select the position of the enlarged focus area before you start adjusting focus. If you use the MF Assist option, the camera will enlarge the display as soon as you start turning the Control ring to adjust focus, and you will not be able to choose the location of the enlarged focus area until the display is already enlarged.

The MF Assist option works well for me, because it operates as soon as I start adjusting focus. However, if you prefer to be able to adjust the location of the frame for the enlarged focus area before starting to adjust focus, the Focus Magnifier option is useful.

The Focus Magnifier feature is easier to use if you assign it to one of the control buttons. For example, you can use the Custom Key Settings option on screen 4 of the Custom menu to assign Focus Magnifier to the Left button. Then, when you are using manual focus or DMF, you can press that button to bring the enlargement frame up on the display. You can then quickly adjust the position of the frame, press the Center button once or twice to enlarge that area, and then adjust the focus and take the picture.

As noted above, Focus Magnifier works differently for movies. If you assign this option to a control button, you can call it up while recording a movie, even if the camera is using autofocus, to check the focus of the area within the frame. The only magnification factor when shooting movies is 4.0x, rather than 8.6x and 17.1x, the factors when shooting still images.

The next menu options, starting with Long Exposure Noise Reduction, are found on screen 5 of the Shooting menu, which is shown in Figure 4-105.

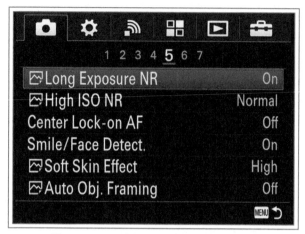

Figure 4-105. Screen 5 of Shooting Menu

Long Exposure Noise Reduction

This option uses processing to reduce the "noise" that affects images during exposures of 1/3 second or longer. This option is turned on by default. When it is turned on, the camera processes your shot for a time equal to the time of the exposure. So, if your exposure is for 2 seconds, the camera will process the shot for an additional 2 seconds, creating a delay before you can shoot again.

In some cases, this processing may remove details from your image. In addition, in certain situations you may prefer to leave the noise in the image because the graininess can be pleasing in some cases. Or, you may prefer to remove the noise using post-processing software. If you want to turn off this option, use this menu item to do so.

This option is not available for adjustment when the camera is set for continuous shooting, exposure bracketing, or in the Auto, Sweep Panorama, or Scene modes. The camera will select a setting for Long Exposure Noise Reduction in those cases. For example, the camera will turn this option off with the Sports Action and Hand-held Twilight Scene mode settings, but turn it on with the Portrait and Macro settings.

I recommend you make this setting based on the type of shooting you are doing. If you're taking casual shots or don't want to do post-processing, I suggest you leave this option turned on. But, if you are shooting with Raw quality and want to do processing with software, I recommend turning it off.

High ISO Noise Reduction

This next menu entry has 3 settings: Normal, Low, or Off; the default is Normal. This option removes noise caused by the use of a high ISO level. One problem with this sort of noise reduction is that it takes time to process your images after they are captured. You may want to set this option to Low or Off to minimize the delay before you can take another picture. If Quality is set to Raw, this option will be unavailable on the menu because this processing is not available for Raw images. It also is not available in the Auto, Scene, or Sweep Panorama modes.

Center Lock-on AF

This menu option is similar to the Lock-on AF option discussed earlier in this chapter, but there are differences. Lock-on AF is a setting that is available for Focus Area on screen 3 of the Shooting menu. That option is available only with continuous autofocus. When it is activated, the camera places a frame of the chosen type on the display. When you center your subject in that frame and half-press the shutter button, the camera will try to keep the subject in focus as it moves.

The option being discussed here, Center Lock-on AF, is a separate menu option. It is not available when the Lock-on AF option has been selected for Focus Area. However, unlike the other option, Center Lock-on AF is available with both single autofocus and continuous autofocus.

To use Center Lock-on AF, select this menu option and turn it on. Then, from the shooting screen, locate the subject you want to focus on in the center of the screen and press the Center button. The camera will display a message like that in Figure 4-106, saying it will track the subject in the center when you press the Center button.

Then, press the Center button again, and the camera will display a double-bordered frame that will move around the display as needed to keep the subject inside the frame and in focus. When you are ready to take the picture, press the shutter button.

This option is more convenient to use than the Lock-on AF option, because you can use it with either type of autofocus and you don't have to select a particular type

of focus frame. You can just press the Center button and the tracking function will start.

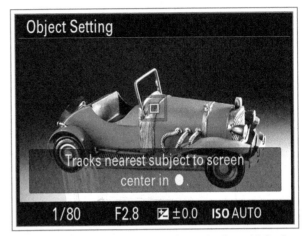

Figure 4-106. Message for Using Center Lock-on AF Option

Smile/Face Detection

This menu option gives you access to 2 functions with fairly different features. There are 4 separate entries on the vertical menu that pops up when this menu item is selected, shown in Figure 4-107.

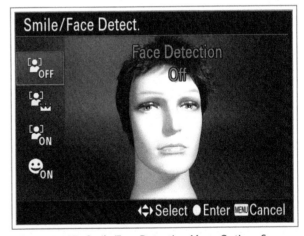

Figure 4-107. Smile/Face Detection Menu Options Screen

You can select the top setting, Off, which leaves all options turned off, or you can select one of the other 3 that operate as follows:

Face Detection On (Registered Faces)

This option is designated on the menu screen by an icon of a person's head and a crown. When you select this choice, the camera searches for faces that you have previously registered using the Face Registration option on the Custom menu, as discussed in Chapter 7. If it detects a registered face, it should consider that face to have priority, in which case it will place a green frame on the face and adjust the Focus Area, Flash Mode, exposure compensation, white balance, and Red Eye Reduction values automatically to produce optimum exposure for that particular face.

In daily shooting, I do not use this feature. It could be useful if you are taking pictures of children in a group setting and you want to make sure your own child is in focus and has his or her face properly exposed. I tried this feature out by registering one face and then aiming the camera at that face along with an unregistered face. In some cases, the camera picked the registered one as the priority face, but at other times it chose the unregistered one. Other users have reported good results with this feature, though, so, if it would be useful to you, by all means explore it further.

FACE DETECTION ON

This setting is similar to the previous one, except that it does not involve registered faces. As shown in Figure 4-108, the camera will detect any human faces, up to 8 in total, and select one as the main face to concentrate its settings on.

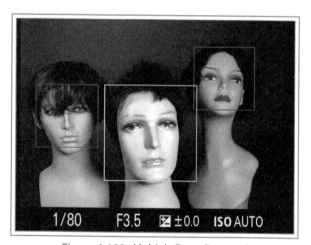

Figure 4-108. Multiple Faces Detected

Before you press the shutter button, the camera will display white or gray frames around any faces it finds. When you press the shutter button halfway to lock focus and exposure, the frame over the face the camera has selected as the main face will turn green. The camera may place multiple green frames if there are multiple faces at the same distance from the camera.

SMILE SHUTTER

The final option for this menu item is the Smile Shutter, which is a sort of self-timer that is activated when the subject smiles. After highlighting this option, use the Left and Right buttons to choose the level of smile that is needed to trigger the camera—Slight Smile, Normal Smile, or Big Smile. Then press the Center button to exit back to the shooting screen, and aim the camera at the subject or subjects. (You can, of course, put the camera on a tripod and aim it at yourself, if you want.)

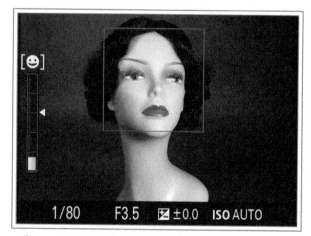

Figure 4-109. Smile Shutter Active on Shooting Screen

As shown in Figure 4-109, the camera will show a meter on the left of the screen with a pointer to indicate how large a smile is needed to trigger a shot. As soon as the camera detects a big enough smile from any person, the shutter will fire. If a person smiles again, the camera will be triggered again, with no limit on the number of shots that can be taken. In effect, this feature acts as a limited kind of remote control with one specific function. I consider this option to be something of a novelty, which can be entertaining but is not necessary for everyday photography.

Soft Skin Effect

This menu option softens skin tones in the faces of your subjects. The option is dimmed and unavailable in some situations, such as when one of the continuous shooting options or the Raw setting for Quality is selected. After you select it and turn it on, you can use the Right and Left buttons to set the level at Low, Mid, or High, as shown in Figure 4-110.

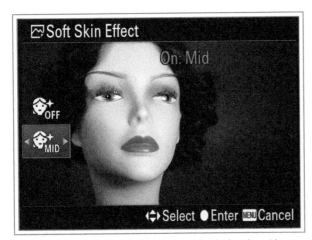

Figure 4-110. Soft Skin Effect Icon Highlighted on Menu

However, even if you turn the Soft Skin Effect option on, it will not produce any changes in your images unless you also have Face Detection turned on in the menu system and the RX100 III has detected a face.

When it works, this setting reduces the sharpness and contrast in areas that the camera perceives as skin tones. It can do a good job of smoothing out wrinkles. Figure 4-111 shows the results of a test I made. The image on the left was taken with the effect turned off; the image on the right had the setting at its High level.

This can be a useful option for doing some basic retouching of your JPEG portraits in the camera.

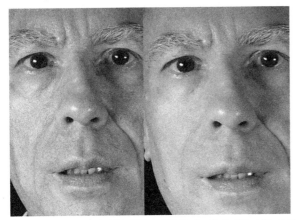

Figure 4-111. Left: Soft Skin Effect Off, Right: Soft Skin Effect High

Auto Object Framing

This menu option provides a somewhat unusual function: It rearranges the composition of your shot based on its own electronic judgment. To activate it, set it to Auto on the menu. Then, when you compose your image, the camera will place a green frame around what it believes to be the subject if it finds that the image can

benefit by being trimmed to fit the subject better. For this feature to work with faces, you need to have Face Detection turned on with the Smile/Face Detection menu option discussed above. Besides faces, Sony says that the feature will work with macro shots and objects tracked with Lock-on AF.

When you take a picture of the face or other subject, the camera may, if it finds it possible, crop the image and produce a new version of the image with the frame trimmed and resized to emphasize the subject in a more pleasing way.

An example is shown in Figure 4-112 and Figure 4-113, which show the uncropped and cropped versions, respectively, of a mannequin head I photographed with Face Detection activated.

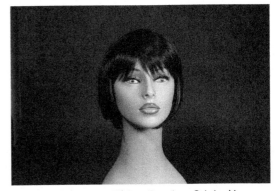

Figure 4-112. Auto Object Framing: Original Image

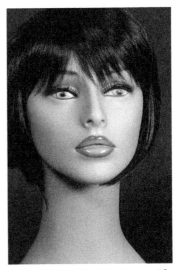

Figure 4-113. Auto Object Framing: Image After Processing

The camera's cropping looks appropriate, but I would rather do the cropping myself in Photoshop or just compose the image in this way to begin with.

The camera saves both versions, so there is no harm in using this feature. It could be useful if you are pressed for time or are unable to get into position to take the shot you want. If you need a more nicely cropped version of the image quickly for a slide show, perhaps, this could be a good way to fill that need.

This feature is available for selection only if the camera is set for autofocus with Quality set to Extra Fine, Fine, or Standard. (This option does not work with Raw images or with certain other settings.)

Next, I will discuss the items on screen 6 of the Shooting menu, shown in Figure 4-114.

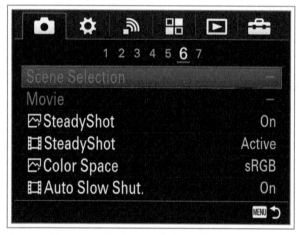

Figure 4-114. **Screen 6 of Shooting Menu**

Scene Selection

As discussed in Chapter 3, this option is used only when the camera is set to Scene mode; you use this menu item to select one of the settings in that shooting mode, including Portrait, Anti Motion Blur, Sunset, Night Scene, and others. Note that you also can use the Control ring to change Scene types, as long as the Control Ring function is set to Standard through the Custom Key Settings option on the Custom menu and you are not using manual focus or DMF. You also can turn the Control wheel to change scene types from the shooting screen. In addition, the Scene Selection menu screen appears automatically when you turn the Mode dial to the SCN position and press the Center button, if the Mode Dial Guide option on the Setup menu is turned on.

Movie

This menu item is available for selection only when the Mode dial is set to Movie mode. It lets you select one of the 4 available exposure settings for recording movies in that mode. I will discuss this option in Chapter 8.

SteadyShot (Still Images)

SteadyShot is Sony's optical image stabilization system, which compensates for small movements of the camera to avoid motion blur, especially during exposures of longer than about 1/30 second. This setting is turned on by default, and I recommend leaving it on at all times, except when the camera is on a tripod. In that case, SteadyShot is not needed, and there is some chance it can "fool" the camera and cause it to try to correct for motion that does not exist, resulting in image blur.

SteadyShot (Movies)

This next option is a separate SteadyShot setting, for movies only. This menu item has a movie film icon in front of its name, while the previous one, for still images, has a landscape icon. I will discuss this video-oriented SteadyShot option in Chapter 8.

Color Space

With this option, you can choose to record your images using the sRGB "color space," the more common choice and the default, or the Adobe RGB color space. The sRGB color space has fewer colors than Adobe RGB; therefore, it is more suitable for producing images for the web and other forms of digital display than for printing. If your images are likely to be printed commercially in a book or magazine or it is critical that you be able to match a great many different color variations, you might want to consider using the Adobe RGB color space. I always leave the color space set to sRGB, and I recommend that you do so as well unless you have a specific need to use Adobe RGB, such as a requirement from a printing company that you are using to print your images.

If you are shooting your images with the Raw format, you don't need to worry so much about color space, because you can set it later using your Raw-processing software.

Auto Slow Shutter

This final item on screen 6 of the Shooting menu is preceded by a movie film icon, meaning it is used only for recording movies. This option lets the camera automatically set a slower shutter speed than normal when shooting a movie, in order to compensate for dim lighting. I will discuss this option in Chapter 8.

Figure 4-115 shows the last screen of this menu.

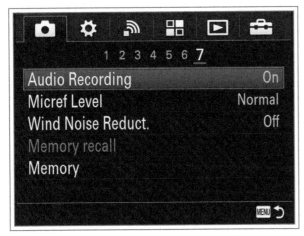

Figure 4-115. Screen 7 of Shooting Menu

Audio Recording, Micref Level, and Wind Noise Reduction

I will discuss these movie-related options in Chapter 8.

Memory Recall

The Memory Recall menu option is used only when the Mode dial is set to MR, for Memory Recall mode. Using this option, you can recall the settings you stored to one of the 3 slots for this mode, as discussed in Chapter 3.

When the Mode dial is first turned to MR, this option's main screen appears with one of the 3 numbers at the upper right highlighted, as shown in Figure 4-116. If the camera is already set to MR mode and you want to change to one of the other memory registers, you can use the menu system to call up this option. Once the Memory Recall screen is displayed, either by turning the Mode dial to MR or by using this menu option, use the direction buttons or turn the Control wheel to select register 1, 2, or 3 at the upper right of the screen. Then press the Center button, and the new set of shooting settings that were stored to that register will take effect.

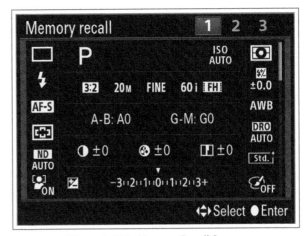

Figure 4-116. Memory Recall Screen

Memory

The final option on the Shooting menu, Memory, was discussed in Chapter 3 in connection with the Memory Recall shooting mode. Once you have set up the RX100 III with the menu options and other settings you want to store to a register of the Memory Recall shooting mode, you select the Memory menu option and choose one of the numbered registers, as shown in Figure 4-117.

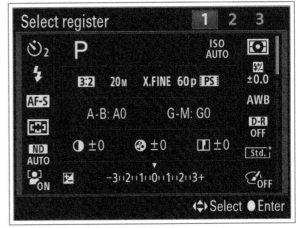

Figure 4-117. Memory Menu Option - Select Register Screen

Press the Center button, and all of the current settings will be stored to that register for the Memory Recall mode. You can recall those settings at any time by turning the Mode dial to the MR position (or selecting the Memory Recall menu option if the Mode dial is already at that position) and selecting register 1, 2, or 3.

With either the Memory Recall or Memory option, you can scroll to additional screens using the Down button to see other settings currently in effect, such as ISO Auto Maximum and Minimum, Red Eye Reduction, High ISO NR, Center Lock-on AF, and several others.

CHAPTER 5: OTHER CONTROLS

The Sony RX100 III, like other compact cameras, does not have very many physical controls. It relies to a large extent on its menus for changing settings. But the RX100 III is at the upper end of the scale of high-quality compact cameras, and one aspect of its quality is that its controls can be configured to adjust many settings on the camera. It is helpful to make settings with a button or a dial for speed of access, and Sony has made it possible to set up the camera's controls to suit your preferences. In this chapter, I'll discuss each of the camera's physical controls and how they can be used to best advantage, starting with the controls on top of the camera, shown in Figure 5-1.

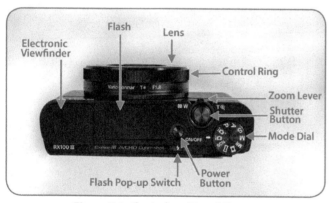

Figure 5-1. Controls on Top of Camera

Mode Dial

The Mode dial has just one function—to select a shooting mode. I discussed the shooting modes in Chapter 3. To take a quick still picture, turn this dial to the green camera icon and fire away. To record a video sequence, turn the dial to that same position and press the red Movie button, just below the Mode dial at the top of the camera's back. It is important to remember that you can record a movie with the Mode dial set to any position. There is a Movie mode on this dial, marked by a movie-film icon, but you do not have to select that icon to record movies.

Note, though, that screen 4 of the Custom menu has an option for locking out the use of the Movie button unless the camera is in Movie mode. If the Mode dial is set to any position other than Movie mode, the Movie button will not work if the Movie Button menu option is set to Movie Mode Only.

Shutter Button

The shutter button is the most important control on the camera. When you press it halfway, the camera evaluates and locks focus and exposure, if you're using standard settings, including single autofocus. You can change this behavior in various ways. For example, as discussed in Chapter 4, you can use manual focus and adjust the focus yourself. You also can go to screen 3 of the Custom menu and set the AEL w/ Shutter option to Off, in which case the camera will not lock exposure when you press the shutter button halfway. I discuss that option in Chapter 7.

In Manual exposure mode, the camera still evaluates exposure when you press the shutter button, but it does not change the aperture or shutter speed settings you have made. If Auto ISO is in effect, the camera will adjust the ISO to achieve a normal exposure if possible.

Once you are satisfied with the settings, press the button all the way to take the picture. When the camera is set for continuous shooting, you hold this button down while the camera fires repeatedly. You also can press this button halfway to exit to the live view from playback mode, menu screens, and help screens.

Zoom Lever

The zoom lever is a small ring with a short handle surrounding the shutter button. Its primary function is to vary the focal length of the lens between its wide-angle setting of 24mm and its telephoto setting of 70mm. If you have the camera set for Clear Image

Zoom or Digital Zoom through screen 3 of the Custom menu, the lever will take the zoom to higher levels, as discussed in Chapter 7.

You can also zoom the lens using the Control ring, if you have assigned the zoom function to the Control ring using the Custom Key Settings option on screen 4 of the Custom menu. You also can set the Control ring to use the Step Zoom function, which causes the lens to zoom in a predefined step each time you operate the ring. (That function is controlled by the Zoom Function on Ring option on screen 4 of the Custom menu.) The Step Zoom function does not work with the zoom lever, though. When you use the zoom lever, the lens zooms continuously, even if Step Zoom is turned on for the Control ring.

In playback mode, moving the zoom lever to the left produces an index screen, and moving the lever to the right enlarges the current image. Those operations are discussed in Chapter 6.

Power Button

This button is used to turn the camera on and off. An orange light in the center of the button glows when the battery is being charged in the camera. You also can turn the camera's power on by pressing the Playback button, which places the camera into playback mode, or by popping up the EVF with the Finder switch.

Built-in Flash and Flash Pop-up Switch

The camera's built-in flash unit is normally retracted and hidden in the center area of the camera's top. If you want the flash to be available for use, you first have to pop it up using the flash pop-up switch, located directly behind the power button.

Once you have popped up the flash unit, if you want it to fire, you need to make an appropriate setting using the Flash Mode menu. You can find the Flash Mode option on screen 2 of the Shooting menu, or you can bring up that menu by pressing the Flash button, which is the Right button on the Control wheel.

Once you have popped up the flash unit and selected a flash mode, the flash may fire when you press the

shutter button, depending on the settings that are in effect and the lighting conditions.

If you want the flash to be stowed away again, you need to press it gently back down into the camera until it clicks into place. If you want to use "bounce flash," which causes the flash to be reflected by the ceiling or wall to reduce its intensity, you can pull the flash unit back carefully with your finger and hold the flash so that it is aiming upward while it fires.

Electronic Viewfinder

Possibly the most striking innovation with the Sony RX100 III is its retractable electronic viewfinder, or EVF. With this feature, the camera can be used in bright conditions without having the LCD display washed out by sunlight. In addition, you can hold the camera up to your eye and keep it steady against your forehead while viewing a high-resolution image that includes the same information that is available with the LCD display.

To use the EVF, first pop it up by pressing down on the Finder switch on the left side of the camera.

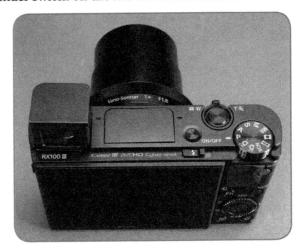

Figure 5-2. Electronic Viewfinder Popped Up but Not Extended

Once the EVF has popped up, as shown in Figure 5-2, you need to grasp the sides of the eyepiece, without grabbing the upper lid of the viewfinder assembly, and gently pull the eyepiece out of the assembly, as shown in Figure 5-3.

Adjust the EVF for your vision using the diopter adjustment lever on top of the eyepiece, shown in Figure 5-3. How you use the EVF, of course, is a matter of personal preference. You can hold it up to either your left or right eye, depending on which feels most comfortable to you. If you wear glasses, as I do, you may find it more comfortable to take them off and use the diopter adjustment lever to compensate. I can see clearly through the finder with a minor adjustment, with my glasses off.

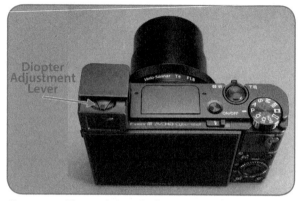

Figure 5-3. Electronic Viewfinder Popped Up and Extended

By default, the camera switches automatically between the EVF and the LCD. That is, when the EVF is popped up and your head is against the EVF, the EVF is active and the LCD is turned off. When you move your head away from the EVF, the LCD screen becomes active and the EVF is turned off. If you want the EVF to be active whenever it is popped up, regardless of the position of your head, use the Finder/Monitor option on screen 3 of the Custom menu; set that option to Viewfinder to keep the EVF active.

To adjust the brightness of the EVF, use the Viewfinder Brightness option on screen 1 of the Setup menu, as discussed in Chapter 7.

The information displayed in the EVF is independent of what is displayed on the LCD screen. That is, with one exception, you can have the EVF display all of the same information that can be shown on the LCD, but you don't have to do that. (The one exception is the For Viewfinder display, which is available only on the LCD screen, as discussed in Chapter 7.)

To set the information displays for the LCD and EVF, use the Display Button option on screen 2 of the Custom menu to choose from the possible displays. Cycle from one display to another by pressing the Display button. I will discuss that menu option and the available information displays in Chapter 7.

When you have finished using the EVF, stow it inside the camera by pressing the eyepiece into the housing and then pushing the EVF down until it clicks into

place. When you do that, the camera will turn off. As of this writing, there is no menu option that will change that behavior. You can quickly turn the camera back on if you want to keep using it with the EVF retracted.

It is possible that Sony will change this situation with a future firmware revision, but as of the initial release of the camera, pushing down the EVF turns off the camera. Of course, you can leave the EVF popped up even when you have stopped using it. In fact, you can even turn the camera off and leave the EVF popped up if you want to, though that may interfere with putting the camera into a case, and it will leave the EVF vulnerable to damage.

Finally, if you pop up the EVF without pressing the power button, the camera will turn on automatically, saving you a step. So, if you know you will be using the EVF, you can just pop it up and you will be ready to start shooting with it in place.

Next, I will discuss 2 items on the front of the camera, as seen in Figure 5-4, before turning to the controls on the back.

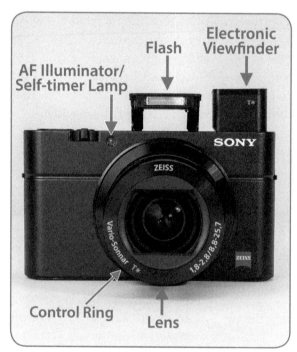

Figure 5-4. Items on Front of Camera

AF Illuminator/Self-Timer Lamp

The light on the front of the camera near the Control ring blinks to signal the operation of the self-timer, and it turns on in dark environments to assist with autofocusing. You can control its function for helping with autofocus through the AF Illuminator item on screen 3 of the Shooting menu, as discussed in Chapter 4. If you set that menu item to Auto, the lamp will light as needed for autofocus; if you set it to Off, the lamp will never light for that purpose, though it will still illuminate for the self-timer.

Control Ring

Whenever the camera is set to manual focus or DMF (direct manual focus) using the Focus Mode menu option on screen 3 of the Shooting menu, the Control ring adjusts focus. The ring also has other functions, depending on the settings you make.

To assign functions to the Control ring, use the Custom Key Settings menu option, the third item on screen 4 of the Custom menu. The first sub-option for this menu item is Control Ring, whose options are shown in Figure 5-5.

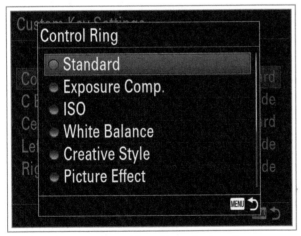

Figure 5-5. Control Ring Menu Options Screen

By default, the Control Ring item is set to Standard. When the Standard setting is in effect, the Control ring controls just one function in any given shooting mode; the function it controls depends on which shooting mode the camera is set to. For example, if the camera is set to the Aperture Priority mode, the Control ring controls aperture; in Shutter Priority mode, the ring controls shutter speed. In the Scene shooting mode, the ring controls selection of scene types.

I usually leave the Control Ring menu item set to Standard because the functions the ring controls in the various shooting modes in that case are quite useful. However, if you want to use the ring for one dedicated

function no matter what shooting mode is in effect, you can use the Control Ring menu item to choose one of the following items that will stay assigned to the ring until you make another change: Exposure Compensation, ISO, White Balance, Creative Style, Picture Effect, Zoom, Shutter Speed, or Aperture. You also can choose Not Set, in which case turning the ring will have no effect (unless you activate a function, such as manual focus, that requires use of the ring).

A function assigned to the ring only works if the context permits it. For example, if you assign Aperture to the Control ring, the ring will control aperture if the camera is set to Aperture Priority or Manual exposure mode. In any other shooting mode, turning the ring will have no effect (except for adjusting manual focus) because aperture cannot be controlled manually in other modes. Also, when you are using the Photo Creativity option in Intelligent Auto or Superior Auto mode, any function assigned to the ring through the Custom menu will not operate, because that operation could conflict with the Photo Creativity settings.

Table 5-1 lists the functions that are assigned to the Control ring with the Standard setting.

Table 5-1. **Control Ring: Standard Setting—**
Shooting Modes vs. Assigned Functions

Shooting Mode	Assigned Function
Intelligent Auto	Zoom
Superior Auto	Zoom
Program	Program Shift
Aperture Priority	Aperture
Shutter Priority	Shutter Speed
Manual Exposure	Aperture
Scene	Scene Selection
Sweep Panorama	Direction
Memory Recall	Depends on Saved Setting

The Control ring also is used in a few other situations regardless of how you have set its assigned function. When you press the Function button (discussed later in this chapter) in shooting mode, the camera activates a menu that shows several options—including items such as white balance, ISO, exposure compensation, etc.—depending on the settings you have chosen for that menu. Once you have pressed the Function button to display that menu, you can turn the Control ring (or the Control wheel) to select the value for the setting that is highlighted on the menu. The Control ring also is used to adjust settings using the Quick Navi menu, which is also called up with the Function button.

Whenever the camera is set to manual focus or DMF (direct manual focus), you use the Control ring to adjust focus. If the MF Assist option is turned on through screen 1 of the Custom menu, the display will be magnified to assist with focusing as soon as you start turning the Control ring. (With DMF, you have to half-press the shutter button while turning the Control ring to use MF Assist.) When the camera is set to either of those focus modes, you cannot use the Control ring for any other function.

The controls on the back of the RX100 III are seen in Figure 5-6.

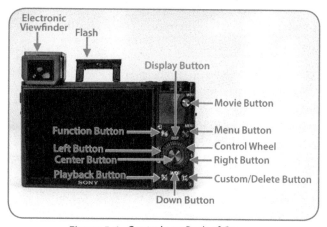

Figure 5-6. Controls on Back of Camera

Playback Button

This button to the lower left of the Control wheel, marked with a small triangle, is used to put the camera into playback mode, which allows you to view your images on the LCD screen (or in the EVF). It also can be used instead of the power button to turn the camera on, placing the RX100 III immediately into playback mode with the lens retracted. When the camera is in playback mode, you can press the shutter button halfway or press the Playback button again to switch the camera into shooting mode.

Movie Button

The red button at the upper right of the camera's back has just one function—to start and stop the recording of a movie sequence. As I noted in discussing the Mode dial earlier in this chapter, you can control how the Movie button operates. If you want to be able to start recording a movie in any shooting mode, go to the Custom menu and select the fifth option on screen 4, called Movie Button. If you set that menu option to Always (the default setting), then the Movie button will operate in any shooting mode. If you set the option to Movie Mode Only, then the Movie button will not operate unless the camera is set to Movie mode using the Mode dial. (Movie mode is the mode marked by a movie-film icon.)

This is a fairly important decision to make, and it depends on your preferences and likely uses of the camera. If you want to be able to start recording a video at any time without delay, leave the Movie Button option set to Always. The reason you might not want to do this is that it is easy to press the Movie button by mistake.

I have done that often myself. When you press the button by mistake, you have to press it again to stop the recording, and then wait for the camera to finish processing the movie before you can use any other controls. And, of course, the camera will have an unwanted file cluttering the memory card, until you delete it.

My preference is to limit use of the Movie button to when the camera is in Movie mode, but if I were going on a vacation and wanted to be able to start recording a movie in Intelligent Auto mode without delay, I would enable the button for use in all modes.

There are differences in how the camera operates for video recording in different shooting modes. I will discuss movie making in detail in Chapter 8.

Menu Button

The Menu button, to the upper right of the Control wheel, is straightforward in its basic function. Press it to enter the menu system, and press it once more to return to whatever mode the camera was in previously (shooting mode or playback mode). The button also cancels out of sub-menus, taking you back to the main menu screen. In playback mode, when an image has been enlarged using the zoom lever, you can press the Menu button (or the Center button) to return it to the normal-sized view.

Function Button

The button marked Fn, for Function, has different functions in shooting mode and playback mode.

SHOOTING MODE: FUNCTION MENU

When the camera is in shooting mode, the Function button gives you flexibility for setting up the RX100 III according to your own preferences. Using the Function Menu Settings option on screen 4 of the Custom menu (discussed in Chapter 7), you can assign up to 12 functions to the Function menu from 27 possibilities, including settings such as ISO, Drive Mode, White Balance, Metering Mode, and Picture Effect.

Once you have assigned up to 12 options to this button, it is ready for action. To use an option, press the Function button when the camera is in shooting mode, and a menu will appear at the bottom of the display in 2 rows with 6 choices each, as shown in Figure 5-7.

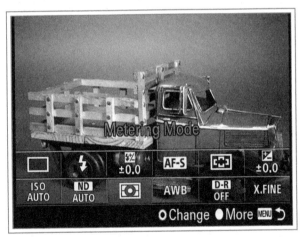

Figure 5-7. Function Menu on Shooting Screen

Use the 4 direction buttons to move to and highlight an option to adjust. Then turn either the Control wheel or the Control ring to change the value of that option. For example, if you have moved the orange highlight block to the Quality item, turn the Control wheel or the Control ring until the setting you want to make appears, as shown in Figure 5-8, where Fine is selected.

Then, press the Function button to confirm the setting and exit from the Function menu screen. Or, if you want to make multiple settings from the Function

menu options, after changing one setting you can press the Center button to go back to the Function menu and make more settings before you press the Function button to exit to the shooting screen.

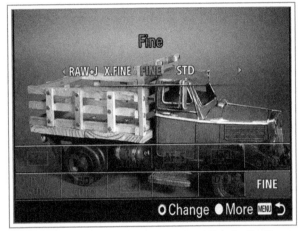

Figure 5-8. Function Menu Setting of Fine for Quality

If the setting you are adjusting needs to have a sub-option set, you can press the Center button to go directly to the menu screen for that setting. For example, suppose you want to set a particular color temperature for white balance. First, from the shooting screen press the Function button to bring up the Function menu, and use the 4 direction buttons to scroll to the White Balance block. Then, instead of choosing a value with the Control wheel or Control ring, press the Center button, and the camera will display the regular White Balance menu screen, as shown in Figure 5-9.

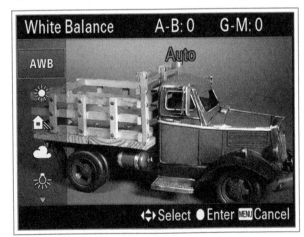

Figure 5-9. White Balance Menu Selected from Function Menu

From that screen, you can navigate to the Color Temperature/Filter option and select the color temperature you want to set. When you have finished, press the Menu button to return to the Function menu.

From there, you can press the Function button to return to the shooting screen.

There may be some items on the Function menu whose icons are dimmed because the item is unavailable for selection in the current context. If you move the orange highlight block to one of those items and then try to change the setting, the camera will display an error message.

Also, the selections I discussed above may not be available because they have not been assigned to the Function menu. If that is the case, you can use the Function Menu Settings menu option to assign them if you want to follow the examples.

The Function menu system on the RX100 III is well thought out and convenient. I strongly recommend that you develop a group of 12 items to assign to this menu and make use of this speedy way to change important settings.

QUICK NAVI SYSTEM

In shooting mode, the Function button also gives you access to the Quick Navi system for changing settings rapidly. This system has similarities to the Function menu system I just discussed, but there are significant differences.

The Quick Navi system comes into play only in one situation—when you have called up the special display screen shown in Figure 5-10, which Sony calls the "For Viewfinder" display.

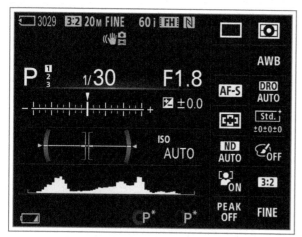

Figure 5-10. For Viewfinder Display Screen

This is the only shooting mode display that does not include the live view. It is called "For viewfinder"

because the idea is that you will use this option when you are using the viewfinder, so you can see the live view through the viewfinder and see the details of your settings on this display, which appears only on the LCD screen.

The For Viewfinder display is summoned by pressing the Display button, but only if you have selected it for inclusion in the cycle of display screens. You select it using the Display Button option on screen 2 of the Custom menu. From that menu option, select the sub-option for Monitor, and then check the box for the For Viewfinder item on the next screen, as shown in Figure 5-11.

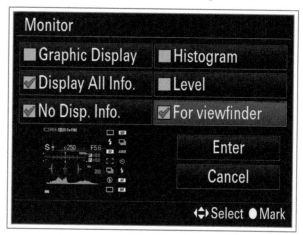

Figure 5-11. For Viewfinder Item Selected on Display Button Screen for Monitor

As seen in Figure 5-10, the For Viewfinder screen displays a lot of information at the right, including Drive Mode, White Balance, Focus Area, DRO, Picture Effect, and several others.

Normally, these items are displayed for information; you cannot adjust them. But, if you press the Function button, an orange highlight appears at the right, as shown in Figure 5-12.

Use the direction buttons to move through the settings. You also can move the highlight to the left, to settings such as ISO, SteadyShot, and Image Size. When you have highlighted a setting to adjust, turn the Control wheel or the Control ring to scroll through the available values and make the adjustment quickly.

When you use the Control wheel or Control ring to adjust a setting, such as Aspect Ratio, a secondary window opens in the top part of the display, as shown in Figure 5-13, showing the options available for the setting.

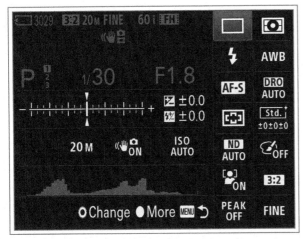

Figure 5-12. Main Screen of Quick Navi System

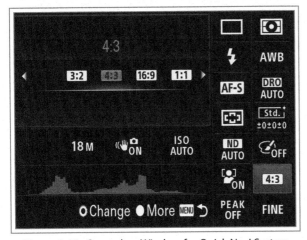

Figure 5-13. Secondary Window for Quick Navi System

After changing a setting, you can move to other settings using the direction buttons. Once you have made all your changes, press the Function button again to exit to the static For Viewfinder display, which will now show the new settings in place.

If you select an option that requires a sub-setting, the steps are slightly different. For example, suppose you want to turn on Auto HDR using the maximum setting of 6.0EV. From the Quick Navi screen, highlight the DRO option and, instead of turning the Control wheel or Control ring to change the setting, press the Center button. You will be taken to a special menu screen for the DRO option, as shown in Figure 5-14.

On that screen, you can select AUTO HDR and set it to 6.0EV. Then press the Menu button to exit to the Quick Navi screen, and press the Function button to return to the For Viewfinder display.

You also can press the Center button when an option is highlighted, even if a sub-setting is not needed, if you

prefer to use a menu screen to make the adjustment. For example, when Aspect Ratio is highlighted on the Quick Navi screen, you can press the Center button to call up a menu, rather than just turning the Control wheel or Control ring.

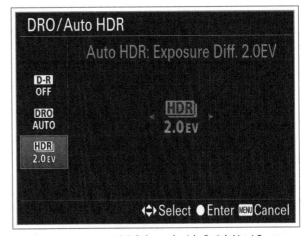

Figure 5-14. Auto HDR Selected with Quick Navi System

The Quick Navi system can streamline your ability to change settings once you get used to it. I recommend you devote some time to practicing with it, if speed is important to you.

Wheel Lock

The Function button also can carry out one other operation in shooting mode, depending on how a Custom menu option is set. The final item on screen 4 of that menu is the Wheel Lock option. If that option is set to Lock, then, when you press and hold the Function button for several seconds when the shooting screen is displayed, the shooting-related operations that are adjusted by turning the Control wheel are locked. The wheel will still operate to navigate through menu screens and menu settings, but turning it will not set items such as ISO, shutter speed, and scene types. The buttons at the edges of the wheel will still operate. I will discuss that menu option in Chapter 7.

Playback Mode: Send to Smartphone

When the RX100 III is in playback mode, pressing the Function button activates the Send to Smartphone option, just as if you had chosen this menu option from the Wi-Fi menu. So, if you have just taken a photo and want to transfer it to your phone for sharing with friends or posting to Facebook, you can just press the Function button in playback mode and make the transfer quickly. I will discuss that menu option in Chapter 9.

Custom/Delete Button

The button marked with a C, to the right of the Playback button, is called the Custom/Delete button. This button can be programmed to perform any one of 41 functions. To make this choice, use the Custom Key Settings option on screen 4 of the Custom menu, and then select the C Button sub-option. I will discuss that menu option in Chapter 7.

By default, the C button is assigned the In-Camera Guide function. With that option, when the camera is displaying a menu you can press the button to display a brief help screen with guidance or tips about the menu option that is highlighted or selected. The help screen varies depending on the context.

If the camera is displaying the main page of a menu screen with the highlight on a particular feature, pressing the C button will bring up a screen with a brief message explaining the use of that feature. For example, Figure 5-15 shows the message that is displayed when the camera is displaying screen 2 of the Shooting menu, with the Drive Mode item highlighted.

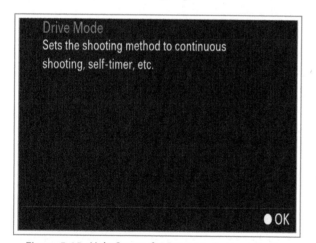

Figure 5-15. Help Screen for Drive Mode Menu Option

If you select a sub-option for a menu item and press the C button, the camera will display a message with details about that particular option. For example, Figure 5-16 shows the help screen that was displayed when I pressed the C button after highlighting the Speed Priority Continuous Shooting option for the Drive Mode item.

This help system is quite detailed; for example, it provides guidance even for different ISO settings, such as ISO 100, 160, and 1600, with tips about when to use each setting. The help function operates with all of the RX100 III menu systems, including Custom, Playback,

Setup, and the others, not just the Shooting menu. It also works with the Function menu and the Quick Navi system to give information about a highlighted option.

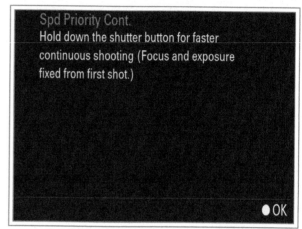

Figure 5-16. Help Screen for Speed Priority Continuous Menu Option

The C button has a special function when the camera is in the Intelligent Auto or Superior Auto mode, regardless of any function assigned to the button using the Custom Key Settings option. When you are using the Photo Creativity option in either of those modes and you have moved the indicator along the curved scale on the screen to change a setting (such as Brightness or Color), you can press the C button to reset the option to its default value.

When the camera is in playback mode, displaying a recorded image or movie (and not a menu screen), this button becomes the Delete button, as indicated by the trash can icon to the lower right of the button. If you press the button, the camera displays the message shown in Figure 5-17, prompting you to select Delete or Cancel.

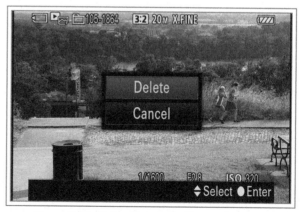

Figure 5-17. Delete Button Confirmation Screen

If you highlight Delete and press the Center button, the camera will delete the image or video that was displayed. If you choose Cancel, the camera will return to the playback mode screen. This operation also works when an image is being displayed briefly with the Auto Review option, right after the image was captured.

How you program the C button is, of course, a matter of personal preference. The In-Camera Guide option is quite useful, especially when you are first learning the operation of the camera. Once you are more confident with the camera's functions, you might want to use this button for an operation that is not available through the menu system, or not readily available through a menu, such as AF/MF Control Toggle. I will discuss all of the options in Chapter 7.

Control Wheel and Its Buttons

Several controls are within the perimeter of the Control wheel, the ridged wheel with icons around its outer edges. In the middle of the wheel is the Center button, a much-used control. The 4 edges of the wheel (up, down, left, and right) act as buttons. If you press the wheel's rim at any of those 4 points, you are, in effect, pressing a button. Each button has at least 2 functions—as a direction control along with one or more other specific assignments. When they act as direction controls, the buttons are used to navigate through menu options and other choices for controlling the camera's settings. The other main functions of the buttons are indicated by one or more icons at each button's position on the Control wheel. I will discuss all of these controls in turn.

CONTROL WHEEL

In many cases, to choose a menu item or a setting, you can turn this wheel. In some cases, you have the choice of using this wheel or pressing the direction buttons. One helpful feature of the RX100 III is that it places a round icon on the screen representing the Control wheel when there is a value that can be adjusted at that point by the wheel. (If you don't see the icon, press the Display button until it appears.)

For example, in Figure 5-18, the icon, which looks like a gray ring lying flat on the screen in the lower right corner, is positioned next to the Av indicator, meaning the Control wheel can now control aperture. (The more

3-dimensional icon to the right of that one shows that the Control ring also can control aperture at this time.)

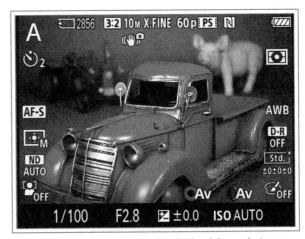

Figure 5-18. Icon Showing Control Wheel Controls Aperture

Figure 5-19 shows the camera in Manual exposure mode, and the icon for the Control wheel is next to the Tv indicator, standing for time value or shutter speed, indicating that you can adjust the shutter speed by turning the Control wheel.

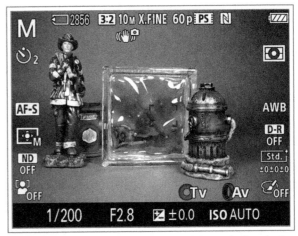

Figure 5-19. Icon Showing Control Wheel Controls Shutter Speed

(The icon to the right shows that the Control ring now adjusts aperture.) In Aperture Priority mode, the wheel controls aperture, and in Shutter Priority mode it controls shutter speed. When the camera is in Scene mode, you can turn the Control wheel to change the scene type, such as Portrait, Landscape, and the like. In Sweep Panorama mode, turning the wheel changes the direction of the panorama. In Program mode, it controls Program Shift.

The Control wheel has several other functions. When you are viewing a menu screen, you can navigate through the lists of options by turning the wheel. When you are adjusting items using the Function menu or Quick Navi system, you can change the value for the selected setting by turning the Control wheel. When you are using manual focus and you have the Focus Magnifier option turned on, you can turn the Control wheel to vary the area of the scene that is being magnified. With the Focus Area menu option, you can turn the Control wheel to adjust the size of the focus frame when the frame is activated for moving around the display.

In playback mode, you can turn the Control wheel to navigate through images. Also, when a video is being played on the screen and has been paused, you can turn the Control wheel to play the video slowly, frame-by-frame, either forward or in reverse.

CENTER BUTTON

This button in the center of the Control wheel has many uses. On menu screens that have additional options, such as the Image Size screen, this button takes you to the next screen to view the other options. It also acts as a selection button when you choose certain options. For example, after you select Focus Mode from screen 3 of the Shooting menu and then navigate to your desired focus option, you can press the Center button to confirm your selection and exit from the menu screen back to the shooting screen.

The Center button also has several other possible uses depending on how it is set up. Screen 4 of the Custom menu (discussed in Chapter 7) has an item called Custom Key Settings, with a sub-option for setting the function of the Center button. Using that option, you can set the Center button to have its normal default functions by selecting the Standard option.

If you select the Standard option, then, if the Focus Area is set to Flexible Spot, pressing the Center button activates the screen for adjusting the location of the focus frame. If Center Lock-on AF is turned on, this button activates focus tracking. When the camera is set to manual focus and MF Assist or Focus Magnifier is turned on, pressing the Center button changes the magnification factor of the display.

If you prefer not to use the Standard option, you can use the Custom Key Settings option to set this button to carry out one of 41 other functions. I will discuss that menu option in Chapter 7.

In playback mode, you press the Center button to start playing a video whose first frame is displayed on the camera's screen. Once the video is playing, press the Center button to pause the playback and then to toggle between play and pause. When a panoramic image is displayed, press the Center button to make it scroll on the screen at a larger size using the full expanse of the display screen. When you have enlarged an image using the zoom lever, you can return it immediately to its normal size by pressing the Center button. When you are selecting images for deletion, protection, or printing using the appropriate Playback menu options, you use the Center button to mark or unmark an image for that purpose.

DIRECTION BUTTONS

Each of the 4 edges of the Control wheel is a button you can press to get access to a setting or operation. This is not immediately obvious, and sometimes it can be tricky to press in exactly the right spot, but these 4 buttons are important to your control of the camera. You use them to navigate through menus and screens for settings, whether moving left and right or up and down.

You also use these buttons in playback mode to move through your images and, when you have enlarged an image using the zoom lever, to scroll around within the magnified image.

In addition to navigation, the direction buttons are used for miscellaneous functions in connection with various settings. For example, when the camera is set to Manual exposure mode, you can press the Down button to toggle the action of the Control wheel between setting aperture and setting shutter speed. And, as with the Center button, the Right and Left buttons can be assigned to carry out other functions through the Custom Key Settings option on screen 4 of the Custom menu, as discussed in Chapter 7.

Finally, each of the direction buttons has its own separate identity, as indicated by the 1 or 2 icons that appear on or near each of the buttons, as discussed below.

Up Button: Display

The Up button, marked "DISP," switches among information displays on the LCD screen and in the viewfinder, in both shooting and playback modes. As discussed in Chapter 7, you can change the contents of the shooting mode screens using the Display Button option on screen 2 of the Custom menu. The various display screens for playback mode are discussed in Chapter 6.

The Up button cannot be reassigned using the menu system; it is permanently assigned as the Display button.

Right Button: Flash Mode

When the camera is in shooting mode, pressing the Right button brings up a menu on the left of the display showing the options for setting the behavior of the flash unit. The options are Flash Off, Autoflash, Fill-flash, Slow Sync, and Rear Sync, although not all of them are available in any one shooting mode. This menu can also be summoned from screen 2 of the Shooting menu. I discussed the use of these settings in Chapter 4.

One important point is that you have to use the flash pop-up switch to pop up the flash before it can be used, no matter what option you have selected from the Flash Mode menu.

You can reassign the function of the Right button using the Custom Key Settings option on screen 4 of the Custom menu. You can choose any one of 37 options, including Flash Mode, Focus Mode, and others; I will discuss that menu option in Chapter 7.

Down Button: Photo Creativity/Exposure Compensation

The Down button has 2 icons directly below it, indicating that it has 2 different functions depending on the shooting mode. In the Intelligent Auto and Superior Auto modes, pressing this button brings up the Photo Creativity options, which I discussed in Chapter 2. In the Program, Aperture Priority, Shutter Priority, Movie, and Sweep Panorama modes, this button controls exposure compensation, discussed below.

In Manual exposure mode, this button toggles the Control wheel's function between controlling aperture and controlling shutter speed. In that mode, you can use the Exposure Compensation item on screen 3 of the Shooting menu to adjust exposure compensation, or you can use the Custom Key Settings menu option to assign a control button or the Control ring to adjust that setting. (Exposure compensation can be adjusted in Manual exposure mode only if ISO is set to Auto ISO.)

In Scene mode, the Down button has no function other than as a direction button. If you press it when the shooting screen is displayed, you will see an error message.

Exposure Compensation

Here is an example of the use of exposure compensation to adjust for an unusual, or non-optimal, lighting situation. Figure 5-20 is a photo of a miniature fire hydrant against a white background, taken using the Program shooting mode.

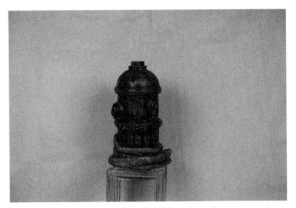

Figure 5-20. Image in Need of Exposure Compensation

The camera's metering system measured the large, white area, and because of that background, it reduced the exposure, making the hydrant appear too dark.

One solution to this problem is to use exposure compensation to increase the overall exposure of the image, so the subject will not be underexposed. To accomplish this with the RX100 III, press the Down button to bring the exposure compensation scale up on the display, as shown in Figure 5-21.

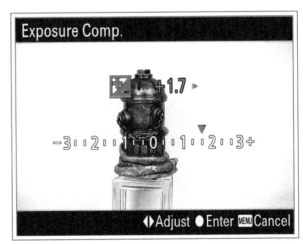

Figure 5-21. Exposure Compensation Adjustment Screen

Turn the Control wheel or press the Left and Right buttons to move the orange triangle above the scale, so it points to a value to the left or right of the zero point.

As you do this, the numbers near the top of the display will change. With a negative value, the image will be darker than it otherwise would; with a positive value, it will be brighter. The camera's display will grow brighter or darker to indicate the effect of the adjustment, if the Live View Display item on screen 2 of the Custom menu is set to Setting Effect On.

In this case, with exposure compensation increased by 1.7 EV (exposure value) units, the hydrant becomes lighter and is no longer underexposed, as shown in the final image in Figure 5-22.

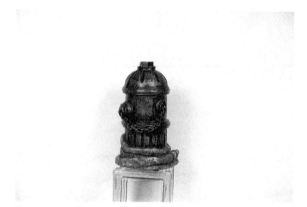

Figure 5-22. Image After Exposure Compensation Applied

Some photographers follow the practice of generally leaving exposure compensation set at a particular amount, such as negative 0.7 EV. You might do this if you find your images generally are slightly overexposed or if you see that highlights are clipping in many cases. (You can tell if highlights are clipping by checking the histogram, as discussed in Chapter 6. If the histogram is bunched all the way to the right, with no space between the data lines and the right side of the chart, highlights are clipping, or reaching the maximum value.) It is difficult to recover details from images whose highlights have clipped, so it can be a safety measure to underexpose images slightly to avoid that situation.

If you don't plan to leave a permanent exposure compensation setting in place, you should return the setting to the zero point when you are finished with it, so you won't inadvertently change the exposure of later images that don't need the adjustment. (The exposure compensation setting will remain in place even after the camera has been turned off and back on again.)

If you use exposure compensation often, you can assign it to the Control ring using the Custom Key Settings menu option. Then you can turn the ring to start adjusting exposure compensation with a circular scale on the screen, as shown in Figure 5-23.

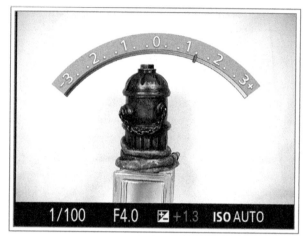

Figure 5-23. Display When Exposure Compensation Adjusted by Control Ring

(The ring will not adjust exposure compensation if the camera is set for manual focus or DMF, because the ring is used to adjust focus with those settings.)

There is one other duty performed by the Down button. In playback mode, when a movie is displayed as ready to play, you can press this button to move to a screen for adjusting the sound level for playback of movies, as shown in Figure 5-24.

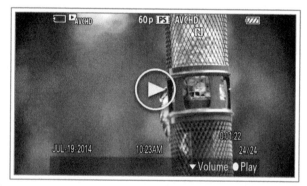

Figure 5-24. Icon Showing to Press Down Button to Adjust Volume

This function also works for still images, if the View Mode option on the Playback menu is set to a view that includes movies, such as Date View. When a movie is playing, you can press this button to get to the full panel of playback controls, as shown in Figure 5-25.

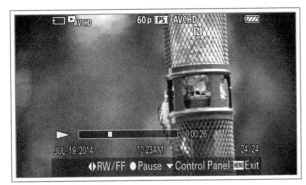

Figure 5-25. Icon Showing to Press Down Button for Control Panel

The Down button is permanently assigned to control exposure compensation and Photo Creativity and cannot be reassigned.

Left Button: Self-Timer/Drive Mode

The Left button is labeled with the timer dial icon for the self-timer and the stack-of-frames icon for continuous shooting. When you press this button, the camera brings up the Drive Mode menu with its options for self-timer, continuous shooting, and several types of bracketing. I discussed these options in Chapter 4 in connection with the Drive Mode option on the Shooting menu.

You can reassign the function of the Left button using the Custom Key Settings option on screen 4 of the Custom menu. You can choose any one of 37 options, as discussed in Chapter 7.

Tilting LCD Screen

The next item to be discussed is the tilting LCD screen on the back of the camera. This screen, even without its tilting ability, is a notable feature of the camera. It has a diagonal span of 3 inches (7.5 cm) and provides a resolution of 1.2 million dots using Sony's "WhiteMagic" technology, which adds a white sub-pixel to the normal red, green, and blue ones, giving a clear and sharp view of your images before and after you capture them.

The screen can tilt to assist with various types of shots. First, it can tilt downward as much as 45 degrees, as shown in Figure 5-26. When the LCD is tilted this way, you can hold the camera above your head and view the scene as if you were an arm's length taller or were standing on a small ladder. If you attach the camera to a monopod or other support and hold it up in the air, you can extend the height even farther and still view the LCD screen quite well. You can activate the self-timer before raising the camera up in the air to take the photo.

You also can use a smartphone or tablet connected to the camera by Wi-Fi to trigger the camera by remote control while it is raised overhead, as discussed in Chapter 9, or you can use Sony's wired remote control, discussed in Appendix A.

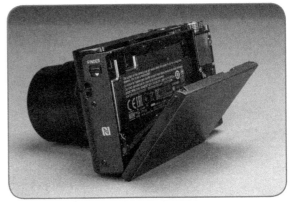

Figure 5-26. LCD Screen Tilted Down for Overhead Shots

On the other hand, if you need to take images from a vantage point near ground level, you can rotate the screen so it tilts upward toward your eye, as shown in Figure 5-27, and hold the camera down as far as you need to get a mole's-eye view of the world.

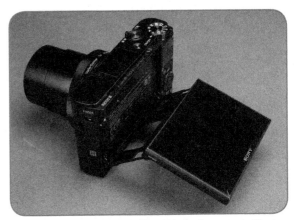

Figure 5-27. LCD Screen Tilted Up for Low-angle Shots

It can be helpful to shoot upward like this when your subject is in an area with a busy, distracting background. You can hold the camera down low and shoot with the sky as your background to reduce or eliminate the distractions. (Similarly, you may be able to shoot from a high angle to place your subject against the ground or floor to have a less-cluttered background.)

The tilting display also is useful for street photography: You can fold the screen upward and look down at the camera while taking photos of people without drawing undue attention to yourself.

Finally, you can rotate the screen 180 degrees so it faces in the same direction as the lens, as shown in Figure 5-28.

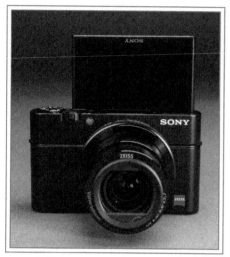

Figure 5-28. LCD Screen Flipped Forward for Self-portraits

With this orientation, you can take self-portraits. If you turn on the self-portrait timer option on screen 3 of the Custom menu, then, when the screen is in this position, the camera will count down from 3 to 1 with large numbers on the screen, as shown in Figure 5-29, to help you prepare for the taking of the self-portrait. This orientation also is quite useful if you are doing a video blog or review and you need to see yourself as you record the video.

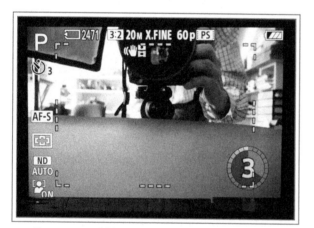

Figure 5-29. Self-portrait Timer Countdown Screen

Ports and Other Items on Right and Left Sides of Camera

Next, I will discuss the ports on the right side of the camera. Figure 5-30 shows this side of the camera with the protective flaps closed.

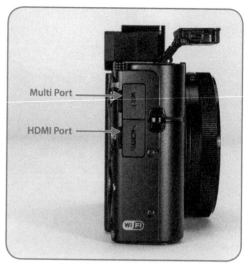

Figure 5-30. Port Covers on Right Side of Camera

Figure 5-31 shows the ports when the flaps are open.

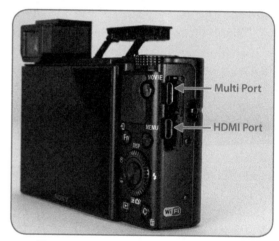

Figure 5-31. Ports on Right Side of Camera

The top port is the Multi port. This is where you plug in the USB cable for charging the battery, uploading images and videos to your computer, or connecting the camera directly to a printer to print images. You also can plug in other accessories that are compatible with this special terminal, including Sony's wired remote control, model RM-VPR1, which I discuss in Appendix A.

The lower port is the HDMI port, where you plug in an optional micro-HDMI cable to connect the camera to an HDTV for viewing images and videos. You also can view the shooting display from the camera through this connection, so you can connect the camera to an HDTV to act as a monitor for your shooting of still images or videos. I will discuss this process in Chapter 9.

The left side of the camera, shown in Figure 5-32, is where the Finder switch is located. Press down on this switch to release the electronic viewfinder so it will pop up. If the camera is turned off, popping up the viewfinder will turn the camera on. Pressing the viewfinder back into the camera's body will power the camera off.

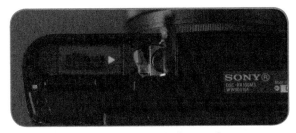

Figure 5-34. Red Access Lamp in Battery Compartment

This red lamp lights when the camera is writing data to the memory card. When the lamp is lit, it's important not to remove the card or the battery from the compartment.

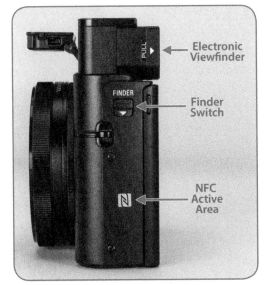

Figure 5-32. Items on Left Side of Camera

Below the Finder switch is a decorative letter N, which marks the NFC active area for the RX100 III. This is where you touch the camera against the similar area on a compatible Android smartphone or tablet that uses the near field communication protocol. As discussed in Chapter 9, when the 2 devices are touched together at their NFC active areas, they should automatically connect through a Wi-Fi connection. Once the connection is established, they can share images and the phone or tablet can control the camera in some ways.

Finally, the bottom of the RX100 III is shown in Figure 5-33.

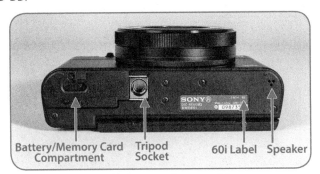

Figure 5-33. Items on Bottom of Camera

The most significant items here are the tripod socket and the battery/memory card compartment. There is an access lamp inside this compartment, as seen in Figure 5-34.

CHAPTER 6: PLAYBACK AND PRINTING

You may not spend a lot of time viewing images and videos in the camera, but it's still useful to know how the various playback functions work. You may need to examine an image closely in the camera to check focus, composition, and other aspects, or you may want to share images with friends and family. So it's worth looking at the playback functions of the RX100 III. I'll also discuss options for printing images in this chapter.

Normal Playback

I'll start with an overview of basic playback. First, you should be aware of the setting for Auto Review on screen 1 of the Custom menu. This setting determines whether and for how long the image stays on the screen for review when you take a new picture. If your major concern is to check images right after they are taken, this setting is all you need to use. As discussed in Chapter 7, you can leave Auto Review turned off or set it to 2, 5, or 10 seconds.

To control how images are viewed later on, you need to use the options available in playback mode. For plain review of images, press the Playback button, marked by a small triangle to the lower left of the Control wheel. Once you press that button, the camera is in playback mode, and you will see the most recent image saved to the memory card. To move back through older images, press the Left button or turn the Control wheel to the left. To see more recent images, use the Right button or turn the wheel to the right. To speed through the images, hold down the Left or Right button.

INDEX VIEW AND ENLARGING IMAGES

In normal playback mode, you can press the zoom lever to view an index screen of images and videos or to enlarge a single image. When you are viewing an individual image, press the zoom lever once to the left, and you will see a screen showing either 9 or 25 images,

one of which is outlined by an orange frame, as shown in Figure 6-1. (You can choose whether this screen shows 9 or 25 images using the Image Index option on the Playback menu, discussed later in this chapter.)

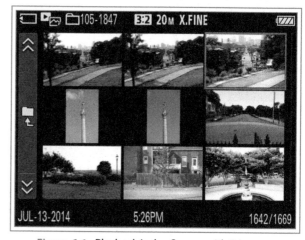

Figure 6-1. Playback Index Screen with 9 Images

You can press the Center button to view the outlined image, or you can move through the images on the index screen by pressing the 4 direction buttons or by turning the Control wheel. If you move the orange highlight to the far left of the display, as seen in Figure 6-2, you then can use the Up and Down buttons to move through the images a screen at a time.

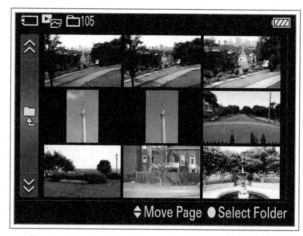

Figure 6-2. Strip at Left of Index Screen Highlighted

On the 9-image or 25-image index screen, one more press of the zoom lever to the left brings up another screen. For example, if View Mode, discussed later in this chapter, is set to Date View, this next screen will be a calendar display, as shown in Figure 6-3.

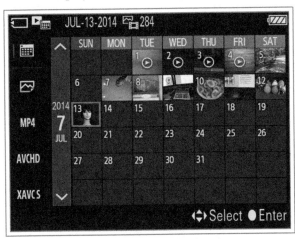

Figure 6-3. Calendar Screen

On that screen, you can move the orange frame to any date and press the Center button to bring up a view with all images from that date. If you move the orange highlight to the narrow strip to the left of the calendar, as seen in Figure 6-4, you can move through the images by months with the Up and Down buttons.

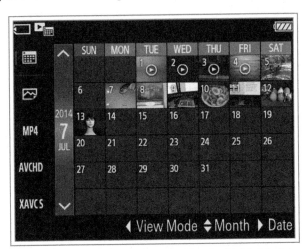

Figure 6-4. Strip to Navigate by Months Highlighted

If you move the highlight to the far left of the screen, as in Figure 6-5, you can use the Up and Down buttons to move through the 5 icons, from which you can choose the date view, still-images view, MP4 videos view, AVCHD videos view, or XAVC S videos view. I will discuss those options later in this chapter, in connection with the View Mode menu option on the Playback menu.

When you are viewing a single image, one press of the zoom lever to the right enlarges that image. You will then see a display in the lower left corner of the image showing a thumbnail with an inset orange frame that represents the portion of the image that is now filling the screen in enlarged view, as shown in Figure 6-6.

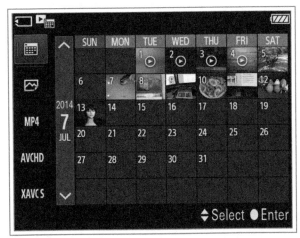

Figure 6-5. Strip to Select View Mode Highlighted

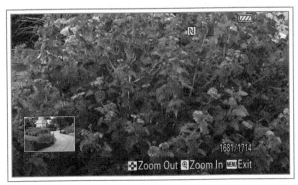

Figure 6-6. Enlarged Image with Inset Block at Lower Left

If you press the zoom lever to the right repeatedly, the image will be enlarged to increasing levels. While it is magnified, you can scroll in it with the 4 direction buttons; you will see the orange frame move around within the thumbnail image. To reduce the image size again, press the zoom lever to the left as many times as necessary or press the Center button or the Menu button to revert immediately to normal size. To move to other images while the display is magnified, turn the Control wheel.

PLAYBACK SCREENS

When you are viewing an image in single-image display mode, pressing the Display (Up) button repeatedly cycles through the 3 screens that are available: (1) full image with no added information; (2) full image with basic information, including date and time taken, image number, aspect ratio, aperture, shutter speed, ISO, and image size and quality, as shown in Figure 6-7; and (3) thumbnail image with detailed recording information, including aperture, shutter speed, ISO, shooting mode, white balance, and other data, plus a histogram, as shown in Figure 6-8.

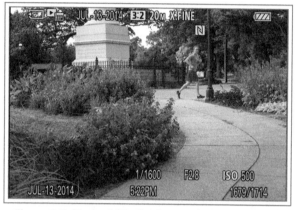

Figure 6-7. Playback Display Screen - Basic Information

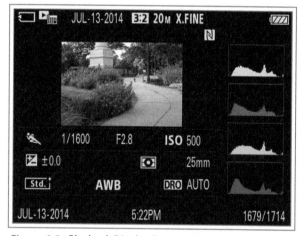

Figure 6-8. Playback Display Screen - Detailed Information

A histogram is a graph showing the distribution of dark and bright areas in the image displayed on the screen. The darkest blacks are represented by peaks on the left and the brightest whites by peaks on the right, with continuous gradations in between. With the RX100 III, the histogram displayed in playback mode includes 4 boxes with information. The top box provides information about the overall brightness of the image. The 3 lower boxes provide information about the brightness of the basic colors that make up the image: red, green, and blue.

If a histogram has peaks bunched at the left, there are too many dark areas and few bright and white areas. If the graph runs into the left side of the chart, it means

shadow areas are "clipped" so that details have been lost in the dark areas. The histogram in Figure 6-9 illustrates this degree of underexposure.

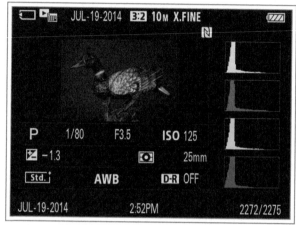

Figure 6-9. Playback Histogram - Underexposed Image

A histogram with its high points bunched to the right means the opposite—too bright, as in Figure 6-10. If the lines of the graph run into the right side of the chart, that means highlights are clipped and the image has lost some details in the bright areas.

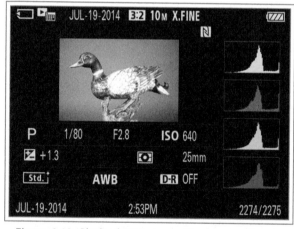

Figure 6-10. Playback Histogram - Overexposed Image

A histogram that is "just right" has high points arranged evenly in the middle of the chart. That pattern, as illustrated by Figure 6-11, indicates a good balance of light, dark, and medium tones.

When the playback histogram is displayed, areas containing highlights that are excessively bright will blink to indicate possible overexposure, alerting you that you may need to take another shot with the exposure adjusted to correct that situation.

The histogram can give you helpful feedback about the exposure of images. Also, there may be instances in which it is appropriate to have a histogram skewed to the left or right for intentionally "low-key" (dark) or "high-key" (brightly lit) scenes.

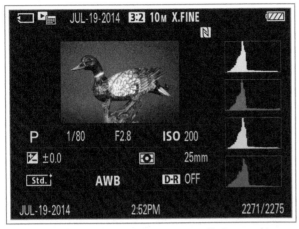

Figure 6-11. Playback Histogram - Normally Exposed Image

To turn on the histogram for the live view in shooting mode, use the Display Button option on screen 2 of the Custom menu.

DELETING IMAGES WITH THE DELETE BUTTON

As I mentioned in Chapter 5, you can delete individual images by pressing the Delete button, also known as the Custom (C) button. If you press this button when a still image or a video is displayed, whether individually or highlighted on an index screen, the camera will display the Delete/Cancel box shown in Figure 6-12.

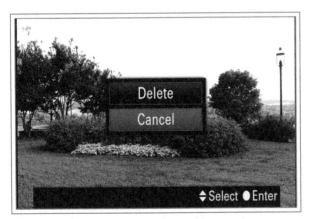

Figure 6-12. Delete Button Confirmation Screen

Highlight your choice and press the Center button to confirm. To delete multiple items, you need to use the Delete option on the Playback menu, discussed later in this chapter. You also can use the Delete button to delete an image when it is displayed immediately after it was taken, with the Auto Review option.

Playback Menu

Other options for playback on the RX100 III appear as items on the Playback menu, whose first screen is shown in Figure 6-13.

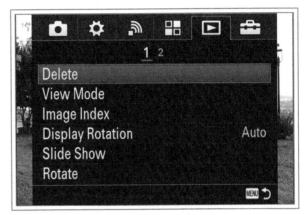

Figure 6-13. Screen 1 of Playback Menu

You get access to this menu by pressing the Menu button. The camera does not have to be in playback mode to get access to this menu, but, in playback mode, pressing the Menu button will take you directly to the Playback menu. Otherwise, you may need to navigate to this menu. You enter playback mode by pressing the Playback button when the camera is turned on in shooting mode. If the camera is turned off, you can turn it on in playback mode by pressing the Playback button instead of the Power button.

Here is information about the items on the Playback menu:

DELETE

The Delete command is used to delete multiple images in one operation. (If you just want to delete 1 or 2 images, it's easier to display each image on the screen, then press the Delete button and confirm the erasure.) When you select the Delete command, the menu offers you various choices, as shown in Figure 6-14.

These choices may include Multiple Images, All in Folder, or All with this Date, depending on the current setting for the View Mode option, discussed below.

If you choose Multiple Images, the camera will display images or videos with a check box at the left side, as shown in Figure 6-15.

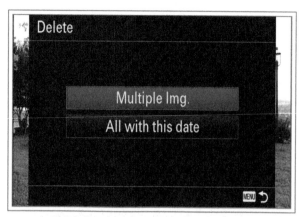

Figure 6-14. Delete Menu Options Screen

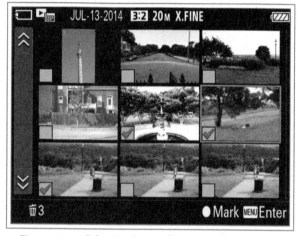

Figure 6-15. Selection Screen for Delete Menu Option

The images and videos may be shown individually or on an index screen, depending on current settings. You can change between full-screen and index views using the zoom lever.

Scroll through the images and videos with the Control wheel or the direction buttons. When you reach an image you want to delete, press the Center button to place a check mark in the check box on that image. Continue with this process until you have marked all images you want to delete. Then press the Menu button to move to the next screen, where the camera will prompt you to highlight OK or Cancel, and press the Center button to confirm. If you select OK, all of the marked images will be deleted.

If, instead of Multiple Images, you choose All in Folder, the camera will display a screen asking you to confirm deletion of all files in the current folder. If you select All with This Date, you will have the opportunity to delete all images and videos from the selected date. If any images have a key icon displayed at the top, those images are protected, and cannot be deleted using this

option unless you first unprotect them, as discussed later in this chapter.

VIEW MODE

This second option on the Playback menu lets you choose which images or videos are currently viewed in playback mode. The options are Date View, Folder View (Still), Folder View (MP4), AVCHD View, and XAVC S View, as shown in Figure 6-16.

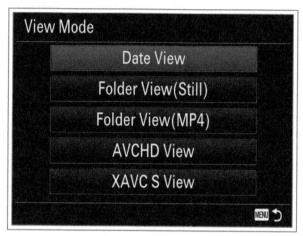

Figure 6-16. View Mode Menu Options Screen

If you select Date View, the camera will display the calendar screen shown earlier in Figure 6-3. You can navigate through that screen using the Control wheel or the direction buttons. Highlight a date and press the Center button; the camera will display all images and videos from that date. When the calendar screen is displayed, you can move to other months by highlighting the gray strip to the left of the calendar and using the Up and Down buttons.

If you select Folder View (Still), the camera will display the screen shown in Figure 6-17, which displays the folders available for selection.

Highlight the folder you want (there may be only one) and press the Center button; the camera will display all still images in that folder. You can navigate through the index screens for those images and select the image or images you want to view.

If you select Folder View (MP4), the camera will display only the MP4 videos from the folder you select, if there are any such videos.

If you select AVCHD View, the camera will display a calendar screen with thumbnail images indicating which dates have AVCHD files associated with them. You can select any date with a thumbnail to display AVCHD videos from that date.

If you select XAVC S View, the camera will display a calendar showing the dates on which videos in that format were recorded.

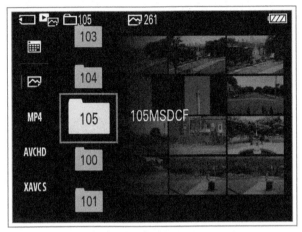

Figure 6-17. Folder View (Still) Screen

My usual preference is to use the Date View option, because then I can view both images and videos from a given date. However, if I want to locate a particular video, it can be quicker to choose one of the video views so I can limit my search to videos only.

You can select a view option from an index screen without using the Playback menu. After moving the zoom lever to the left to call up the calendar display or folder display, move the highlight to the extreme left of the screen to the line of icons that represent the 5 view modes, as shown in Figure 6-5, and select one of the modes from that display.

IMAGE INDEX

This menu option, shown in Figure 6-18, gives you the choice of having the camera include either 9 images or 25 images when it displays an index screen. When you make this selection, the camera displays the index screen you chose, and it will display that screen whenever you call up the index screen using the zoom lever, as discussed earlier.

Whether you choose the 9-image screen or the 25-image screen depends on your personal preference as well as some other factors, including how many images and videos you have on your memory card and how easy it is to distinguish one from another by

looking at the small thumbnail images. The thumbnails on the 9-image screen are considerably larger than those on the 25-image screen, and it may make sense to choose the 9-image screen unless you have so many images that it would be burdensome to scroll through them 9 at a time.

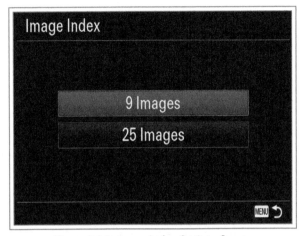

Figure 6-18. Image Index Options Screen

DISPLAY ROTATION

This next item on the Playback menu controls whether images shot with the camera held vertically appear that way when you play them back on the camera's screen. By default, this option is set to Auto, meaning images taken vertically are automatically rotated so that the vertical shot appears in portrait orientation on the horizontal display, as shown in Figure 6-19.

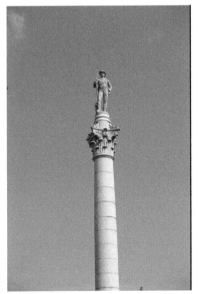

Figure 6-19. Image Auto-rotated on Screen

With this setting, if you tilt the camera sideways so one side is up, a vertical image will rotate to fill the screen. In this way, you get the best of both worlds: Vertical images display in proper orientation (but smaller than normal) within the horizontal display, and, when you tilt the camera, they display at full size.

If you change the setting to Manual, a vertical image will appear vertically on the horizontal screen, in the same way as shown in Figure 6-19. The difference with this setting from Auto is that, if you tilt the camera, the image will not change its orientation.

If you set this option to Off, a vertical image will display horizontally on the display, as shown in Figure 6-20, so you would have to tilt the camera to see it in its proper orientation.

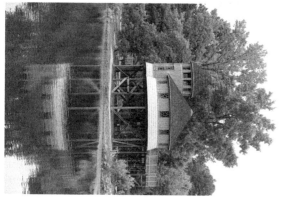

Figure 6-20. Image with Display Rotation Turned Off

With all of these settings, you can use the Rotate option on the Playback menu, discussed later in this chapter, to rotate an image manually to a different orientation.

SLIDE SHOW

This feature lets you play still images and videos in sequence at an interval you specify. This option will be dimmed and unavailable if the View Mode option on the Playback menu is set to either Folder View (MP4), AVCHD View, or XAVC S View. If that is the case, use the View Mode menu option to select either Date View or Folder View (Still). The Slide Show option will display all of your movies, in all 3 formats, along with your still images, if you select Date View from the View Mode menu option. Each movie will play in full before the show advances to the next item, unless you interrupt it with one of the controls.

When you select the Slide Show option, the next screen has 2 options you can set: Repeat and Interval, as seen in Figure 6-21.

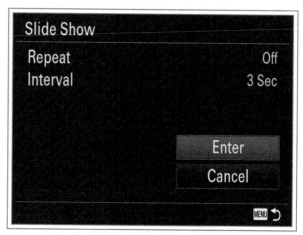

Figure 6-21. Slide Show Menu Options Screen

If Repeat is turned on, the show will keep repeating; otherwise, it will play only once. The camera will not power off automatically in this mode, so be sure to stop the show when you are done with it. The Interval setting, which controls how long each image stays on the screen, can be set to 1, 3, 5, 10, or 30 seconds. (The Interval setting does not apply to movies, which play to the end.)

Once the options are set, navigate to the Enter box at the bottom of the screen using the Control wheel or the direction buttons, and press the Center button to start the show. You can move forward or backward through images (and videos, if included) with the Right and Left buttons. Hold the buttons down to fast-forward or fast-reverse through the images and videos.

You can stop the show by pressing the Menu button or the Playback button. There is no way to pause the show and resume it. When a movie is playing as part of the show, you can control its volume by pressing the Down button and then adjusting the sound with the Left and Right buttons or the Control wheel. Each movie plays fully before the next movie or image is displayed, but you can skip to the next movie or image using the Right button.

The Slide Show option does not provide settings such as transitions, effects, or music. You cannot select which images to play; this option just lets you play all of your still images from the selected folder, if you are using Folder View, or all still images and videos starting from the selected date, if you are using Date View.

ROTATE

The Rotate option is a way to rotate an image manually. Select this menu item, and you will see a screen like that in Figure 6-22, prompting you to press the Center button to rotate the image.

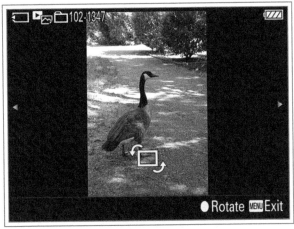

Figure 6-22. Screen for Rotating Image

Each time you press the button, the image will rotate 90 degrees counter-clockwise. You can use this option for images taken vertically, when Display Rotation, discussed above, is turned off.

The remaining options on the Playback menu are on its second and final screen, shown in Figure 6-23.

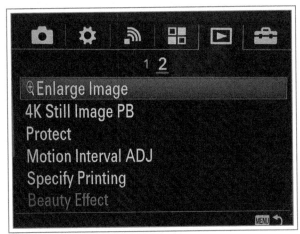

Figure 6-23. Screen 2 of Playback Menu

ENLARGE IMAGE

This option does the same magnification discussed earlier in this chapter, which you can also do with the zoom lever. When you select this option, the enlarged image will appear on the screen; you can use the zoom lever to change the enlargement factor.

4K STILL IMAGE PLAYBACK

This option is dimmed and cannot be selected unless the camera is connected to a TV set that supports 4K resolution. The standard known as 4K is a relatively recent option for HDTVs. The 4K stands for 4,000, meaning each frame has a horizontal resolution of about 4,000 pixels. A standard HD (high-definition) TV set outputs frames with a horizontal resolution of 1920 pixels and a vertical resolution of 1080 pixels. A 4K TV frame has a horizontal resolution of 3840 and a vertical resolution of 2160. The overall resolution of the 4K TV image is about 8 megapixels, while the resolution of full HDTV is about 2 megapixels, so a 4K picture has 4 times the resolution of full HDTV. So, if you have a 4K TV available, you can connect your RX100 III using an optional HDMI cable and enjoy your still images at the highest possible resolution.

PROTECT

With the Protect feature, you can "lock" selected images or videos so they cannot be erased with the normal erase functions, including using the Delete button and using the Delete option on the Playback menu, discussed above. However, if you format the memory card using the Format command, all data on the card will be erased, including protected images.

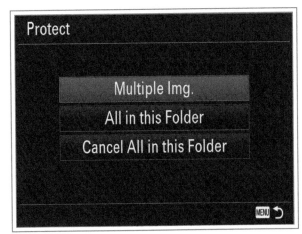

Figure 6-24. Protect Menu Options Screen

To protect images or videos using this menu item, the procedure is similar to the one for deleting images, discussed above. When you select this option, the camera will display a screen similar to that shown in Figure 6-24, with choices to select multiple images; all from the same date or folder as the current image; or to cancel protection for all images with this date or from this folder. (The current View Mode setting will determine whether the choices are for the current date or the current folder.)

If you select Multiple Images, the camera will present you with either index screens or individual images. As with the Delete option, you can scroll through your images and mark any image's check box for protection by pressing the Center button. When you have finished marking images, press the Menu button and the camera will display a confirmation screen. If you select OK to confirm, the marked images and videos will be protected. Any item that is protected will have a key icon in the upper right corner to the left of the battery icon, as shown in Figure 6-25.

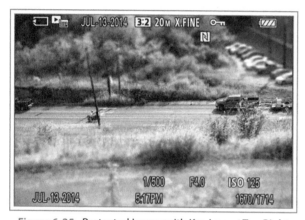

Figure 6-25. Protected Image with Key Icon at Top Right

The key icon will be visible when the image is viewed with the detailed information screen or the basic information screen, but it will not appear in the image-only view.

To unprotect all images or videos in one operation, select the appropriate Cancel option from the Protect item on the Playback menu. That option will prompt you to Cancel All with this Date or to Cancel All in this Folder, depending on the View Mode setting.

MOTION INTERVAL ADJUSTMENT

This menu option gives you a way to adjust the length of time the camera uses for the interval between frames when it creates the Motion Shot effect in playing back a movie. The adjustment screen for this option is shown in Figure 6-26. The default value is 4; you can set the interval to any value from 1 to 7. The higher the number, the greater the spacing between images in the motion shot. I will discuss this option in Chapter 8, where I discuss movie playback features.

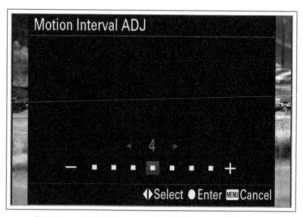

Figure 6-26. Motion Interval Adjustment Screen

SPECIFY PRINTING

This menu option lets you use the DPOF (Digital Print Order Format) function, a standard printing protocol that is built into the camera. The DPOF system lets you mark various images on your memory card to be added to a print list, which can then be sent to your own inkjet or laser printer. Or, you can take the memory card to a commercial printing company to print out the selected images.

To add images to the DPOF print list, select the Specify Printing option from the Playback menu. On the next screen, shown in Figure 6-27, choose the option for Multiple Images.

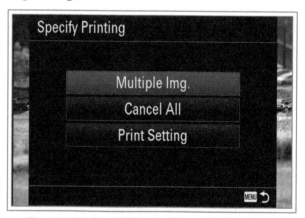

Figure 6-27. Specify Printing Menu Options Screen

The camera will display the first image with a check box at the left, as shown in Figure 6-28, or an index screen with an orange frame around the currently selected image and a check box in the lower left corner of each image thumbnail, as with the Delete and Protect functions discussed earlier.

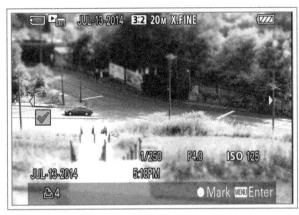

Figure 6-28. Specify Printing Selection Screen

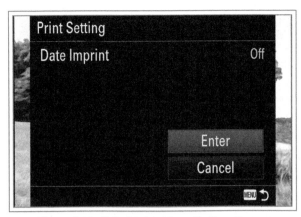

Figure 6-29. Print Setting Menu Options Screen

You can choose to display individual images or index screens using the zoom lever. There will be a small printer icon in the lower left with a zero beside it at first, meaning no copies of any images have been set for printing yet. Use the Control wheel or direction buttons to move through the images. When an image you want to have printed is displayed, press the Center button to mark it for printing or to unmark it. You can then keep browsing through your images and adding them to (or subtracting them from) the print list. As you add various images to the print list, the counter in the lower left corner of the display will show the total number of images selected for printing. You can only select JPEG images; you will see an error message if you try to select a Raw image.

When you have finished selecting images to be printed, press the Menu button to move to a screen where you can confirm your choices by selecting OK.

You also can turn the Date Imprint option on or off to specify whether or not the pictures will be printed with the dates they were taken. To do this, go to the first screen of the Specify Printing menu option and select Print Setting. On the next screen, shown in Figure 6-29, the camera will let you turn Date Imprint on, to specify that the date should be printed on each image.

You can take the memory card with the DPOF list to a service that prints photos using this system, or you can connect the camera to a PictBridge-compatible printer to print the images. If you want to cancel a Specify Printing order, go to the Specify Printing menu item and select the Cancel All option.

Beauty Effect

This final option on the Playback menu gives you a set of tools for retouching photographs of faces that you have previously taken. To use this feature, navigate to an image of a face in playback mode and select this option from the Playback menu. The camera will display the image with an orange frame or a white frame around any face it detects. If there are multiple faces, use the Left and Right buttons to select the one you want to retouch; the selected face will be marked with the orange frame.

After selecting the chosen face, press the Center button to move to the next screen, shown in Figure 6-30.

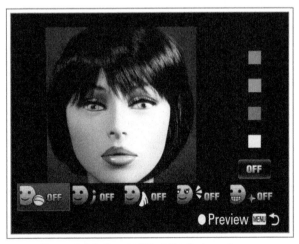

Figure 6-30. Beauty Effect Controls on Screen

On this screen, the camera displays 5 controls, from left to right: Skin Toning, Skin Smoothing, Shine Removal, Eye Widening, and Teeth Whitening. Highlight an adjustment you want to make using the Left and Right buttons, and adjust each of these settings using the Up and Down buttons or the Control wheel. When they are all adjusted as you want, press the Center button to

generate a preview. The camera will display Before and
After images on a screen like that shown in Figure 6-31.

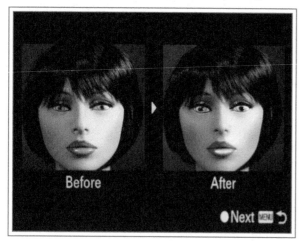

Figure 6-31. Beauty Effect Before and After Images

If you are satisfied, press the Center button, and select
OK to confirm on the next screen. Then, if you need to
adjust another face in the same image, select that image
again and make adjustments for the next face.

Chapter 7: Custom and Setup Menus

In earlier chapters, I discussed the options available in the Shooting and Playback menu systems. The Sony RX100 III has 2 other menu systems – Custom and Setup -- that help you set up the camera and customize its operation. In this chapter, I will discuss all of the options on those menus. I'll discuss menu options for Movie mode in Chapter 8 and I'll discuss the Wi-Fi and Application menus in Chapter 9.

Custom Menu

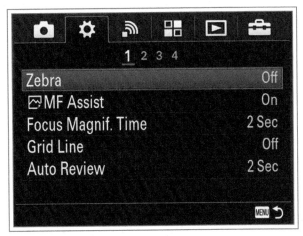

Figure 7-1. Screen 1 of Custom Menu

The Custom menu, whose first screen is shown in Figure 7-1, gives you control over items that affect the ways you use the camera to take pictures and videos, but that do not change photographic settings such as white balance, ISO, focus modes, and matters of that nature. With this menu, the items to be adjusted are more in the categories of control and display options. Details about the options on the 4 screens of this menu follow.

Zebra

This first Custom menu option helps you gauge whether your image or video will be overexposed. When you turn this menu option on, you can select a value from 70 to 100 in 5-unit increments, or 100+ for values

greater than 100. Figure 7-2 shows the screen for turning the option off or selecting a value up to 90.

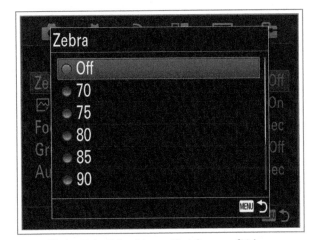

Figure 7-2. Zebra Menu - First Screen of Values

When you turn this option on to any level, you very likely will see, in some parts of the display, the black-and-white "zebra" stripes that give this feature its name.

The numerical units from 70 to 100+ are IRE units, named for the Institute for Radio Engineers, an organization that later merged into the Institute of Electrical and Electronics Engineers (IEEE). The IRE units are a measure of relative brightness or exposure, with 0 representing black and 100 representing white.

Zebra stripes originally were created for professional video cameras, so the videographer could check exposure of a scene. This tool often is used in the context of taping an interview, when proper exposure of a human face is the main concern.

There are various approaches to using these stripes. Some videographers like to set the zebra function to 90 IRE and adjust the exposure so the stripes just barely start to appear in the brightest parts of the image. Another recommendation is to set the option to 75 IRE for a scene with Caucasian skin, and expose so that the stripes just barely appear in the area of the skin.

In Figure 7-3, I set IRE to 75 and exposed to have the stripes barely begin to appear on the mannequin's face.

As the brightness of the lighting increases for a subject, there may be no stripes at first, then they will gradually appear until they cover the subject, then they will seem to disappear, because the exposure is so bright that the subject is surrounded by an outline of "marching ants" rather than having stripes in its interior.

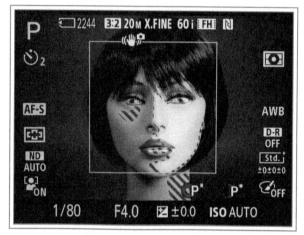

Figure 7-3. Zebra Feature in Use at IRE 75

Zebra is a feature to consider, especially for video recording, but the RX100 III has an excellent metering system, including both live and playback histograms, so you can manage without this option if you don't want to deal with its learning curve.

MF ASSIST

The MF Assist option is for use with still images when manual focus or DMF is in effect. With MF Assist turned on in manual focus mode, the camera enlarges the image as soon as you start turning the Control ring to adjust focus, as shown in Figure 7-4.

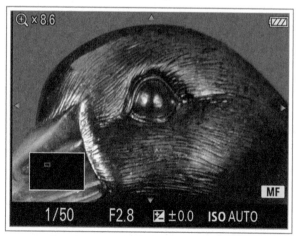

Figure 7-4. Enlarged Image with MF Assist

This feature helps show whether a particular area is in sharp focus. If you turn this option off, you can use another focusing aid, such as Focus Magnifier, discussed in Chapter 4, or Peaking Level, discussed later in this chapter. Or, you can use this option and Peaking Level at the same time, to provide even more assistance.

When DMF is in effect, you have to keep the shutter button pressed halfway down while turning the Control ring to use the MF Assist enlargement feature.

I find MF Assist very helpful, especially because I can set the camera to leave the enlarged screen in place indefinitely using the Focus Magnification Time option, discussed immediately below. However, the Focus Magnifier option also is helpful, and may be preferable in one way because the screen does not become magnified until you press the Center button, select the area to be magnified using the orange frame, and then magnify the screen.

In some cases, if a subject (like the moon) does not have edges or other features to focus on, enlarging the view may not be very helpful. In those situations, Peaking Level may be more useful. Or, you may find that using Peaking Level in conjunction with MF Assist is the most useful approach of all. You should experiment with the various options to find what works best for you.

FOCUS MAGNIFICATION TIME

This option controls how long the display stays magnified with the MF Assist option, discussed above, or the Focus Magnifier option, discussed in Chapter 4. The choices are 2 or 5 seconds or No Limit, as seen in Figure 7-5. The default is 2 seconds.

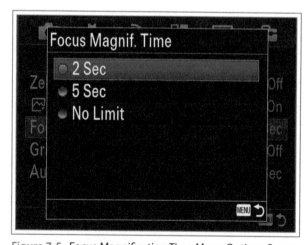

Figure 7-5. Focus Magnification Time Menu Options Screen

If you select No Limit, the image will stay magnified until you press the shutter button all the way to take the picture or press it halfway to dismiss the enlarged view. My preference is to use No Limit so I can take my time to adjust manual focus precisely. Note, though, that with the No Limit option, whenever you turn the Control ring when using MF Assist, the image will be enlarged, and you may want to be able to keep adjusting focus with a view of the unenlarged subject. If that is the case, select one of the options with a time limit or use the Focus Magnifier option.

GRID LINE

With this option, you can select one of 4 settings for a grid to be superimposed on the shooting screen. By default, there is no grid. If you choose one of the grid options, the lines will appear in your chosen configuration whenever the camera is showing the live view in shooting mode, whether the detailed display screen is selected or not. Of course, the grid does not appear when the For Viewfinder display, with its black screen full of shooting information, is displayed. The 4 options are seen in Figure 7-6.

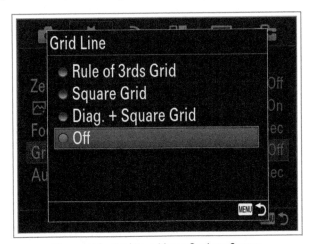

Figure 7-6. Grid Line Menu Options Screen

Following are descriptions of these choices, other than Off, which leaves the screen with no grid.

Rule of Thirds Grid

This arrangement displays 2 vertical and 2 horizontal lines, dividing the screen into 9 blocks, as shown in Figure 7-7. This grid reflects a rule of composition that calls for locating an important subject at an intersection of these lines, which will place the subject one-third of the way from the edge of the image. This arrangement can add interest and asymmetry to an image.

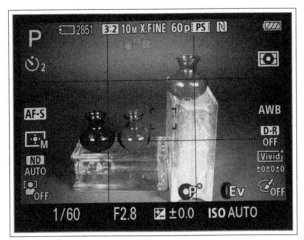

Figure 7-7. Rule of Thirds Grid in Use

Square Grid

With this setting, the grid uses 5 vertical lines and 3 horizontal lines, dividing the display into 24 blocks, as seen in Figure 7-8.

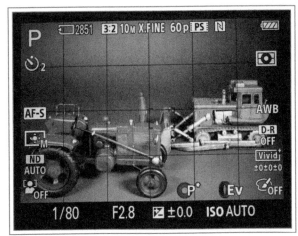

Figure 7-8. Square Grid in Use

In this way, you can still use the Rule of Thirds, but you have additional lines available for lining up items, such as the horizon or the edge of a building, that need to be straight.

Diagonal Plus Square Grid

The last option gives you a square grid of 4 blocks in each direction and adds 2 diagonal lines, as shown in Figure 7-9. The idea is that placing a subject or, more likely, a string of subjects along one of the diagonals can add interest to the image by drawing the viewer's eye into the image along the diagonal line.

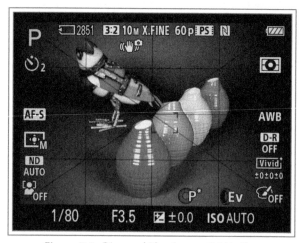

Figure 7-9. Diagonal Plus Square Grid in Use

AUTO REVIEW

With the Auto Review option, shown in Figure 7-10, you can set the length of time that an image appears on the display screen immediately after you take a still picture.

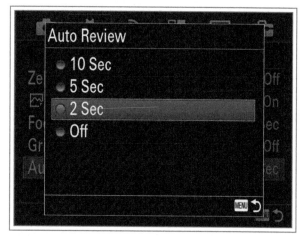

Figure 7-10. Auto Review Menu Options Screen

The default is 2 seconds, but you can set the time to 5 or 10 seconds, or you can turn the function off. If you turn it off, the camera will return to shooting mode as soon as it has saved a new image to the memory card. When this option is in use, you can always return to the live view by pressing the shutter button halfway. The Auto Review option does not apply to movies; the camera does not display the beginning frame of a movie that was just recorded until you press the Playback button.

While a new image is being displayed, you can use the various functions of playback mode, such as enlarging the image, bringing up index screens, and moving to other images. If you start one of these actions before

the camera has reverted to shooting mode, the camera will stay in playback mode.

The second screen of the Custom menu is shown in Figure 7-11.

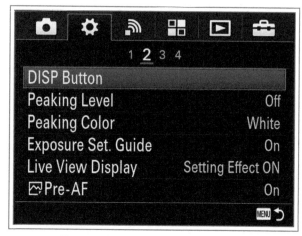

Figure 7-11. Screen 2 of Custom Menu

DISPLAY BUTTON

This option lets you choose what screens appear in shooting mode as you press the Display button. There are sub-options for the monitor (LCD) and viewfinder, as seen in Figure 7-12.

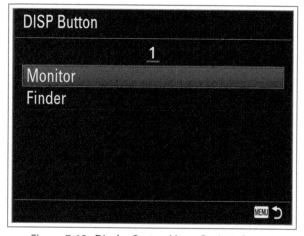

Figure 7-12. Display Button Menu Options Screen

You can make different choices for the LCD and the viewfinder, so pressing the Display button when you are using the monitor may bring up a different set of screens than when you are using the viewfinder.

After you decide to choose display screens for the monitor or the viewfinder, you will see a screen like that shown in Figure 7-13.

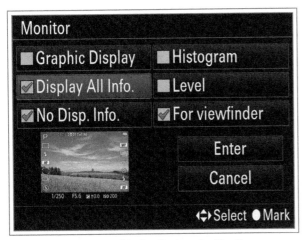

Figure 7-13. Display Options for Monitor

This screen shows the 6 display screens you can select for the monitor. The selection screen for the viewfinder is identical to this one, except that the sixth choice, For Viewfinder, is not available as a choice to appear in the viewfinder. That display screen is designed to appear on the monitor to provide shooting information when you are viewing the live view through the viewfinder.

Five of the 6 display screens available for the monitor are shown in Figure 7-14 through Figure 7-18. The screen displaying just the image with no information is not shown here.

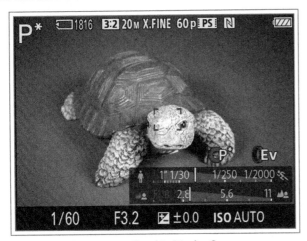

Figure 7-14. Graphic Display Screen

Figure 7-14 shows the screen with the Graphic Display in the lower right corner; that display illustrates the use of faster shutter speeds to stop action and wider apertures to blur backgrounds. I find it distracting and not especially helpful, but if it is useful to you, by all means select it.

I find the Display All Information screen, shown in Figure 7-15, to be cluttered, but it has useful information.

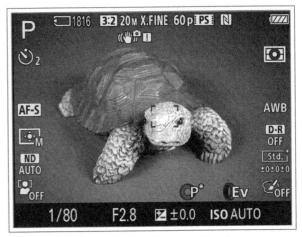

Figure 7-15. Display All Information Screen

You can always move away from this screen by pressing the Display button (if there is at least one other display screen available), and I like to have it available for times when I need to see what settings are in effect. In addition, if you don't have this screen available, you won't be able to see icons that indicate the status of certain features, such as the ND Filter.

The third option, displaying only the image, isn't shown here. That display is helpful for focusing and composing your shot, and I always include it in the cycle of display screens.

The fourth option, shown in Figure 7-16, displays the histogram.

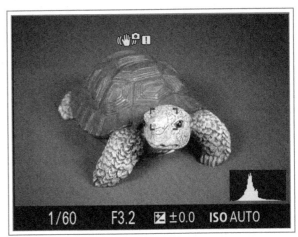

Figure 7-16. Histogram Display Screen

This shooting mode histogram, unlike the one displayed in playback mode, shows only basic exposure information with no color data. However, it helps you decide whether your image will be well exposed, letting you adjust exposure compensation and other settings as appropriate while watching the live histogram on the screen. If you can make the histogram display look like a triangular mountain centered in the box, you are likely to have a good result.

You should try to keep the body of the histogram away from the right and left edges of the graph, in most cases. If the histogram runs into the left edge, that means shadow areas are clipping and details in those areas are being lost. If it hits the right edge, you are losing details in highlights. If you have to choose, it is best to keep the graph away from the right edge because it is harder to recover details from clipped highlights than from clipped shadows.

The fifth available display screen, shown in Figure 7-17, shows the RX100 III's level, which is a useful tool for leveling the camera both side-to-side and front-to-back.

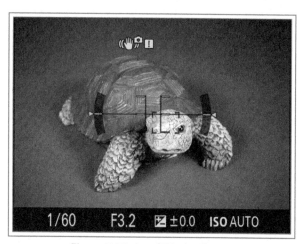

Figure 7-17. Level Display Screen

Watch the small orange lines on the screen; when the outer 2 ones have turned green, the camera is level side-to-side; when the inner 2 lines are green, the camera is level front-to-back.

The sixth choice, shown in Figure 7-18, which is available only for the monitor, is called For Viewfinder. This option is the only one that does not include the live view in shooting mode. Instead, it displays a black screen with detailed information about the camera's settings, so you can check your settings after (or before) you look at the live view in the viewfinder. In addition, as I discussed in Chapter 5, this screen includes the Quick Navi system. When you press the Function

button, the settings on the screen become active. You can navigate through the settings using the direction buttons and adjust them using the Control wheel or the Control ring.

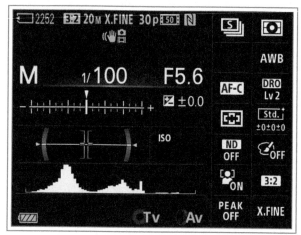

Figure 7-18. For Viewfinder Display Screen

Once you select the Display Button option and choose whether to select screens for the monitor or viewfinder, you can scroll through the 6 (monitor) or 5 (viewfinder) choices using the Control wheel or the direction buttons. When a screen you want to have displayed is highlighted, press the Center button to put an orange check mark in the box to the left of the screen's label, as seen in Figure 7-13.

You can also press that button to unmark a box. The camera will let you un-check all 6 of the items (or all 5 for the viewfinder), but if you do that, you will see an error message as you try to exit the menu screen. You have to check at least one box so that some screen will display when the camera is in shooting mode.

After you select 1 to 6 screens for the monitor and 1 to 5 for the viewfinder, highlight the Enter block and press the Center button. Then, when the camera is in shooting mode, those screens will be displayed; cycle through them by pressing the Display button. If you have selected only one screen, pressing that button will have no effect in shooting mode when the live view is displayed.

Even if you select only the screen with no information, the LCD always displays shutter speed, aperture, exposure compensation, and ISO in the black strip below the image. With the viewfinder, the camera always displays those values at the bottom and displays

Aspect Ratio, Image Size, Quality, File Format, and a few other values in a strip at the top of the screen.

PEAKING LEVEL

The Peaking Level option, shown in Figure 7-19, controls the camera's use of the Peaking display to assist with manual focus.

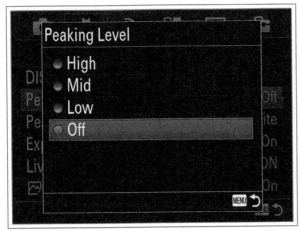

Figure 7-19. Peaking Level Menu Options Screen

By default, this option is turned off. You can turn the feature on with a level of Low, Mid, or High. When it is on and you are using manual focus or DMF, the camera places an outline with the selected intensity around any areas of the image that have edges the camera can distinguish. As focus becomes sharper, the lines become thicker. Figure 7-20 illustrates this feature with a composite image in which Peaking Level is turned off for the left image and set to Mid for the right image.

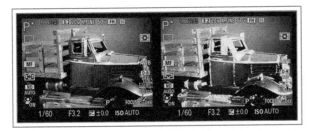

Figure 7-20. Left: Peaking Level Off, Right: Peaking Level Mid

The idea is that these lines provide a clearer indication that focus is sharp than just relying on your judgment of sharpness. When I first used a camera with this feature, I found it distracting and not as useful as options such as MF Assist and Focus Magnifier that enlarge the screen for a clearer view when using manual focus. However, after further experience, I have come to appreciate the usefulness of the Peaking feature for some situations.

For example, as discussed in Chapter 9, I took some shots of the moon through a telescope connected to the RX100 III. I used manual focus and fine-tuned the focus using the controls on the telescope. The image on the camera's screen was unsteady because of the high magnification, and the moon did not have any features with edges that I could see clearly in the enlarged view. When I turned on Peaking Level with the red color selected, I found it much easier to focus; the camera displayed a broad band of red around the edge of the moon when focus was sharp.

Some photographers set Creative Style to black and white while focusing so the Peaking color will stand out, and some like to set Peaking Level to Low so the color is not overwhelming, letting them see when the color just starts to appear. Some like to turn on MF Assist to enlarge the screen when using Peaking. You should experiment to find what approach works best for you.

For an excellent demonstration of how Peaking works, see this YouTube video posted by a participant in the Sony Cyber-shot Talk forum at dpreview.com at http://youtu.be/jMAlMQev7Kw.

Note that Peaking also works with DMF, even if you are using the autofocus function of that setting.

PEAKING COLOR

This option lets you choose red, yellow, or white for the color of the lines that the Peaking Level feature places around the edges of in-focus areas of the image. The default color is white. The Peaking Level feature is likely to be most useful when the color you choose for the effect contrasts with the main colors in your subject. As noted above, I found that the red color worked very well for shots of the moon; yellow or white may work well with darker subjects.

EXPOSURE SETTINGS GUIDE

The next option on the Custom menu, when turned on, places a circular display on the screen to simulate 1 or 2 rotating wheels showing the settings for aperture, shutter speed, or both, when you adjust those settings using the Control wheel. (When you adjust any of the above values using the Control ring, the camera always displays a circular scale in the top half of the screen.)

The display varies according to the shooting mode. In Program mode, 2 wheels display aperture and shutter speed when you activate Program Shift using the Control wheel. In Shutter Priority and Manual exposure modes, a single wheel displays shutter speed as you adjust it using the Control wheel. In Aperture Priority mode, a single wheel shows the aperture as you adjust it using the wheel. Figure 7-21 shows the display when shutter speed is being adjusted. I find this display distracting, so I leave it turned off, but it might be useful to see this display to let you know what value is being set, in some circumstances.

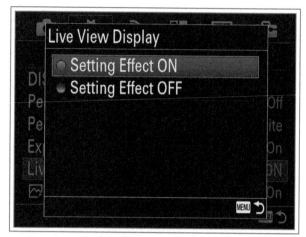

Figure 7-22. Live View Display Menu Options Screen

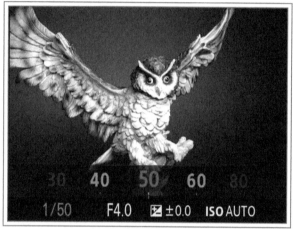

Figure 7-21. Exposure Settings Guide Option in Use for Shutter Speed

LIVE VIEW DISPLAY

This menu option can be important for getting results that match your expectations. It lets you choose whether or not the camera displays the effects that certain settings will have on your final image, while you are composing the image.

With this option, there are 2 sub-options on the next screen: Setting Effect On and Setting Effect Off, as seen in Figure 7-22. With Setting Effect On, when you are using Program, Aperture Priority, Shutter Priority, or Manual exposure mode, the camera's display in shooting mode will show the effects of exposure compensation, white balance, Creative Style, and Picture Effect settings. In addition, it will show the effects of exposure changes in Manual exposure mode and the other 3 advanced modes.

In some cases, it may be helpful to see what effect a particular setting will have on the final image, and in other cases that display might be distracting or might make it difficult to take the shot.

For example, when you are setting white balance, it can be helpful to see how various options will alter the appearance of your images. If you have selected Setting Effect On, then, as you scroll through the white balance options, you will instantly see the effect of each setting, such as Daylight, Shade, and Incandescent. That change in the display is informative and not distracting.

However, if you are using the Picture Effect option and experimenting with a setting such as Posterization, which drastically alters the appearance of your images, you might find it difficult to compose the image with Setting Effect On selected.

There is one use for the Live View Display menu option that I find practically indispensable. On occasion, I use the RX100 III to trigger external flash units using optical slaves, with the camera set to Manual exposure mode. For some of these shots, I may use settings such as f/11.0, 1/200 second, and ISO 80. Such a shot will be exposed properly with the flash units I am using, but, with Setting Effect On selected, the camera's screen is completely dark as I compose the shot. That is because the camera's programming does not account for the fact that flash units will be fired.

If I use the Setting Effect Off setting, then the camera displays the scene using the available ambient light, ignoring the settings I have made. In this way, I can see the scene on the camera's display in order to compose the shot properly.

The Setting Effect On option, though, can be useful when using Aperture Priority, Shutter Priority, or Manual exposure mode when you are shooting in unusually dark or bright conditions, because the camera's display screen will change its brightness to alert you that a normal exposure may not be possible with the current settings. (You should see the aperture, shutter speed, ISO, or other value flashing to alert you to this situation, also.)

With the Picture Effect setting, some of the options will not change the appearance of the display, even with this setting activated, because the effects are added while the image is being processed. Those options are Soft Focus, HDR Painting, Rich-tone Monochrome (the display will appear black and white, but without the rich-tone processing), Miniature, Watercolor, and Illustration.

When the Setting Effect Off option is selected, the camera will display a VIEW icon on the screen, as shown in Figure 7-23, to remind you that you the camera's display is not showing the effects of all your settings.

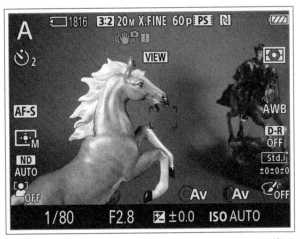

Figure 7-23. VIEW Icon on Screen when Setting Effect Off is in Effect

My recommendation is to leave this option at Setting Effect On unless it is difficult to compose a shot, either because the display is too dark or light, or because a setting such as Picture Effect interferes with your ability to view the subject clearly.

In Intelligent Auto, Scene, Sweep Panorama, and Movie modes, this option is forced to Setting Effect On and cannot be changed.

Pre-AF

The Pre-AF setting affects the way the RX100 III uses autofocus. When this option is turned on and the focus mode is single or continuous autofocus, the camera continuously tries to focus on a subject, even before you

press the shutter button halfway. With this setting, the camera's battery is depleted more quickly than normal, but the final focusing may be speeded up because the camera can reach an approximate focus adjustment before you press the shutter button to evaluate focus and take the picture. If this setting is turned off, the camera makes no attempt to focus until you press the shutter button halfway to check focus.

I usually leave this setting off to avoid running the battery down too soon. But, if I were taking pictures of moving subjects, I might activate this setting to speed up the focusing process.

Screen 3 of the Custom menu is shown in Figure 7-24.

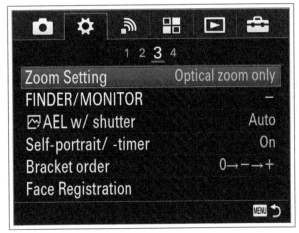

Figure 7-24. Screen 3 of Custom Menu

Zoom Setting

The first option on screen 3 of the Custom menu, Zoom Setting, provides 2 ways to give the RX100 III extra zoom range, using features called Clear Image Zoom and Digital Zoom. To explain these features in context, I will discuss all 3 zoom methods that the camera offers—optical zoom, Clear Image Zoom, and Digital Zoom. I will also discuss a fourth feature that is related to these, called Smart Zoom.

Optical zoom is the camera's "natural" zoom capability—moving the lens elements so they magnify the image, just as binoculars do. You can call optical zoom a "real" zoom because it increases the information that the lens gathers. The optical zoom of the RX100 III operates within a range from 24mm at the wide-angle setting to the fully zoomed-in telephoto setting of 70mm.

To complicate matters a bit, the actual optical zoom range of the RX100 III's lens is 8.8mm to 25.7mm; you can see those numbers on the end of the lens. But the numbers that are almost always used to describe the zoom range of a compact camera's lens are the "35mm-equivalent" figures, which translate the actual zoom range into what the range would be if this were a lens on a camera that uses 35mm film. This translation is done because many photographers are familiar with the zoom ranges and focal lengths of lenses for traditional 35mm cameras, on which a 50mm lens is considered "normal." I use the 35mm-equivalent figures throughout this book.

The Digital Zoom feature of the RX100 III magnifies the image electronically without any special processing to improve the quality. This type of zoom does not really increase the information gathered by the lens; rather, it just increases the apparent size of the image by enlarging the pixels within the area captured by the lens. On some cameras, the amount of digital zoom can be very large, such as 50 times normal, but such a large figure can be considered as a marketing ploy to lure customers, rather than a feature of real value to the photographer.

The other option on the RX100 III, Clear Image Zoom, is a special type of digital zoom developed by Sony. With this feature, the RX100 III does not just magnify the area of the image; rather, the camera analyzes the image and adds pixels through interpolation. This system produces a smoother, more realistic enlargement than the Digital Zoom feature. With Clear Image Zoom, the camera achieves greater quality than with Digital Zoom, though not as much as with the "pure" optical zoom.

Finally, there is another way the RX100 III can have a zoom range greater than the normal optical zoom range with no reduction in image quality. The standard range of 24mm to 70mm is available when Image Size is set to Large. However, if Image Size is set to Medium or Small, the camera needs only a portion of the pixels on the image sensor to create the image at the reduced size. It can use the "extra" pixels to enlarge the view of the scene. This process, which Sony calls Smart Zoom, is similar to what you can do using software such as Photoshop. If the image size does not need to be Large, you can crop out some pixels from the center (or other area) of the image and enlarge that area, thereby

retaining the same overall image size with a magnified view of the scene.

With Smart Zoom, if you set Image Size to M or S, the camera can zoom to a greater range than with Image Size set to L and still keep the full quality of the optical zoom. You will end up with lower-resolution images, but that may not be a problem if you are going to post them on a website or share them via e-mail.

In short, optical zoom provides the best quality for magnifying the scene; Clear Image Zoom gives excellent quality; and Digital Zoom produces magnification with reduced image quality. Smart Zoom gives you greater zoom range with no image deterioration, but at the expense of resolution.

Here is how to use these settings. I will assume for this discussion that you are leaving Image Size set to L, because that is the best setting for excellent results in printing and editing your images.

When you select the Zoom Setting menu option and press the Center button, the camera displays the screen shown in Figure 7-25, giving you the choice of Optical Zoom Only; On: Clear Image Zoom; or On: Digital Zoom. If you turn on Digital Zoom, Clear Image Zoom will automatically be activated also. Optical Zoom is always available, no matter what settings are used.

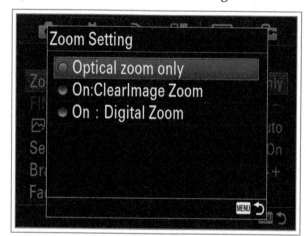

Figure 7-25. Zoom Setting Menu Options Screen

If you turn on only Clear Image Zoom, you will have greater zoom range than normal, as discussed above, with minimal quality loss. If you also turn on Digital Zoom, you will get even greater zoom range, but quality will suffer as the lens is zoomed past the Clear Image Zoom range. When these various settings are in effect, you will see different indications on the camera's display.

In Figure 7-26, Image Size is set to L and both Clear Image Zoom and Digital Zoom are turned off. The zoom indicator at the top of the screen goes only as far as 70mm.

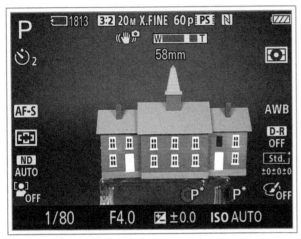

Figure 7-26. Zoom Scale - Optical Zoom Only

In Figure 7-27, Clear Image Zoom is turned on. The zoom indicator shows the lens can zoom to 2.0 times the normal range.

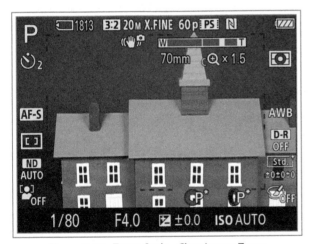

Figure 7-27. Zoom Scale - Clear Image Zoom

There is a small vertical line in the center of the zoom scale showing where the zoom changes from optical-only to expanded (Clear Image Zoom or Digital Zoom, depending on the settings). The magnifying glass icon with the "C" beneath the scale means Clear Image Zoom is turned on. Also, once the lens zooms past the optical zoom range, the sound of the zoom mechanism stops, so you can tell by listening when the camera has entered the range of Clear Image Zoom and Digital Zoom.

In Figure 7-28, both Clear Image Zoom and Digital Zoom are turned on, and the zoom indicator can go up to 4 times normal magnification. The magnifying glass icon beneath the scale has a "D" beside it, indicating that Digital Zoom is now in effect.

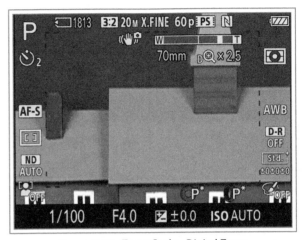

Figure 7-28. Zoom Scale - Digital Zoom

With an Image Size setting smaller than Large, the zoom indicator will use a letter S to show that the camera is using Smart Zoom, as the zoom range extends beyond the standard optical zoom range. For example, in Figure 7-29, with Image Size set to Small, the lens is zoomed in to 1.7 times the optical range, and the zoom indicator displays an S to indicate that Smart Zoom is in effect.

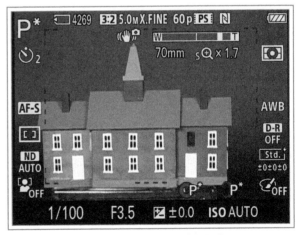

Figure 7-29. Zoom Scale - Smart Zoom

With smaller image sizes, the ranges of Clear Image Zoom and Digital Zoom also are expanded. For example, as shown in Figure 7-30, with Image Size set to Small and Digital Zoom turned on, the lens can be zoomed in to 8.0 times the normal optical range.

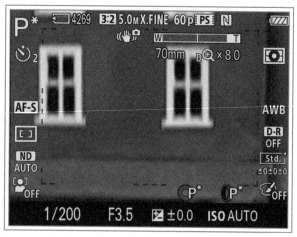

Figure 7-30. Zoom Scale - Digital Zoom with Image Size Small

Table 7-1 shows the zoom ranges that are available when Image Size is set to Large, Medium, and Small, with settings of Optical Zoom, Clear Image Zoom, and Digital Zoom. In all cases, Aspect Ratio is set to 3:2; with other Aspect Ratio settings, results would be different.

Table 7-1. **Maximum Zoom Range at Various Image Sizes**

	Large	Medium	Small
Optical Zoom (with no deterioration)	70mm	98mm	140mm
Clear Image Zoom (with minimal deterioration)	140mm	196mm	280mm
Digital Zoom (with significant deterioration)	280mm	392mm	560mm

To summarize the situation with zoom, when Image Size is set to Large, you can zoom up to 70mm with no deterioration using optical zoom; you can zoom to about 140mm with minimal deterioration using Clear Image Zoom; and you can zoom to about 280mm using Digital Zoom but with significant deterioration.

My preference is to limit the camera to optical zoom and avoid any deterioration. However, many photographers have found that Clear Image Zoom yields surprisingly good results, and it is worth using when you cannot get close to your subject. I do not like to use Digital Zoom to take a picture. However, it can be useful to zoom in to meter a specific area of a distant subject, or to check the composition of your shot before zooming back out and taking the shot using Clear Image Zoom or optical zoom.

Clear Image Zoom and Digital Zoom are not available when shooting Raw images, when the Smile Shutter or face detection is in use, or in Sweep Panorama mode. They also are unavailable when Record Setting for movies is set to 120p 50M.

Whenever the lens is zoomed into the range of Clear Image Zoom or Digital Zoom, the Focus Area option is disabled and the camera uses a broad focus frame, which is represented by the dotted area seen in Figures 7-27 through 7-30. Metering Mode is set to Multi when non-optical zoom is in use.

FINDER/MONITOR

This next option on the Custom menu, shown in Figure 7-31, lets you choose whether to view menus and shooting and playback displays on the RX100 III's LCD screen or in the viewfinder.

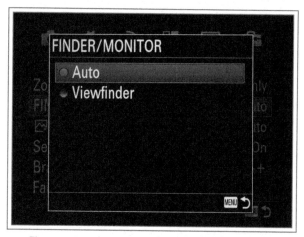

Figure 7-31. Finder/Monitor Menu Options Screen

The viewfinder can provide the same information as the LCD screen (depending on menu settings), but its display is viewed inside an eye-level window that is shaded from daylight, giving you a clear view of the shooting, playback, and menu screens.

By default, this menu option is set to Auto, which means the camera switches the view to the viewfinder automatically when you move your head near the camera, if the viewfinder has been popped up. The camera turns on the viewfinder display and blacks out the LCD. (The viewfinder has an eye sensor at its left side that detects the presence of an object nearby.)

If you prefer to use the viewfinder at all times, set this option to Viewfinder. With that setting, the camera will turn off the LCD and will activate the viewfinder only when your head approaches it.

To put this another way, with the Auto setting the camera will activate the LCD screen when you are not using the viewfinder; with the Viewfinder setting, the camera will never activate the LCD screen, unless you retract the viewfinder. In that case, the camera will always use the LCD screen.

My preference is to use the Auto setting because I find it convenient to view the image on the LCD unless conditions are quite bright. With the Viewfinder setting, though, you might be able to save some battery power by not activating any display unless your head is near the viewfinder.

AEL WITH SHUTTER

This menu item, whose options screen is shown in Figure 7-32, controls how the shutter button handles autoexposure lock. There are 3 possible settings for this feature: Auto, On, and Off.

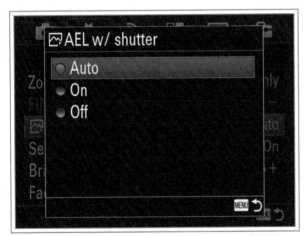

Figure 7-32. AEL w/Shutter Menu Options Screen

With the default option, Auto, pressing the shutter button halfway locks exposure when Focus Mode is set to AF-S for single-shot autofocus or DMF for direct manual focus. When the focus mode is set to AF-C for continuous autofocus or MF for manual focus, pressing the shutter button halfway does not lock exposure.

If AEL with Shutter is On, pressing the shutter button halfway locks exposure in all situations, regardless of what focus mode is in effect. So, for example, if the focus mode is set to continuous autofocus, pressing the shutter button halfway locks exposure, though the focus mechanism will continue adjusting focus.

If this menu option is set to Off, pressing the shutter button halfway never locks exposure, in any focus mode. You may want to use this setting when you need to press the shutter button halfway to lock focus and then move the camera to change the composition somewhat. You might want the camera to re-evaluate the exposure, even though you have already locked the focus.

If this option is set to Off or Auto and continuous autofocus is in use, a half-press of the shutter button locks the aperture setting but does not lock the overall exposure.

Another use for this option is with the continuous shooting settings of Drive Mode. As I discussed in Chapter 4, if you want the camera to adjust exposure for each shot in a burst, you need to set AEL with Shutter to Off, or Auto if using continuous AF. Otherwise, the camera will lock exposure with the first shot and will not adjust it if the lighting changes during the burst.

Of course, you may not want to use those settings in that scenario, because exposure adjustment can slow the burst of shots, and, depending on the situation, it may not be likely that lighting will change during a brief burst of shots. But this option is available for times when you want the camera to keep evaluating and adjusting exposure while you take a burst of shots.

SELF-PORTRAIT TIMER

This next Custom menu option can be turned either on or off. If it is turned on, then, when you flip the LCD screen up and around so it faces forward, the camera will display a large 3-step countdown timer when you press the shutter button, so you can get ready for a self-portrait. The timer screen is shown in Figure 7-33.

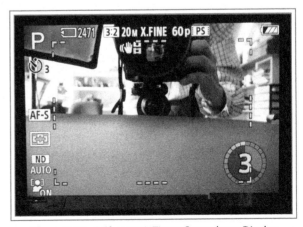

Figure 7-33. Self-portrait Timer Countdown Display

If this option is left off, you can still take a self-portrait, but without the on-screen timer.

When you use this option, a possible problem is that the camera locks focus when you press the shutter button to start the timer, and, if your position changes during the countdown, the focus may be incorrect. To avoid this problem, you can turn off this option and take the picture with no delay. Another approach is to use the Smart Remote Embedded app or another remote-control app to control the camera, as discussed in Chapter 9.

BRACKET ORDER

As I discussed in Chapter 4, the RX100 III offers several varieties of bracketing. When you turn on one of those settings, the camera takes multiple shots with different values for the setting being bracketed—exposure, white balance, or DRO. The Bracket Order option lets you change the order in which the bracketed exposures are taken for exposure bracketing and white balance bracketing. This option has no effect on the order of shots for DRO bracketing.

The default option, seen on the first line in Figure 7-34, uses the order: normal, low, high. When the camera is set to take 5 shots, it records them as: normal, low, high, even lower, even higher.

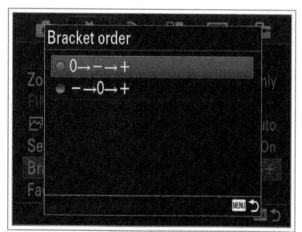

Figure 7-34. Bracket Order Menu Options Screen

If you choose the second option, the camera records 3 shots as follows: low, normal, high. When it takes 5 shots, it records them as follows: low, normal, high, higher, highest.

I do not use bracketing all that much, and I have never had occasion to change the bracket order. If you do a lot

of bracketing, you might prefer to have the exposures arranged in ascending order of settings, rather than having the normal shot come first.

FACE REGISTRATION

This last option on screen 3 of the Custom menu lets you register human faces so the RX100 III can give those faces priority when it uses face detection. You can register up to 8 faces and assign each one a priority from 1 to 8, with 1 being the highest. Then, when you set the Shooting menu option for Smile/Face Detection to On (Registered Faces), the camera will try to detect the registered faces first in the order you have assigned them. This feature is not one I find a need for, but it could be useful if, for example, you take pictures at school functions and you want to make sure the camera focuses on your own children.

To use this menu option, select it and on the next screen, shown in Figure 7-35, select New Registration. Press the Center button, and the camera will place a square frame on the screen.

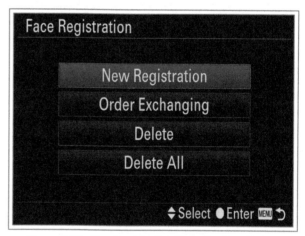

Figure 7-35. Face Registration Menu Options Screen

Compose a shot with the face to be registered inside that frame, as shown in Figure 7-36, and press the shutter button to take a picture of that face. If the process works, the camera will display that face with the message "Register face?" Highlight the Enter bar on that screen and press the Center button to complete the registration process. Later, you can use the Order Exchanging option to change the priorities of the registered faces, and you can delete registered faces individually or all at once using other menu options.

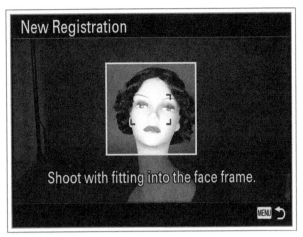

Figure 7-36. Face Inside Registration Frame

The final screen of the Custom menu is shown in Figure 7-37.

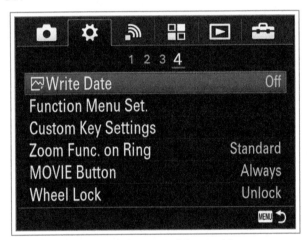

Figure 7-37. Screen 4 of Custom Menu

WRITE DATE

This first setting on screen 4 of the Custom menu embeds the date in the lower right corner of your images, as shown in Figure 7-38.

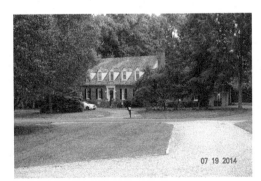

Figure 7-38. Image with Write Date Information in Lower Right Corner

This embedding is permanent, so the information cannot be deleted other than through cropping or other

editing procedures. Use this option only if you want the date recorded permanently on your images, perhaps for a scientific research project.

When you are shooting with this option activated, the word "DATE" appears in the upper part of the screen as you compose your shot if you are using a shooting screen that displays detailed information. This option is not available when Quality is set to Raw or Raw & JPEG, with panoramas, bracketing, continuous shooting, or in Movie mode.

FUNCTION MENU SETTINGS

When you press the Function button in shooting mode, the camera displays up to 12 options in blocks at the bottom of the display, as shown in Figure 7-39.

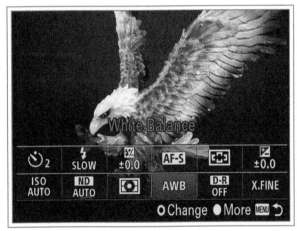

Figure 7-39. Function Menu on Screen

You move through those options with the direction buttons. Adjust the main settings with the Control wheel or the Control ring. To make secondary settings, press the Center button to go to the regular menu screen for the option being adjusted.

You use the Function Menu Settings menu item to assign options to the Function menu. When you select this option, the camera displays the screen shown in Figure 7-40, showing the assignments for the upper 6 blocks of the Function menu.

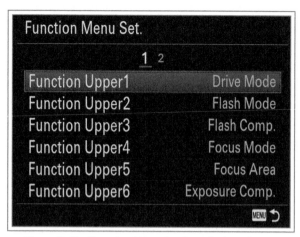

Figure 7-40. Function Menu Settings Options Screen

When you press the Center button on any one of those lines, you will see a screen like that in Figure 7-41, listing the options that can be assigned to that block.

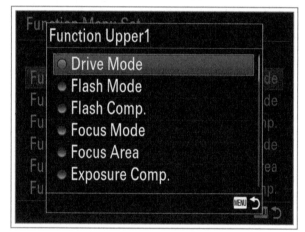

Figure 7-41. List of Settings for Function Menu Slot

For each menu block, these options can be assigned:
- Drive Mode
- Flash Mode
- Flash Compensation
- Focus Mode
- Focus Area
- Exposure Compensation
- ISO
- ND Filter
- Metering Mode
- White Balance
- DRO/Auto HDR
- Creative Style
- Shoot Mode
- Picture Effect

- Center Lock-on AF
- Smile/Face Detection
- Soft Skin Effect
- Auto Object Framing
- Image Size
- Aspect Ratio
- Quality
- SteadyShot (Still Images)
- SteadyShot (Movies)
- Zebra
- Grid Line
- Peaking Level
- Peaking Color
- Not Set

Press the Center button when the option you want to assign is displayed, and the camera will place an orange dot on that line to indicate that that feature is assigned to that block. I recommend you assign a function to each of the 12 blocks and experiment to find the best setup. You can use the Control ring and the Custom, Center, Left, and Right buttons for your most important settings, such as, perhaps, ISO, AEL Toggle, Drive Mode, ND Filter, and Focus Area, so you can reserve these 12 blocks for other options.

CUSTOM KEY SETTINGS

I described this menu option in Chapter 5, in discussing physical controls that can have settings assigned to them. Now I will discuss the settings that can be assigned to these controls. When you select the Custom Key Settings menu option, you will see the screen shown in Figure 7-42.

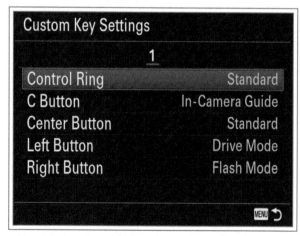

Figure 7-42. Custom Key Settings Menu Options Screen

Navigate to the line for a control and press the Center Button. You will see a screen listing all the options that can be assigned to that control. In most cases, these assignments are self-explanatory. When you assign a function, such as ISO, to a button, pressing the button calls up the menu screen for the option, which lets you adjust it just as if you had selected it from the Shooting menu. However, there are differences for some controls, and there are some items that can be assigned through this option that are not available through any menu. I will discuss these details below.

Control Ring

The first control on the Custom Key Settings menu screen is the Control ring. This control is a special case, because, of course, it is not a button but a ring. The options that can be assigned to the ring are Standard, Exposure Compensation, ISO, White Balance, Creative Style, Picture Effect, Zoom, Shutter Speed, Aperture, or Not Set, the first 6 of which are shown in Figure 7-43.

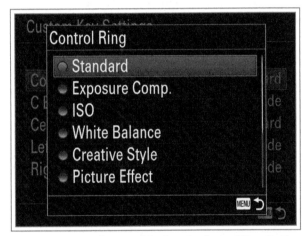

Figure 7-43. First Screen of Options for Control Ring Setting

This feature is powerful because, when you assign a setting such as ISO to this ring, you can use the ring to adjust the setting instantly. For example, if you choose ISO, then, when the camera is in shooting mode, all you have to do is turn the Control ring and the ISO setting will change. You can then immediately press the shutter button to take a picture with the new setting.

However, you cannot get access to all aspects of these settings by turning the ring. For example, if you assign ISO to the ring, you can select a numerical ISO value or Auto ISO, but you cannot set the Minimum and Maximum settings for Auto ISO, and you cannot select a value for the Multi Frame Noise Reduction setting.

Similarly, if you assign white balance to the Control ring, you can select a white balance setting, including Custom or Color Temperature, but you cannot set a new Custom White Balance or choose a new Color Temperature setting, and you cannot fine-tune the white balance using the color axes. For those options, you need to use the White Balance menu option. Likewise, with Creative Style assigned to the ring, you cannot adjust the contrast, sharpness, and saturation parameters of a selected setting.

However, with Picture Effect, you can select any of the settings or sub-settings, because the Control ring will cycle through all of the options, including, for example, the sub-settings for Toy Camera, which are Normal, Cool, Warm, Green, and Magenta.

When the Control ring has been assigned to a function, the camera puts an icon representing the ring in the bottom right of the screen next to an icon or label indicating the setting currently assigned to the ring. For example, Figure 7-44 shows the screen as it appears when ISO has been assigned to the Control ring.

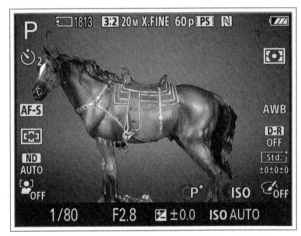

Figure 7-44. Icon Showing Control Ring Controls ISO

By default the Control ring's function is set to Standard. In that case, the ring controls various functions in the various shooting modes, as shown in Table 7-1.

Table 7-1. **Control Ring: Standard Setting—Shooting Modes vs. Assigned Functions**

Shooting Mode	Assigned Function
Intelligent Auto	Zoom
Superior Auto	Zoom
Program	Program Shift

Table 7-1. **Control Ring: Standard Setting—**
Shooting Modes vs. Assigned Functions

Aperture Priority	Aperture
Shutter Priority	Shutter Speed
Manual Exposure	Aperture
Scene	Scene Selection
Sweep Panorama	Direction
Movie	[No function]
Memory Recall	Depends on Saved Setting

Or you can choose the final option, Not Set, in which case the ring will control only manual focus from the shooting screen. (It also will select items with the Function menu and Quick Navi system.) In my opinion, the Standard option is the most useful, but you might prefer to use the Control ring for one specific purpose, such as controlling exposure compensation, ISO, or zoom for all shooting modes.

C (Custom) Button

If you select C Button from the Custom Key Settings menu screen, the camera will display a screen like that shown in Figure 7-45, which lists the first 6 of the many options that can be assigned to the Custom button.

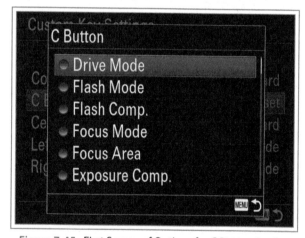

Figure 7-45. First Screen of Options for C Button Setting

The complete list, which is much longer than a single screen, includes all of the following choices, any one of which can be assigned to this button:

- Drive Mode
- Flash Mode
- Flash Compensation
- Focus Mode

- Focus Area
- Exposure Compensation
- ISO
- ND Filter
- Metering Mode
- White Balance
- DRO/Auto HDR
- Creative Style
- Picture Effect
- Smile/Face Detection
- Soft Skin Effect
- Auto Object Framing
- SteadyShot (Still Images)
- SteadyShot (Movies)
- Image Size
- Aspect Ratio
- Quality
- In-Camera Guide
- Memory
- AEL Hold
- AEL Toggle
- Spot AEL Hold
- Spot AEL Toggle
- AF/MF Control Hold
- AF/MF Control Toggle
- Center Lock-on AF
- Eye AF
- Focus Magnifier
- Deactivate Monitor
- Zebra
- Grid Line
- Peaking Level
- Peaking Color
- Send to Smartphone
- Download Application
- Application List
- Monitor Brightness
- Not Set

Scroll through the list and press the Center button to make your selection. The dot next to the chosen option will turn orange to mark the choice.

Many of these options are self-explanatory because, when the button has the option assigned, pressing the button will simply call up the menu screen for that option, if the option is available in the current shooting mode. For example, if the Custom button is assigned to Drive Mode, then, when you press the button, the camera displays the Drive Mode menu, just as if you had used the Menu button to get access to that option. (In some cases the screen looks different from the menu screen called up with the Menu button, but the regular menu options are available in every case.) I will not discuss those options here; see Chapter 4 for discussion of the Shooting menu, Chapter 7 for discussion of the Custom and Setup menus, and Chapter 9 for discussion of the Wi-Fi and Application menus.

However, there are several other selections for the Custom button (and the other control buttons) that do not call up a menu screen. Instead, they perform a function that does not come from a menu option. I will discuss those selections below.

AEL Hold

If you set the Custom button to the AEL Hold (Autoexposure Lock Hold) option, then, when the camera is in shooting mode, pressing this button will lock exposure at the current setting as metered by the camera, as long as you hold down the button. When exposure is locked in this way, a large asterisk will appear in the lower right corner of the display and remain there until the AEL button is released.

You might want to use AEL Hold to calibrate exposure for an object that is part of a larger scene, such as a dark painting on a light wall. You could lock exposure while holding the camera close to the painting, then move back to take a picture of the wall with the locked exposure ensuring the painting will be properly exposed.

Assuming the camera is in Program mode, hold the camera close to the painting until the metered aperture and shutter speed appear on the screen. Press and hold the Custom button and an asterisk (*) will appear in the lower right corner of the screen, as shown in Figure 7-46, indicating that exposure lock is in effect.

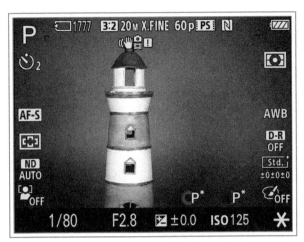

Figure 7-46. Asterisk in Lower Right Corner for AEL Hold

Now you can move back (or anywhere else) and take the photograph using the exposure setting that you locked in. Once you have finished using the locked exposure setting, release the Custom button to make the asterisk disappear. The camera is now ready to measure a new exposure reading.

If the camera is set to Manual exposure mode, pressing a control button assigned to AEL Hold activates Manual Shift, which I discussed in Chapter 3. While you hold down the button for AEL Hold, if you change the aperture or shutter speed, the camera will select a corresponding shutter speed or aperture to maintain the original exposure. This feature operates whether ISO is set to ISO Auto or to a numerical value.

AEL Toggle

If you set the Custom button to the AEL Toggle option, then, in shooting mode, pressing the button will lock exposure just as with AEL Hold. The difference with this setting is that you just press and release the button; the exposure will remain locked until you press the button again to cancel the exposure lock.

Spot AEL Hold

The next option for the Custom button is AEL Hold with a spot icon before the name. The spot icon means that, with this setting, when you press the Custom button and hold it, the camera will lock exposure as metered by the spot-metering area in the center of the display, no matter what metering method is currently in effect. This option can be quite useful if you want to switch to spot-metering just for 1 or 2 shots. You can hold down the Custom button, make sure the center of the display covers the area you want to use for evaluating exposure, and take the shot with the exposure adjusted for that spot.

Spot AEL Toggle

The Spot AEL Toggle option is similar to the AEL Toggle option, except that the camera meters only in the spot area in the very center of the display, as with the Spot AEL Hold option.

AF/MF Control Hold

If you select AF/MF Control Hold for the Custom button's function, pressing the button switches the camera between autofocus and manual focus, but only while you hold down the button. If the camera is set to any autofocus mode, pressing and holding the Custom button will switch the camera into manual focus mode. Releasing it will switch to the autofocus mode that was originally set. If the camera is set to manual focus mode, pressing and holding the button will switch to single-shot AF mode. In this situation, when you press the Custom button, the camera will also evaluate the focus and lock focus, if possible. Releasing the button will switch back to manual focus mode. If the camera is set to DMF mode, pressing the button will toggle between DMF and manual focus.

This function is useful in situations when it is difficult to use autofocus, such as dark areas, extreme closeups, or areas where you have to shoot through obstructions such as glass or wire cages. You can switch quickly into manual focus mode and back again, as conditions warrant.

Also, this capability is helpful if you want to set zone focusing, so you can shoot quickly without having to wait for the autofocus mechanism to operate. For example, if you are doing street photography, you can set the camera to single-shot autofocus mode and focus on a subject at about the distance you expect to be shooting from—say, 25 feet (7.6 meters). Then, once focus is locked on that subject, press and hold the Custom button to switch the camera to manual focus mode, and the focus will be locked at that distance in manual focus mode. You can then take shots of subjects at that distance without having to refocus. If you need to set another focus distance, release the Custom button to go back to autofocus mode and repeat the process.

Finally, it is convenient to quickly get the camera to use autofocus when it is set to manual focus mode. With this function, as noted above, when you press and release the Custom button, the camera will quickly focus using autofocus, and then go back to manual focus mode for any further adjustments you may want to make.

AF/MF Control Toggle

If you select AF/MF Control Toggle for the setting of the Custom button's function, pressing the button switches the camera between autofocus and manual focus. This option works the same as AF/MF Control Hold, except that you do not hold down the button; you just press it and release it. The switched focus mode then stays in effect until you press the button again.

Eye AF

If you assign Eye AF to the Custom button, then, when the camera is set to single-shot autofocus mode, it will look for human eyes and focus on them if possible. If the camera detects an eye, it will display a small green frame to show that it has focused on the eye, as shown in Figure 7-47.

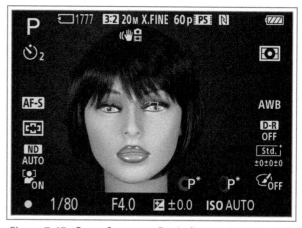

Figure 7-47. Green Square on Eye Indicating Eye AF in Use

Continue to hold down the assigned button to lock focus on the eye while you press the shutter button to take the picture.

This option can be especially useful when depth of field is shallow, such as when the lens is zoomed in to a long focal length or you are shooting a closeup, to make sure the focus is sharpest on the subject's eyes rather than on the nose or some other feature. A portrait generally looks best when the eyes are in sharp focus.

Deactivate Monitor

This is the next non-menu option for the Custom button. (Remember that I'm skipping over settings that are just duplicates of menu options, such as Focus Magnifier.)

If you assign the Custom button to the Deactivate Monitor option, pressing the button while the camera is in shooting mode will turn off the LCD, leaving only a single line of information at the bottom of the screen. You might want to use this option if you are in a darkened area and don't want to distract others or attract attention with the brightness of the monitor. This feature can also help save power if your battery is running down. By pressing the assigned button, you can quickly turn off the monitor temporarily, and recall it just as quickly with the same button.

To deactivate the monitor on a longer-term basis, you can use the Finder/Monitor option on screen 3 of the Custom menu. If you select Viewfinder for that option and pop up the RX100 III's viewfinder, the LCD monitor will be turned off at all times, and will not display even the single line of information that appears when the Deactivate Monitor option is used.

Not Set

The last option that can be assigned to the Custom button is called Not Set. If you choose this option, then the button will not be assigned any special function. I cannot think of any reason to use this option, unless you will be using a limited number of settings and don't want to risk activating a different setting by pressing the button accidentally.

Center Button

Next, you can assign the Center button to any of the same options as for the Custom button. Because of the location and other duties of this button, though, there are a few differences in how this assignment operates.

Most importantly, the first of the possible assignments for the Center button is called Standard, as shown in Figure 7-48. This option is not available for any other control. As I noted in Chapter 5, if you select Standard, the Center button is used for 2 purposes. First, it activates the tracking frame for Center Lock-on AF, if you have turned on that option on screen 5 of the Shooting menu. Second, if Focus Area is set to Flexible Spot on screen 3 of the Shooting menu, pressing the

Center button activates the screen for adjusting the location of the spot-focusing bracket.

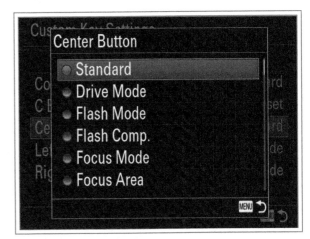

Figure 7-48. List of Options for Center Button Setting

If you don't want to assign the Standard option to this button, you can select one of the other options on the list, which are the same as for the Custom button, discussed above. If you do that, the Center button will no longer do the actions that can be assigned to it with the Standard option. It will select menu options, but it will not lock on a subject when Center Lock-on AF is selected, and it will not activate the focus frame so it can be moved when Flexible Spot is selected for the Focus Area menu option.

If you assign the Center button to one of the AEL functions (locking exposure by holding or toggling the button), then, if you are using manual focus, you will still be able to use the Center button for changing the magnification on the MF Assist screen without affecting the exposure lock function. To activate or cancel the exposure lock, press the Center button when the shooting screen is in its normal mode (that is, when the MF Assist magnification screen is not displayed).

I recommend that you leave the Center button assigned to the Standard option so it will carry out its focus-related duties. There are other controls that can have settings assigned to them without disrupting the normal uses of the Center button.

Left Button

The choices of assignments for the Left button are the same as for the Custom button, except that 4 of the choices are not available. The unavailable options are AEL Hold, Spot AEL Hold, AF/MF Control Hold, and Eye AF. So, if you want to set the Left button to lock exposure or to switch between autofocus and manual focus, the button will act only as a toggle, not as one that you have to hold down. Presumably, Sony made this choice because it would be awkward to hold down the Left button while pressing the shutter button. (Eye AF also requires that you hold down the control button while pressing the shutter button.)

Right Button

The Right button has the same options as the Left button.

ZOOM FUNCTION ON RING

This next item on the Custom menu controls the way the Control ring operates when you are using it to zoom the lens in and out. As I discussed earlier in this chapter, the Control ring controls zoom when its function is set to Standard in Intelligent Auto mode and Superior Auto mode. In any other shooting mode, you have to set the Control ring's function to Zoom to enable it to zoom the lens. You set the ring's function using the Custom Key Settings menu option, discussed above.

When the ring is set to control zoom, you can use the Zoom Function on Ring menu option to choose between Standard and Step for the way the zoom operates, as shown in Figure 7-49.

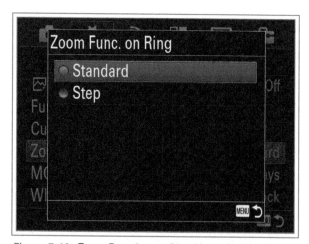

Figure 7-49. Zoom Function on Ring Menu Options Screen

With Standard, when the Control ring is used to zoom the lens, it does so continuously, just as the zoom lever does. That is, as you turn the ring, the lens zooms through all focal lengths that are available. With optical zoom, that means it will zoom from the 24mm wide-angle setting to the 70mm telephoto setting in continuous increments. With Clear Image Zoom and

Digital Zoom, the zoom levels increase beyond the 70mm point.

If you set this menu option to Step, then the Control ring zooms the lens only to certain preset values: 24mm, 28mm, 35mm, 50mm, and 70mm. When you nudge the ring toward the wide-angle or telephoto side, the zoom will move to the next preset focal length. You should give the ring a quick nudge and then release it; if you keep turning it, it will move past the next value and go on to the one after that.

There are some limitations with the Step Zoom function on the RX100 III. First, if you set the camera for manual focus or DMF using the Focus Mode menu option, the Control ring will control manual focus and will not zoom the lens.

Next, the Step Zoom feature works only for the Control ring; the zoom lever will always zoom the lens continuously. Also, the Step Zoom feature does not work when shooting movies.

Finally, if you turn on Clear Image Zoom or Digital Zoom using the Zoom Setting option on screen 3 of the Custom menu, the Step Zoom feature will not include specific increments for the zoom range beyond the optical limit of 70mm. Instead, as shown in Figure 7-50, the camera will display the range of preset increments along with an area at the right side of the scale extending from the 70mm mark to a magnifying glass icon at the far right, showing a general area of extended zoom range.

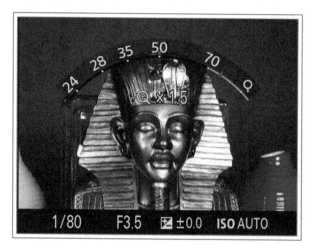

Figure 7-50. Zoom Scale with Step Zoom in Effect

Step zoom is a valuable feature in some situations. For example, if you want to set a specific focal length for a shot, using Step Zoom is an excellent way to make sure you have the lens zoomed to the exact focal length you want. Of course, this feature is of use only if your desired focal length is 28mm, 35mm, or 50mm; it is easy to set the focal length to 24mm or 70mm using the normal zoom method because those focal lengths are at the 2 extremes of the camera's optical zoom range.

You might want to choose a focal length of 35mm, for example, to compare shots from the RX100 III against shots from another camera using that specific focal length.

MOVIE BUTTON

This option, shown in Figure 7-51, lets you lock out the operation of the red Movie button to avoid accidentally starting a video recording. The 2 choices are Always and Movie Mode Only.

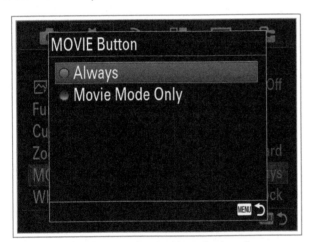

Figure 7-51. Movie Button Menu Options Screen

If you want to be able to start recording a video at any time without delay, you should leave the Movie Button option set to Always. With that setting, you can start recording a movie by pressing this button, no matter what shooting mode is set on the Mode dial. This is a convenient system, because you can start shooting a video at a moment's notice without having to turn the Mode dial to the Movie position.

As I discussed in Chapter 5 in the section on the Movie button, the main reason to choose the Movie Mode Only option is if you are afraid you may press the Movie button by mistake. I have pressed it by mistake several times myself, so, unless I am on a trip when I may want to record movies quickly, I leave this menu option set to Movie Mode Only, to avoid having to stop and delete unwanted recordings.

WHEEL LOCK

This final option on the Custom menu has 2 possible settings, Lock and Unlock, as seen in Figure 7-52.

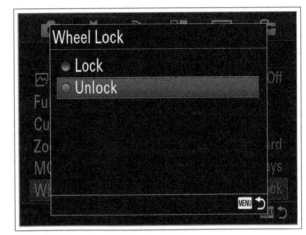

Figure 7-52. Wheel Lock Menu Options Screen

If you select Lock, you can lock the functioning of the Control wheel. To engage the actual lock, after this menu item is set to Lock, press and hold the Function button for several seconds until a Locked message appears on the screen. After that, you will see an icon in the lower right corner of the display indicating that the lock is in effect, as shown in Figure 7-53.

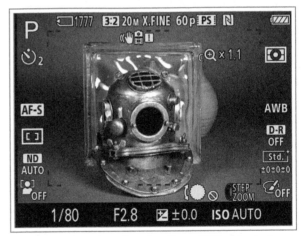

Figure 7-53. Icon Showing Control Wheel Locked

Once the lock is in effect, turning the Control wheel will not change the camera's settings. For example, in Shutter Priority or Manual exposure mode, turning the Control wheel will not change the shutter speed as it normally would. In Scene mode, turning it will not change to a different scene setting. However, the wheel will still navigate through menus, and the buttons at the edges of the wheel will operate, even with the lock in effect.

If you have made an important adjustment to your settings, you can lock the wheel so the setting will stay in place. When you are ready to change settings, press and hold the Function button again to remove the lock.

Even when the Lock option is turned on, the Function button can call up the Function menu. A quick press of the button will call up the menu; a longer press-and-hold will lock or unlock the wheel.

Setup Menu

The next menu to be discussed is the Setup menu, whose first screen is shown in Figure 7-54.

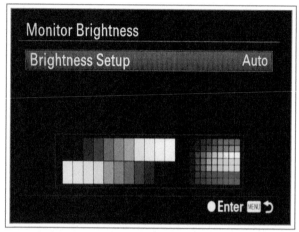
Figure 7-55. Monitor Brightness Menu Options Screen

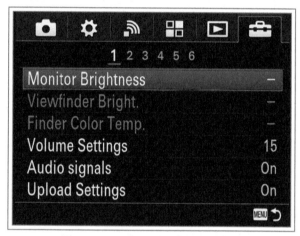
Figure 7-54. Screen 1 of Setup Menu

This 6-screen menu has options for matters like USB connections, display brightness, audio volume, file numbering, formatting a memory card, and others. I will discuss each menu item below.

MONITOR BRIGHTNESS

When you select this option, the camera displays a screen showing the current setting, as seen in Figure 7-55. If you press the Center button on that screen, you will see a screen where you can choose 1 of 3 available settings for controlling the brightness of the LCD display: Auto, Manual, or Sunny Weather, as shown in Figure 7-56. If you choose Auto, the camera adjusts the screen's brightness using a small light sensor at the lower left corner of the LCD screen to gauge the amount of ambient light. As the ambient light grows dimmer, the screen grows dimmer also, and vice-versa.

With Manual, the camera displays the screen in Figure 7-57.

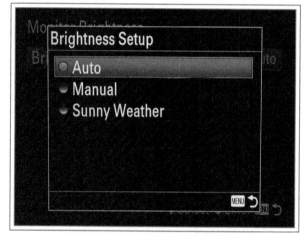
Figure 7-56. Brightness Setup Options Screen

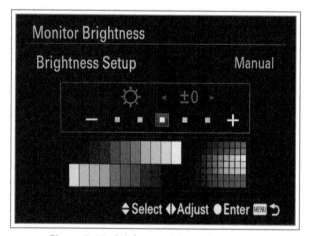
Figure 7-57. Brightness Adjustment Screen

Using the controls on the adjustment screen, you can vary brightness to 1 or 2 units above or below normal. After moving the orange block into the scale, press the Left or Right button to make the adjustment. If your battery is running low and you don't have a spare, you may want to set the monitor to its minimum brightness to conserve power. Conversely, you can increase brightness if you're finding it difficult to compose the image on the screen.

If you are shooting outdoors in bright conditions, you can choose Sunny Weather, which sets the display to a very bright level. Of course, you can switch to using the viewfinder in bright conditions, but there may be times when you want to hold the camera away from your head as you compose the shot, even in bright sunlight. Or, you may want to play back your images for friends while outdoors. The Sunny Weather setting drains the camera's battery fairly rapidly, so you should turn it off when it is no longer needed.

VIEWFINDER BRIGHTNESS

This second option on the Setup menu is similar to Monitor Brightness, with some differences. With this option, you have to look into the viewfinder to make adjustments. There is no Sunny Weather setting, because the viewfinder is shaded from the sun and there is no need for a super-bright setting. You can set the brightness to Auto or Manual. If you select Manual, you can make the same adjustments as with the LCD screen.

FINDER COLOR TEMPERATURE

This option lets you adjust the color temperature of the view through the viewfinder. As with the Viewfinder Brightness setting, you have to look into the viewfinder to make the adjustments. You can use the camera's controls to adjust the color temperature downward by 1 or 2 units, which will make the view appear slightly more reddish, or "warmer," or you can adjust upward by 1 or 2 units to make it more bluish, or "cooler." I have not found a reason to take advantage of this adjustment, but it is easy to use and it may be helpful to you.

VOLUME SETTINGS

This option, whose settings screen is shown in Figure 7-58, lets you set the volume for playback of movies at a level anywhere from 0 to 15. You can also set this level when a movie is playing by pressing the Down button to get access to the detailed controls, which include a volume setting option. When a movie is displayed on the screen in playback mode before playback starts, pressing the Down button calls up the volume adjustment screen immediately. Pressing that button when a still image is displayed in playback mode also

calls up the volume screen, if View Mode is set to Date View or any other view that includes videos.

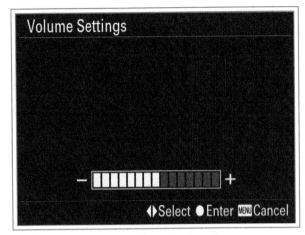

Figure 7-58. Volume Settings Screen

AUDIO SIGNALS

This option, whose main screen is shown in Figure 7-59, lets you choose whether or not to activate the various sounds the RX100 III makes when an operation takes place, such as pressing the shutter button, confirming focus, or pressing a control button.

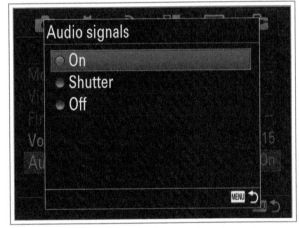

Figure 7-59. Audio Signals Menu Options Screen

By default, the sounds are turned on, but it can be helpful to silence them during a religious ceremony, or when you are doing street photography and want to avoid alerting your subjects. There is a separate entry for Shutter, so you can leave the shutter sound on while silencing sounds such as focus beeps if you want.

UPLOAD SETTINGS

This last item on the first screen of the Setup menu, shown in Figure 7-54, appears only when an Eye-Fi card is in the camera. If no Eye-Fi card is present, this menu option does not display at all, leaving a blank space at the bottom of the menu screen.

As discussed in Chapter 1, an Eye-Fi card is a memory card with a transmitter to send images to a computer over a Wi-Fi network. This menu item has only 2 settings—On or Off. You might want to use the Off setting if you are on an airplane where you may be required to turn off radio transmitters. Or, if you know you will not be using the Eye-Fi uploading capability for a while, you can turn this menu option off to save some battery power.

Of course, the RX100 III has built-in Wi-Fi capability, which makes it less likely you will use an Eye-Fi card.

The second screen of the Setup menu is shown in Figure 7-60.

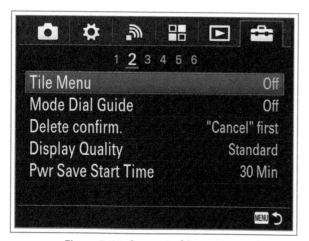

Figure 7-60. Screen 2 of Setup Menu

Following are details about the options on this screen.

TILE MENU

If you turn this option on, the camera displays a screen with 6 tiles representing the various menu systems, as shown in Figure 7-61, when you press the Menu button. This screen gives you a graphic representation of which menu is which, and it lets you get quick access to the menu of your choice. You navigate through the 6 blocks using the direction buttons or the Control wheel.

I prefer to leave this option turned off, because, without it, pressing the Menu button takes me right to the last menu option I was using. From there, I can navigate quickly to any other menu system. But for those who are new to this camera or who like having a large display

to show the menu choices clearly, the Tile Menu option may be worth using.

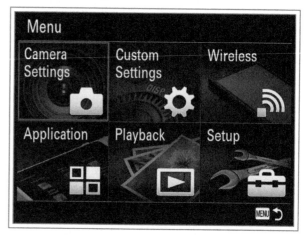

Figure 7-61. Tiled Menus

MODE DIAL GUIDE

This menu item lets you turn on or off the Mode dial guide, a graphic display that appears on the camera's screen when you turn the Mode dial to select a shooting mode, as shown in Figure 7-62.

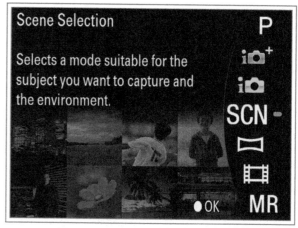

Figure 7-62. Mode Dial Guide Display

This guide is helpful when you first get the camera, but it can be annoying if you don't need the reminders, and you have to press the Center button or press the shutter button halfway to dismiss the screen. I leave this option turned off to speed up my shooting.

DELETE CONFIRMATION

This menu item has 2 possible settings, as shown in Figure 7-63: "Delete" First or "Cancel" First. This option lets you fine-tune how the menu system operates for deleting images. Whenever you press the Delete button to delete an image in playback mode, the camera displays a confirmation screen, as shown in Figure 7-64, with 2 choices: Delete or Cancel.

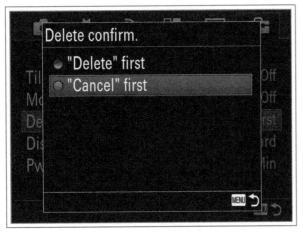

Figure 7-63. Delete Confirmation Menu Options Screen

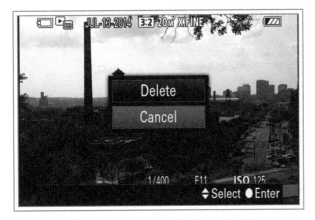

Figure 7-64. Delete Button Confirmation Screen

One of those choices will be highlighted when the screen appears; you can then press the Center button to accept that choice and the operation will be done. You also can use the Control wheel or the Up or Down button to highlight the other option before you press the Center button to carry out your choice.

Which setting you choose for this menu item depends on how careful you want to be to guard against the accidental deletion of an image. If you like to move quickly in deleting images, choose "Delete" First. Then, as soon as the confirmation screen appears, the "Delete" option will be highlighted and you can press the Center button to carry out the deletion. If you prefer to have some assurance of avoiding an accidental deletion, choose "Cancel" First, so that, if you press the Center button too quickly when the confirmation screen appears, you will only cancel the operation, rather than deleting an image.

Unless you use this process often and need to save time, I recommend you leave this menu item set at the "Cancel" First setting to be safe.

DISPLAY QUALITY

This menu item lets you choose Standard or High for the quality of the display. According to Sony, with the High setting the camera displays the live view on the LCD screen or in the viewfinder at a higher resolution than with the Standard setting, at the expense of additional drain on the battery.

I have tried several experiments with these settings, viewing small print from a catalog using both the viewfinder and the LCD display with both Display Quality settings, and I have not found a noticeable difference. There may be situations in which this option has a more noticeable impact on the display, but my recommendation is to leave it at Standard to conserve battery life.

POWER SAVE START TIME

This option lets you set the interval before the camera turns off automatically to save power, when no controls have been operated. The default is 2 minutes; with this option you can also choose 1, 5, or 30 minutes, as shown in Figure 7-65.

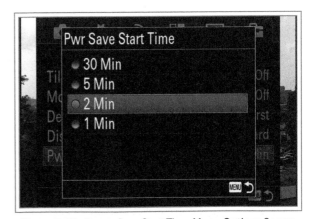

Figure 7-65. Power Save Start Time Menu Options Screen

After the designated time, the camera does not just go into a "sleep" mode, it powers off. You have to turn it back on by pressing the power button, the Playback button, or the Finder switch. The setting you use depends on your preferences. I am usually well aware of the camera's status, and I like to use the maximum 30-minute period for this option so the camera does not power down just when I am about to use it again.

I always have extra batteries available and I'm not too concerned if I have to replace the battery. If you are out in the field and running low on battery power, you might want to choose a shorter time for this option, to conserve battery life.

PAL/NTSC SELECTOR

This menu option appears only on cameras that are sold in areas that use the PAL video standard and that therefore use the 1080 50i video format rather than the 1080 60i format that is used in the United States, Canada, and other areas with the NTSC standard. As I noted in the Introduction, I live in the United States and have the NTSC version of the RX100 III, so my information about this menu option is secondhand.

The 50i version of the camera, which has a "50i" label on the bottom, can be switched to record video with the NTSC/60i standard by means of this PAL/NTSC Selector menu option. So, if you purchased your camera in Europe or another area where the PAL version is sold, you will have the option to record your videos in either the PAL (50i) or NTSC (60i) format. However, if, like me, you have the 60i (NTSC) version of the camera, you can record and play back video only in the NTSC format.

If you have the PAL version of the camera, you cannot record NTSC video on a memory card that was previously formatted using the PAL system. If you try to do so, you will receive an error message. You will have to re-format the card with the PAL/NTSC Selector set to NTSC or use a different card that has been formatted under that system.

Screen 3 of the Setup menu is shown in Figure 7-66.

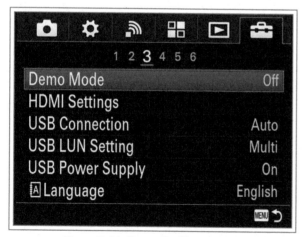

Figure 7-66. Screen 3 of Setup Menu

DEMO MODE

The Demo Mode menu item automatically plays a movie if the camera has not had any controls operated for about one minute. This feature is designed for use by retail stores, so they can leave the camera turned on with a continuous demonstration on its screen. But you can use it for your own purposes, if you want to create a movie that demonstrates the camera's features for friends, for example, or if you just like the idea of having the camera play a movie when it's not otherwise occupied.

For this feature to be available for selection on the menu screen as shown in Figure 7-66, the camera has to be powered by an AC adapter and the battery has to be removed from the camera. Otherwise, this line on the menu will be dimmed. (As noted in Chapter 1 and Appendix A, the charger that ships with the RX100 III does not work as an AC adapter; you can purchase one from Sony as an optional accessory.)

When this option is turned on and the camera is in shooting mode, after one minute of inactivity the camera will enter Demo Mode. At that point, the camera will automatically play a movie, which you have to provide. It cannot be just any movie. The movie the camera will play in Demo Mode must be recorded in the AVCHD format, it must be protected using the Protect option on the Playback menu, and it must be the oldest AVCHD movie on the memory card. So, if you have a reason to use this option, you may want to use a fresh memory card and record a single AVCHD movie on the card, and then use the Protect function to protect it. When the movie plays, it plays audio as well as video, and it will keep repeating in a loop. To exit from Demo Mode, you can press the Center button or just turn the camera off.

HDMI SETTINGS

The HDMI Settings menu option has 3 sub-options: HDMI Resolution, HDMI Information Display, and CTRL for HDMI. I will discuss these below.

HDMI Resolution

The HDMI Resolution option can be set to Auto, 1080p, or 1080i. This setting controls how the camera displays images and videos on an HDTV. Ordinarily, the Auto setting will work best; the camera will set itself for the optimum display according to the resolution of the

HDTV it is connected to. If you experience difficulties with that connection, you may be able to improve the image on the HDTV's screen by trying one of the other settings.

HDMI Information Display

This feature controls the behavior of the camera when you connect it to an HDTV set using an optional HDMI cable. However, unlike other HDMI-related menu options, this one does not control what happens when the camera is in playback mode, playing your images and videos on the HDTV. Instead, it controls what happens in shooting mode when the HDMI connection is active.

If this menu option is set to On, which is the default setting, then, when the camera is connected to an HDTV in shooting mode, the HDTV's screen displays exactly what you would see on the camera's display in that mode if the camera were not connected to the HDTV. With the On setting, the HDTV acts as a large, external monitor for the RX100 III, and the screen of the RX100 III itself is blank. I use this setting a great deal myself, because this is how I capture screen shots for this book. Once the camera is connected, I can capture all of the shooting screens and menu screens of the camera, with a few exceptions for special settings that are not output through the HDMI port, such as the zebra stripes.

If this menu option is set to Off, then, when the camera is connected to an HDTV in shooting mode, the HDTV's screen displays only the image that is being viewed by the camera, with no shooting information displayed at all. If you press the Display button, nothing will happen on the TV; the view will not switch to another display with more information on it. However, at the same time, the camera's screen continues to display all of the shooting information it normally would, including the image and whatever information is chosen by presses of the Display button.

You might use the Off setting when you want to display images from the camera's shooting mode on a large HDTV screen, possibly at a wedding or other gathering, and not have the images cluttered or marred by any shooting information at all. For example, I have seen occasions where a camera is used to focus on an unsuspecting person in the audience, and that person's image suddenly appears on the large screen for everyone to see.

Also, this option is useful for video production when you need to output a "clean" video signal that does not include any shooting information from the camera. That signal could be sent through an HDMI cable to a video recorder for recording to another medium, or for display on a large monitor being viewed by the production team. For example, you can record video directly from the camera to a computer by outputting the clean HDMI signal to a device such as the Intensity Pro by Blackmagic Design. There are similar devices available from companies such as AverMedia, Hauppage, and Elgato.

With the On setting, you can press the Display button to show a screen with very minimal shooting information, but that screen still shows the basic information of aperture, shutter speed, exposure compensation, and ISO value at the very bottom of the screen, and shows the shooting mode in the upper left corner. If you don't want even that minimal level of information to interfere with the video display, choose the Off setting.

This setting does not change the behavior of the camera for playback of images; its only effect is on the display of information in shooting mode through an HDMI connection.

CTRL for HDMI

This sub-option is of use only when you have connected the camera to an HDTV and you want to control the camera with the TV's remote control, which is possible in some situations. If you want to do that, set this option to On and follow the instructions for the TV and its remote control. This option is intended to be used when you connect the camera to a Sony Bravia model HDTV.

USB CONNECTION

This menu item sets the technical standard that the camera uses for transferring images and videos to a computer using the USB cable. This option has 3 choices, as shown in Figure 7-67: Auto, Mass Storage, and MTP, which stands for Media Transfer Protocol, a standard developed by Microsoft for transferring media files over a USB connection.

You ordinarily should select Auto, and the RX100 III should detect which standard is used by the computer you are connecting the camera to. If the camera does not automatically select a standard and start transferring images, you can try one of the other settings to see if it works better than the Auto setting.

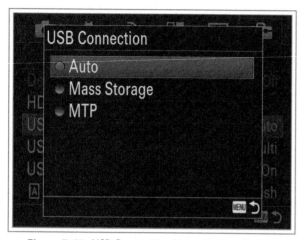

Figure 7-67. USB Connection Menu Options Screen

USB LUN SETTING

This is a technical option that should not often be used. LUN stands for logical unit number. This option has 2 possible settings—Multi or Single. Ordinarily, it should be set to Multi, the default. In particular, it should be set to Multi when the RX100 III is connected to a Windows-based computer and you are using Sony's PlayMemories Home software to manage your images. If you encounter a problem with a USB connection to a computer, you can try the Single setting to see if it solves the problem.

USB POWER SUPPLY

The USB Power Supply option, which can be turned either on or off, controls whether or not the camera's battery will be charged when the camera is connected by its USB cable to a computer or other device. This option also can be used if you have a portable USB charger available—a device that uses battery power to charge your cell phone and other portable gadgets.

Turning this option on gives you another avenue for keeping the RX100 III's battery charged. The only problem is that if your computer is running on its battery, then that battery will be discharged more rapidly than usual. If you are plugging the camera into a computer that is plugged into a wall power outlet, there should be no problem in using this option.

As I will discuss in Appendix A, in my opinion, you should get an external battery charger and at least one extra battery for the RX100 III because even if

you can charge the battery in the camera using the USB cable, you don't have the ability to insert a fully charged battery into the camera when the first battery is exhausted.

I recommend leaving this option at its default setting of On, unless you will be connecting the camera to a battery-powered computer or other device and you don't want to run down the battery on that device.

LANGUAGE

This option gives you the choice of language for the display of commands and information on the camera's LCD screen. Once you have selected this menu item, as shown in Figure 7-68, scroll through the language choices using the Control wheel or the direction buttons and press the Center button when your chosen language is highlighted.

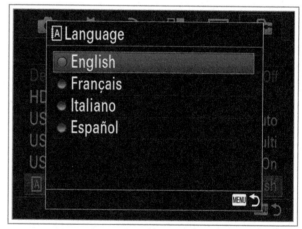

Figure 7-68. Language Selection Screen

Next, I will discuss the items on screen 4 of the Setup menu, shown in Figure 7-69.

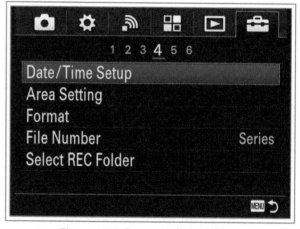

Figure 7-69. Screen 4 of Setup Menu

DATE/TIME SETUP

I discussed this item in Chapter 1. When the camera is new or has not been used for a long time, it will prompt you to set the date and time and will display this menu option. If you want to call up these settings on your own, you can do so at any time.

When you press the Center button on this menu line, you will see a screen like that in Figure 7-70, with the choice of adjusting Daylight Savings Time (On or Off), Date/Time, or Date Format.

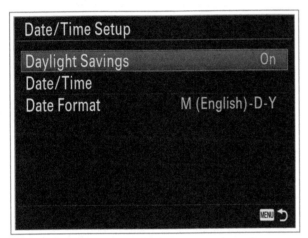

Figure 7-70. Date/Time Setup Menu Options Screen

To adjust Date/Time, select that option and press the Center button. The camera will display a screen like that shown in Figure 7-71.

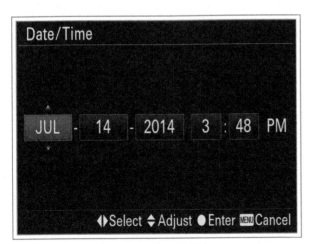

Figure 7-71. Date/Time Settings Screen

Scroll through the options for setting month, day, year, and time by turning the Control wheel or pressing the Left and Right buttons. As you reach each item, adjust its value by using the Up and Down buttons. When all

of the settings are correct, press the Center button to confirm them and exit from this screen.

From the first menu screen, you can also turn Daylight Savings Time on or off depending on the time of year, and you can choose a date format according to your preference.

AREA SETTING

The next option on screen 4 of the Setup menu, Area Setting, lets you select a location so you can adjust the date and time for a different time zone when you are traveling. When you highlight this item and press the Center button, the camera displays the map shown in Figure 7-72.

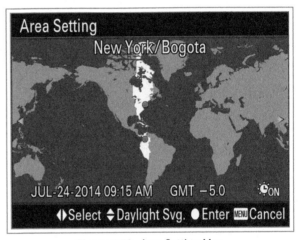

Figure 7-72. Area Setting Map

Turn the Control wheel or press the Left and Right buttons to move the light-colored highlight over the map until it covers the area of the location you want to set. If you want to adjust the setting for Daylight Savings Time, press the Up or Down button to make the adjustment. Then press the Center button and the date and time will be adjusted for that location until you change the location again using this menu item.

FORMAT

The next option on screen 4 of the Setup menu—Format—is used to prepare a new memory card to store images and videos with the correct data format. This command also is useful when you want to wipe all the data off a card that has become full or you have copied a card's images to your computer or other storage device. Choose this process only when you want or need to completely wipe all of the data from a memory card. When you select the Format option, as shown in Figure

7-73, the camera will warn you that all data currently on the card will be deleted if you proceed.

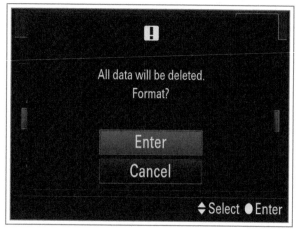

Figure 7-73. Format Confirmation Screen

If you reply by highlighting Enter and pressing the Center button to confirm, the camera will format the card that is in the camera, and the result will be a card that is empty and properly formatted to store new images and videos.

With this procedure, the camera will erase all files, including those that have been protected from accidental erasure with the Protect function on the Playback menu. It's a good idea to periodically save your images and videos to your computer or other storage device and then re-format your card to make sure it is properly set up for recording new images and videos. It's also a good idea to use the Format command on any new memory card when you first insert it into the camera. Even though it likely will work without that procedure, it's best to make sure the card is set up with Sony's method of formatting for the RX100 III.

FILE NUMBER

This option controls how the camera assigns file numbers to images. The choices are Series or Reset, as seen in Figure 7-74. If you choose Series, then the camera continues numbering where it left off, even if you put a new memory card in the camera. For example, if you have shot 112 images on your first memory card, the last image likely will be numbered 100-0112: 100 for the folder number (the first folder number available) and 0112 for the image number. If you then switch to a new memory card with no images on it, the first image on that card will be numbered 100-0113 because the numbering scheme continues in the same sequence. If

you choose Reset instead, the first image on the new card will be numbered 100-0001 because the camera resets the numbering to the first number.

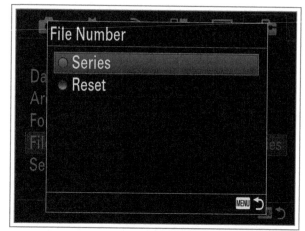

Figure 7-74. File Number Menu Options Screen

SELECT REC FOLDER

When you select this menu item, the camera displays an orange bar with the name of the current folder, as shown in Figure 7-75.

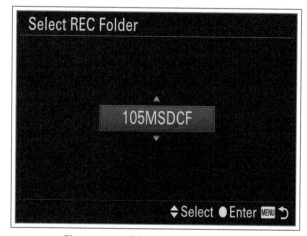

Figure 7-75. Select REC Folder Screen

You can use the Up and Down buttons or turn the Control wheel to choose another folder on the memory card if one exists, so you can store future images in that folder. For example, if you take some photos for business and some for pleasure, you could create a new folder for business shots (see the next menu item, below). The camera would then use that folder. Afterward, you could use the Select REC Folder option to select the folder where your personal images are stored and take more images that will be stored there. This option is not available if you use Date Form for the File Name option, discussed later in this section. This option also selects the folder number for storing MP4 videos, though that folder is different from the one for still images.

The next items to be discussed appear on screen 5 of the Setup menu, shown in Figure 7-76.

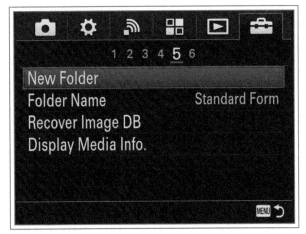

Figure 7-76. Screen 5 of Setup Menu

NEW FOLDER

This first item on screen 5 of the Setup menu lets you create a new folder on your memory card for storing images. After you highlight this item on the menu screen and press the Center button, you will see a message announcing that a new folder has been created, as shown in Figure 7-77.

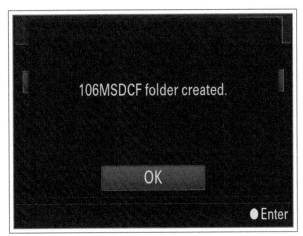

Figure 7-77. New Folder Creation Message

The camera will store new images in that folder until you select another folder with the Select REC Folder option, discussed above, or create another folder using this option. The camera will create a new folder for storing MP4 videos at the same time. The camera also will create a new folder once a folder contains 4,000

images. Folders for still images are created within the DCIM folder, and folders for MP4 videos are created within the MP_ROOT folder.

I find this option useful for organizing images. When I go on a trip to take photos at a particular location, I often create a new folder to store the photos from that trip so I can easily find them and upload them to my computer when I return.

FOLDER NAME

This option gives you a choice of 2 methods for naming folders that store still images on your memory card, as seen in Figure 7-78: Standard Form or Date Form. Standard Form uses the folder number, such as 100, 101, or higher, followed by the letters MSDCF. An example is 100MSDCF. If you choose Date Form, folder names will have the same 100 or higher number followed by the date, in a form such as 10040728 for a folder created on July 28, 2014, using only one digit to designate the year.

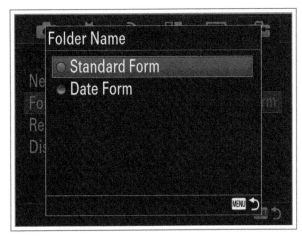

Figure 7-78. Folder Name Menu Options Screen

I find the date format confusing and hard to read, and I am used to the MSDCF format. If you use the date format, you will end up having a folder for every date on which you record still images. You may prefer having your image folders organized in that way so you can quickly locate images from a particular date. I prefer having fewer folders and organizing the images using software on my computer according to my own preferences.

RECOVER IMAGE DATABASE

This menu item activates the Recover Image Database function. If you select this option and press the Center button to confirm it on the next screen, as shown in Figure 7-79, the camera runs a check to test the integrity of the file system on the memory card.

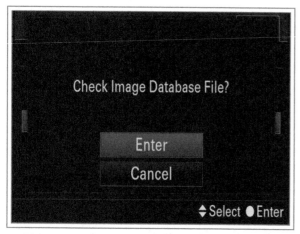

Figure 7-79. Recover Image DB Confirmation Screen

This option displays automatically when you insert into the camera a new memory card or a card that has previously been used in a different camera. I have never used this menu option, but if the camera is having difficulty reading the images on a card, using this option might recover the data.

DISPLAY MEDIA INFORMATION

The final item on this menu screen gives you another way to see how much storage space is remaining on the memory card that is currently in the camera.

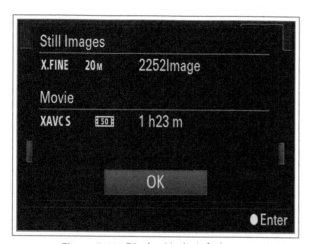

Figure 7-80. Display Media Info Screen

When you select Display Media Information and press the Center button, the camera displays a screen like that in Figure 7-80, with information about the number of still images or the minutes of video that can be recorded using current settings. It is nice to have

this option available, although the number of images that can be recorded is also displayed on the detailed shooting screen, and the number of minutes of video that can be recorded is displayed on the video recording screen once a recording has been started.

The final screen of the Setup menu is seen in Figure 7-81.

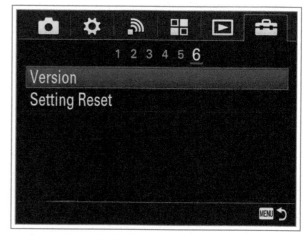

Figure 7-81. Screen 6 of Setup Menu

VERSION

This menu option displays the current version of the firmware installed in your camera. The Sony Cyber-shot DSC-RX100 III, like other digital cameras, is programmed at the factory with firmware, which is a set of computer instructions electronically implanted in the camera. These instructions control all aspects of the camera's operation, including the menu system, functioning of the controls, and in-camera processing of your images. The reason you may want to check to see what version is installed is that, in many cases, the manufacturer will release an updated version of the firmware that may fix problems or bugs in the system, provide minor enhancements, or, in some cases, even provide major improvements, such as adding new shooting modes or menu options.

To determine the firmware version installed in your camera, highlight this menu option and press the Center button, and the camera will display the version number, as shown in Figure 7-82. To see if firmware upgrades have been released, visit Sony's support website at http://esupport.sony.com. Find the link for Drivers and Software, then the link for Cyber-shot Cameras, and then a link to any updated version for the RX100 III (often referred to by Sony as the RX100M3).

The site will provide instructions for downloading and installing the new firmware.

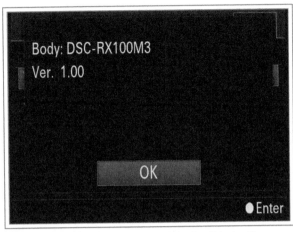

Figure 7-82. Firmware Version Number Display Screen

SETTING RESET

This final option on the Setup menu is useful when you want to reset some or all of the camera's settings to their original (default) values. This action can be helpful if you have been playing around with different settings and you find that something is not working as expected.

With this item, the camera presents you with 2 sub-options: Camera Settings Reset and Initialize, as shown in Figure 7-83.

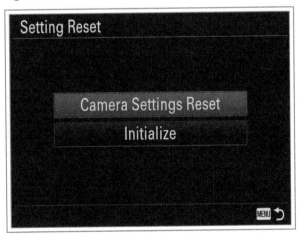

Figure 7-83. Setting Reset Menu Options Screen

If you choose Camera Settings Reset, only the settings that directly affect shooting images and videos are reset. If you select Initialize, all settings, including items such as Audio Signals and Monitor Brightness, are reset to their factory values.

CHAPTER 8: MOTION PICTURES

You may have purchased the Sony RX100 III because of its excellent features for capturing still images, but you should not overlook the camera's options for recording movies. The RX100 III's video abilities are strong for a camera this small; they provide you with excellent flexibility in capturing video. Before I discuss specific settings you can make for your movies, I'll begin with a brief overview of the process.

Movie-Making Overview

In one sense, the fundamentals of making movies with the RX100 III can be stated in 4 words: "Push the red button." (That is, the red Movie button at the upper right corner of the camera's back.) Anytime you see a reason to take some video footage, you can press and release the red button while aiming at your subject, and you will get results that are likely to be quite usable. You do not need to worry about making special settings, particularly if you have set the camera to one of the Auto modes. To stop recording, press the red button again. (If you prefer not to run the risk of recording unwanted movies by pressing the red button accidentally, you can change the button's operation so it activates movie recording only when the camera is in Movie mode, as discussed in Chapter 7.)

If you're mainly a still photographer with little interest in movie making, you don't need to read any further. Be aware that the red button exists, and if a newsworthy event starts to happen, you can capture good footage to post on YouTube or elsewhere with a minimum of effort.

But for those RX100 III users who want to delve further into their camera's excellent motion picture capabilities, there is considerably more information to discuss.

First, there is a requirement that may determine what memory card you will purchase for your camera. If you want to record movies using the highest-quality format, XAVC S, you have to use an SDXC card with a capacity of 64 GB or more and a speed of at least Class 10 or UHS-I. This is not just a recommendation. If you do not use a card that meets those specifications, the camera will display an error message and will not record video using that format. (Sony says you also can use a Memory Stick XC-HG Duo card. I have not found a source for that card, but if you can find one, it should work also.)

Also, it's important to note that the RX100 III, like most cameras in its class, has built-in limitations that prevent it from recording any sequence longer than about 29 minutes (15 minutes for the MP4 HD format). You can, of course, record multiple sequences adding up to any length depending on the amount of storage space available on your memory cards.

So, even if you decide not to get a 64 GB card for recording XAVC S video, if you plan on recording a significant amount of HD video, you should get a high-capacity and high-speed card. For example, a 16 GB card can hold about 75 minutes of the highest quality of AVCHD video, about 2 hours of lower-quality AVCHD video, or about 2 hours 45 minutes of MP4 HD video. (I will discuss these video formats later in this chapter.)

Details of Settings for Shooting Movies

As I noted above, the one step that is a necessity for recording a movie with the RX100 III is to press the Movie button. However, there are numerous settings that affect the way the camera records a movie when that button is pressed.

I will discuss 4 categories of settings: (1) the movie-related selections you make on the Shooting menu; (2) the position of the Mode dial on top of the camera; (3) the other selections you make on the Shooting menu and other menus; and (4) the settings you make with the camera's physical controls.

MOVIE-RELATED SHOOTING MENU OPTIONS

First, I will discuss the movie-related options on the Shooting menu, because those options control the format and several other important settings for the movies you record with the RX100 III. I discussed this menu in Chapter 4, but I did not provide details about the movie-oriented options in that chapter.

As noted above, you can press the Movie button to start a video recording any time and in any shooting mode, as long as the Movie Button option on screen 4 of the Custom menu is set to Always. Because of this ability to shoot movies in any shooting mode, you can always change the settings for movie recording using the Shooting menu, no matter what shooting mode the camera is set to. I will discuss each item on the Shooting menu that has an effect on your shooting of videos.

At this point, I am going to discuss the Shooting menu options that apply only to movies; later in this chapter, I will discuss the options on this menu and other menus that affect movies as well as still images, such as White Balance, ISO, Creative Style, Picture Effect, and others.

File Format

The last item on screen 1 of the Shooting menu, File Format, gives you a choice of the 3 available movie recording formats on the RX100 III—XAVC S, AVCHD, and MP4, as shown in Figure 8-1.

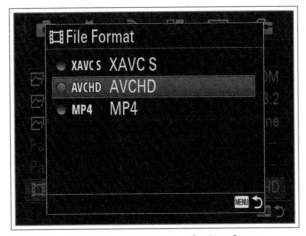

Figure 8-1. File Format Menu Options Screen

This setting determines the format the camera will use to record movies when you press the Movie button. The 3 formats have different characteristics, as discussed below.

XAVC S

The XAVC S format, a relatively new option, is a consumer version of the XAVC format, developed for use with 4K video recording, sometimes known as Ultra HD. (The term "4K" refers to a horizontal resolution of roughly 4,000 pixels, instead of the 1920 pixels in standard HD video.)

The XAVC S format used by the RX100 III does not provide 4K resolution, but it offers high-quality HD recording and compatibility with several video-editing programs, such as Adobe Premiere Pro, Sony Vegas Pro, and others. With this format, you can record movies at a higher bit rate than with other formats and at higher speeds in frames per second, meaning you can record more information and have more options for producing high-quality slow-motion footage.

It is worth repeating that, in order to use this format, you are required to use an SDXC card with a capacity of 64 GB or more and a speed rating of Class 10 or UHS-I, or a Sony Memory Stick XC-HG Duo card.

AVCHD

If you don't want to purchase a 64 GB SDXC or XC-HG Duo card so you can use XAVC S but you still want very high quality for your movies, you can choose AVCHD, which is the default choice with the RX100 III. This format, developed jointly by Sony and Panasonic, has become increasingly common in advanced digital cameras. It provides excellent quality, and movies recorded in this format on the RX100 III can be used to create Blu-ray discs.

MP4

If you want to record movies with excellent video quality but in a format that is easier to edit with a computer than the first 2 options, you can choose MP4. The MP4 format is compatible with Apple Computer's QuickTime software, and the files can be edited with various software programs, including QuickTime, iMovie, Windows Movie Maker, and many others.

Record Setting

The Record Setting item on the Movie menu is another quality-related option for recording video. (The accent is on the second syllable of "Record.") The choices for this item are different depending on whether you choose XAVC S, AVCHD, or MP4 for File Format. I will discuss these options for cameras sold in the United States and other areas that use the NTSC video system, which uses the 1080 60i format. Cameras sold in Europe and other areas that use the PAL video system will have different options, although they can be switched to use NTSC video formats using the PAL/NTSC Selector option on the Setup menu, as discussed in Chapter 7.

XAVC S

If you choose XAVC S, the 4 choices for Record Setting are 60p 50M, 30p 50M, 24p 50M, and 120p 50M, as shown in Figure 8-2. (Cameras sold in countries using PAL video rather than NTSC use 50p, 25p, and 100p formats.)

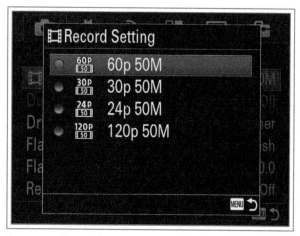

Figure 8-2. Record Setting Options Screen for XAVC S Format

For these choices, the letter "p" stands for progressive, which means the camera records 24, 30, 60, or 120 full video frames per second. (The other option, used with some AVCHD formats, as discussed below, is the letter "i," standing for interlaced. With those options, such as 60i, the camera records 60 fields, or half-frames, per second, which yields lower quality and fewer possibilities for editing.)

The standard speed for recording video in the United States is about 30 frames per second, and using the 30p setting will yield excellent quality. If you use the 60p or 120p option, the camera will record at 2 or 4 four times the normal speed, and will record 2 or 4 times as much video information as with the 30p choice. If you use one of those higher speeds, you will be able to produce a slow-motion version of your footage at very high quality. This possibility exists because, as noted above, the 60p footage is recorded with twice the number of full frames as 30p footage, so the quality of the video does not suffer if it is played back at one-half speed. So, if you think you may want to slow down your footage

significantly for playback, you should choose the 60p setting, or, for even slower motion, the 120p setting.

Video taken with the 120p setting will play back at normal speed in the camera. To play it back in slow motion, you can use a program such as iMovie for the Mac or Movie Maker for Windows. Just set the playback speed to a factor such as 0.25x to play the footage at one-quarter speed.

Note that the 120p selection (100p for PAL cameras) is not available with the Intelligent Auto, Superior Auto, and Scene shooting modes.

If you select 24p 50M, your video will be recorded at 24 fps. This is not a substantially slower rate than for the 60p format, because the video playback rate in the United States is about 30 fps, and the 60p and 120p formats are converted to about 30 fps for playback. The 24p rate is considered by some people to be more "cinematic" than the 60p format. This may be because 24 fps is the standard speed for movie cameras that shoot with film. My preference is to use the 60p format, but if you find that 24p suits your purposes better, you have that option with the RX100 III.

The 50M designation means that each of these formats records video with a bit rate up to a maximum of 50 megabits per second, which is a very high rate that yields excellent quality.

The first 3 options—60p, 30p, and 24p—are recorded in full HD, meaning the pixel count for each video frame is 1920 x 1080. The 120p option is recorded with an HD frame with lower resolution, 1280 x 720.

AVCHD

If you choose AVCHD for File Format, the 5 choices for Record Setting are 60i 24M(FX), 60i 17M(FH), 60p 28M(PS), 24p 24M(FX), and 24p 17M(FH), as shown in Figure 8-3.

60i and 60p Video Formats

First, I will discuss the 3 formats using 60 fields or frames per second. As noted above, the letter "i" or "p" stands for interlaced or progressive. With interlaced video, the camera records 60 fields per second; a field is equal to one-half of a frame, and the 2 halves are interlaced to form 30 full frames. The video frame rate of about 30 frames per second (fps) is the standard video playback rate in the United States.

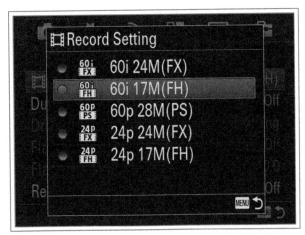

Figure 8-3. Record Setting Options Screen for AVCHD Form

If the letter is "p," for progressive, the camera records 60 full frames per second, which yields higher quality than interlaced video. The 60 frames are later translated into 30 frames for playback at the standard rate of 30 fps. However, as with the XAVC S format, if your video-editing software has this capability, you can play back your 60p footage in slow motion at one-half the normal speed and still maintain full HD quality.

The 28M, 24M, or 17M, states the "bit rate," or volume, of video information that is recorded—either 28, 24, or 17 megabits per second. Not surprisingly, the higher-numbered settings provide greater quality at the cost of using more storage capacity on the memory card and requiring greater computer resources to edit.

The final designations, FH, FX, and PS, are proprietary labels used by Sony for these various qualities of video. They have no particular meanings; they are just labels for various levels of video quality—PS is the highest, then FX, and then FH.

Choose 60p 28M if you want the highest quality (including slow-motion capability), 60i 24M for excellent quality, or 60i 17M for excellent quality that takes up fewer resources.

24p Video Formats

As I discussed for XAVC S, above, the 24p formats are available if you want a more "cinematic" look for your footage. (Cameras with the 50i system offer a 25p format instead of 24p.)

MP4

If, instead of XAVC S or AVCHD, you choose MP4 for File Format, you are presented with just 2 choices for

Record Setting: 1440 x 1080 12M and VGA 3M, as shown in Figure 8-4.

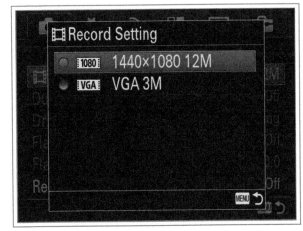

Figure 8-4. Record Setting Menu Options Screen for MP4 Format

The numbers 1440 x 1080 represent the horizontal and vertical pixels in the image. An image with 1440 pixels horizontally and 1080 vertically is considered to be widescreen. The other choice, listed as VGA, has only 640 x 480 pixels; this format produces images in the shape of traditional computer monitors, which are often designated as VGA, for video graphics array. As you can see from the last numbers for these settings, 12M and 3M, they have lower data rates than any of the AVCHD or XAVC S settings. Therefore, the quality is not as great, but the MP4 formats take up less storage space than AVCHD or XAVC S and, as noted above, are easier to manipulate with a computer and to send by e-mail.

If you choose the MP4 file format, I recommend you always select the 1440 x 1080 setting, because the quality of VGA video is quite low. You should use VGA only if you have a shortage of space on your memory card or you are recording the video for a purpose that does not require high quality, such as making an inventory of household possessions.

You also should recall that because of a 2 GB limitation on file size, the RX100 III can record only 15 minutes of MP4 video in the HD format (1440 x 1080) in one continuous file. Of course, you can record any number of 15-minute segments, up to the storage limit of your memory card.

DUAL VIDEO RECORDING

This next menu option, which can be turned either on or off, sets the camera to record an MP4 movie at the same time that it records an XAVC S or AVCHD movie. This feature is like a video version of the Raw & JPEG setting for Quality, for still images. It gives you a video file in a high-quality format for later editing on a computer, along with a lower-quality MP4 version that is easier to manipulate quickly and post to social media sites.

This option is available only when File Format is set to XAVC S or AVCHD. For XAVC S movies, it is available only when Record Setting is set to 30p or 24p; for AVCHD movies, it is available only when Record Setting is set to one of the 60i or 24p formats. It is not available when SteadyShot (Movies) is set to Intelligent Active.

MOVIE (EXPOSURE MODE)

The next movie-related item, on screen 6 of the Shooting menu and somewhat confusingly called simply Movie, is one of the most important options for video shooting with the RX100 III, because it gives you control over aperture and shutter speed.

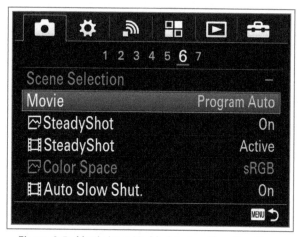

Figure 8-5. Movie Item Highlighted on Shooting Menu

This item, seen in Figure 8-5, can be selected only when the camera's Mode dial is set to Movie mode, as shown in Figure 8-6.

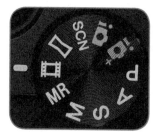

Figure 8-6. Movie Mode

In other shooting modes, this menu option cannot be selected.

When the camera is in Movie mode, the Movie option on the menu lets you select an exposure mode for shooting movies. If you have the Mode Dial Guide option turned on through screen 2 of the Setup menu, the screen with choices for the Movie item, shown in Figure 8-7, will appear automatically when you select Movie mode with the Mode dial and then press the Center button after the initial Mode Dial Guide screen appears.

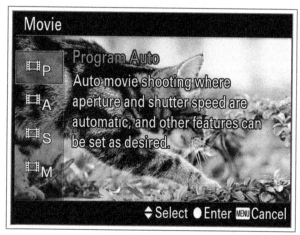

Figure 8-7. Movie Options Screen

If the Mode Dial Guide option is not active, you get to this screen by selecting Movie from the Shooting menu. With the Mode dial set to Movie mode, Navigate to screen 6 of the Shooting menu, select the second item, Movie, and this screen will appear with its 4 options: Program Auto, Aperture Priority, Shutter Priority, and Manual Exposure, the same as shown in Figure 8-7. Move through these choices by turning the Control wheel or by pressing the Up and Down buttons.

You also can call up this screen of 4 Movie options by assigning Shoot Mode to the Function menu using the Function Menu Settings option on screen 4 of the Custom menu. If you do that, then, when the Mode dial is set to Movie, you can press the Function button to activate the Function menu, scroll to the Shoot Mode item, and select your choice of Movie exposure mode.

Following are details about the behavior of the RX100 III when shooting movies with each of these settings.

Program Auto

With the Program Auto setting, the RX100 III handles video recording the same way it does when set to one of the 4 advanced modes for still photography—Program, Aperture Priority, Shutter Priority, or Manual. The camera sets aperture and shutter speed according to its metering, and it uses settings from the Shooting menu that carry over to video recording, including ISO, White Balance, Metering Mode, Face Detection, and DRO.

In this mode, the camera can set the aperture as narrow as f/11.0 and it can use the unusually fast shutter speeds available in Movie mode—as fast as 1/12800 second. In normal conditions, the camera will not use a shutter speed slower than 1/30 second, 1/50 second, or 1/60 second, depending on the settings for File Format and Record Setting. It can use a slightly slower speed if you turn on the Auto Slow Shutter option, discussed later in this chapter.

With one caveat, noted below, I don't recommend using the Program Auto setting for the Movie option. It doesn't provide options for video recording beyond those that are available when the camera is set to a still-shooting mode, such as Program or Shutter Priority. And it has the disadvantage that the Mode dial must be set to the Movie mode. In that mode, you cannot shoot still images; if you press the shutter button, you will see an error message. So, if you want to shoot movies with the camera making all of the exposure decisions for you, I recommend that you set the camera to the P position on the Mode dial. With that setup, you can take still images with the settings you want, and you also can press the red Movie button at any time to record a video.

The one exception to this recommendation is if you use the Movie Button option on screen 4 of the Custom menu to lock out the functioning of the Movie button unless the camera is set to Movie mode. You might do that to avoid recording a movie by pressing the Movie button inadvertently. If you have made that setting, you cannot start recording a movie unless the camera is set to Movie mode. In that situation, you may want to have the Movie (exposure mode) menu option set to Program Auto, so you can turn the Mode dial to Movie mode and start recording a movie with automatic exposure in effect. You also could set one of the 2 Memory Recall slots on the Mode dial to call up Movie mode with the Program Auto setting, for quick access to this setting.

Aperture Priority

With the Aperture Priority setting, shown in Figure 8-8, you can set the aperture, just as in the similar mode for still images, and the camera will set the shutter speed based on its metering.

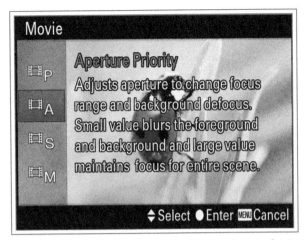

Figure 8-8. Movie Options Screen for Aperture Priority Setting

You can set the aperture anywhere from f/1.8 to the most narrow f/11.0. As with the Program Auto exposure mode, discussed above, the camera will not use shutter speeds slower than 1/30 second (1/60 second for 60i or 60p settings) unless you turn on the Auto Slow Shutter option, discussed later in this chapter.

With this setting, you can adjust the aperture during a video recording. This may not be something you need to do often, but it can be useful in some situations. For example, you may be recording at a garden show, and at some point you may want to open the aperture wide to blur the background as you focus on a small plant. Afterward, you may want to close the aperture down to a narrow value to achieve a broad depth of field to keep a large area in focus.

Also, you can use the aperture setting to accomplish a fadeout. For example, in indoor lighting, you may start with the aperture set to f/1.8 and ISO set to 200, with Auto Slow Shutter turned off. Press the Movie button to start recording. When you're ready, turn the Control ring or the Control wheel to the f/11.0 setting. (I'm assuming the Control ring is set to the Standard option). You should get a nice fade to black. In brighter conditions, you may need to turn on the ND Filter on screen 3 of the Shooting menu, and you may need to reduce ISO to its minimum setting for movies, which is 125.

Shutter Priority

With the Shutter Priority mode for movies, shown in Figure 8-9, you set the shutter speed and the camera will set the aperture.

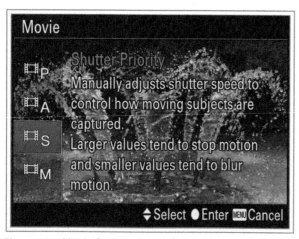

Figure 8-9. Movie Options Screen for Shutter Priority Setting

Unlike the situation with the Aperture Priority exposure mode for movies, in which the camera normally will not set the shutter speed slower than 1/30 second (or 1/60 second for 60i or 60p video formats), you are able to set the shutter speed as slow as 1/4 second in most cases, even if Auto Slow Shutter is turned off. (With the 120p setting for XAVC S, the slowest shutter speed available is 1/125 second.) You can select a shutter speed from 1/4 second all the way to the super-fast maximum shutter speed for movies, which is 1/12800 second. Of course, to expose your video normally at a shutter speed of 1/12800 second, you must have bright lighting, a high ISO setting, or both. Using a fast shutter speed for video can yield a crisper appearance, especially when there is considerable movement, as when shooting sports or other fast-moving events. In addition, having these very fast shutter speeds gives the camera flexibility for achieving a normal exposure when recording video in bright conditions.

With slower shutter speeds, particularly below the normal video speed of 1/30 second (equivalent to 30 fps), footage can become blurry with the appearance of smearing, especially with panning motions. If you are shooting a scene in which you want to have a drifting, dreamy appearance that looks like motion underwater, this option may be appropriate. You will not be able to achieve good lip sync at the slower shutter speeds, so this technique would not work well for realistic recordings of people talking or singing.

One interesting point is that you can preview this effect on the camera's display even before you press the Movie button to start recording. If you have the shutter speed set to 1/4 second in Movie mode, you will see any action on the screen looking blurry as if it had already

been recorded with this slow shutter speed. (The Live View Display option on screen 2 of the Custom menu is forced to the Setting Effect On option in Movie mode, and you cannot change it.)

With the Shutter Priority exposure mode for movies, you also can achieve a fadeout effect, as with Aperture Priority mode, discussed above. Just turn the Control ring or Control wheel smoothly to increase the shutter speed to its fastest speed of 1/12800 second, and the scene may go black, depending on the lighting conditions. You may need to turn on the ND Filter to achieve full darkness.

Manual Exposure

The last setting for the Movie item, shown in Figure 8-10, gives you more complete control over the exposure of your videos.

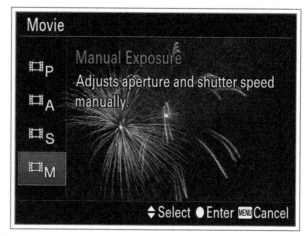

Figure 8-10. Movie Options Screen for Manual Exposure Setting

As with Manual exposure mode for stills, you can adjust both the aperture and the shutter speed to achieve your desired effect. With video shooting, you can adjust the aperture from f/1.8 to f/11.0, and you can adjust the shutter speed from 1/12800 second to 1/4 second. (If Record Setting is set to 120p for XAVC S video, the slowest shutter speed available is 1/125 second.) Using these settings, you can create effects such as fades to and from black as well as similar fades to and from white.

For example, if you begin a recording in normal indoor lighting using settings of 1/60 second at f/3.2 with ISO set to 800, you can start recording the scene, and, when you want to fade out, start turning the Control wheel slowly to the right, increasing the shutter speed smoothly until it reaches 1/12800 second. (You may have to press the Down button to let the Control wheel control shutter speed.) Depending on how bright the lighting is, the result may be complete blackness. Of course, you can reverse this process to fade in from black.

If you want to fade to white, here is one possible scenario. Suppose you are recording video with shutter speed set to 1/400 second and aperture set to f/2.8 at ISO 3200. When you want to start a fade to white, make sure the Control wheel is setting shutter speed, and turn the Control wheel smoothly to the left until the shutter speed decreases all the way to 1/4 second. In fairly normal lighting conditions, as in my office as I write this, the result will be a fade to a bright white screen.

There are, of course, other uses for Manual Exposure mode when recording videos, such as shooting "day for night" footage, in which you underexpose the scene by using a fast shutter speed, narrow aperture, or both, to turn day into night for creative purposes. Also, you might want to use Manual Exposure mode when you are recording a scene in which the lighting may change, but you do not want the exposure to change. In other words, for creative purposes, you may want some areas to remain dark and some to be unusually bright, rather than have the camera automatically adjust the exposure. In some cases, having a constant exposure setting can be preferable to having the scene's brightness change as the metering system adjusts the exposure.

Note that you can set ISO to Auto ISO with the Manual Exposure setting if you want. With the Auto ISO setting, you can maintain a constant aperture and shutter speed, but the camera will adjust exposure using the ISO setting to the extent that it can. You might want to use that setup if you need to maintain a narrow aperture to have a broad depth of field.

STEADYSHOT (MOVIES)

The second SteadyShot item on screen 6 of the Shooting menu, shown in Figure 8-11, is different from the SteadyShot (Still Images) item above it. (The Movies and Still Images designations are indicated by icons on the menu—a movie film icon for Movies and a mountain/landscape icon for Still Images.)

As shown in Figure 8-12, the SteadyShot (Movies) setting offers 4 options: Off, Standard, Active, and Intelligent Active, unlike the Still Images version, which is limited to being turned on or off.

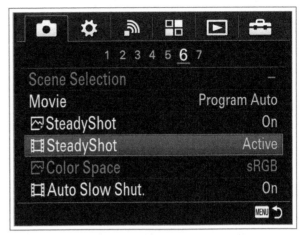

Figure 8-11. SteadyShot (Movies) Item Highlighted on Screen

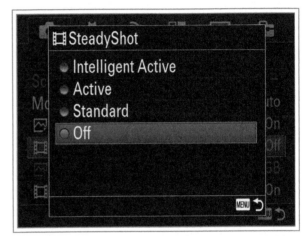

Figure 8-12. SteadyShot (Movies) Menu Options Screen

With the Movies version, if you select Standard, the camera uses the same stabilization system used for shooting stills. If you select Active, the camera uses an additional electronic stabilizing system that can compensate for unwanted camera movement to a greater extent. With this feature, the camera crops out parts of the image at the edges to compensate for the required processing of the image. With Intelligent Active, the camera uses an even stronger stabilizing effect and crops the frame even more heavily.

Figures 8-13 through 8-16 illustrate the cropping that results with the various settings of SteadyShot (Movies), using the same scene in each case. In Figure 8-13, SteadyShot (Movies) was turned off; in Figure 8-14 it was set to Standard; in Figure 8-15 to Active; and in Figure 8-16 to Intelligent Active.

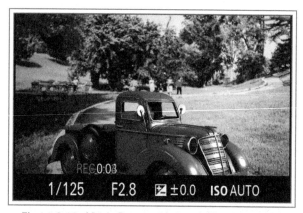

Figure 8-13. Movie Frame with SteadyShot Turned Off

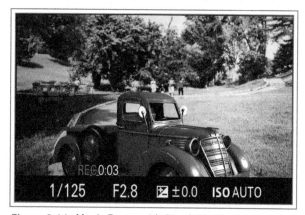

Figure 8-14. Movie Frame with SteadyShot Set to Standard

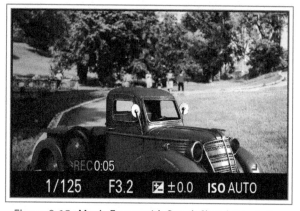

Figure 8-15. Movie Frame with SteadyShot Set to Active

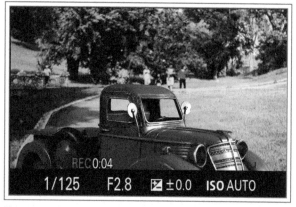

Figure 8-16. Movie Frame with SteadyShot Set to Intelligent
Active

As you can see, the Standard setting does not crop the frame, but the Active setting crops pixels from all 4 sides of the frame, and Intelligent Active crops even more pixels from all 4 sides.

I recommend using Standard in most cases to avoid the cropping that comes from using the Active or Intelligent Active setting. If you need to shoot movies when there is a great likelihood of camera movement, though, those 2 settings can be useful.

AUTO SLOW SHUTTER

This last item on screen 6 of the Shooting menu can be turned either on or off. When this option is turned on and the RX100 III is recording a movie using automatic exposure, the camera will automatically use a slower shutter speed than normal if the lighting is too dim to achieve a proper exposure otherwise.

The details of this option depend on the settings for File Format and Record Setting on screens 1 and 2 of the Shooting menu. If File Format is set to XAVC S or AVCHD and Record Setting is at a 60p or 60i setting, then the camera normally will not use a shutter speed slower than 1/60 second. (This makes sense, because, in order to record 60 fields or frames per second with good quality, a shutter speed of 1/60 second is needed.) If Auto Slow Shutter is on, the camera can use a shutter speed as slow as 1/30 second.

If File Format is set to XAVC S or AVCHD and Record Setting is at one of the 24p settings, the camera ordinarily will use a shutter speed no slower than 1/50 second, but it will go down to 1/25 second with Auto Slow Shutter turned on. If File Format is set to MP4, the slowest shutter speed available without this option is 1/30 second. With the option turned on, the camera can use a shutter speed as slow as 1/15 second.

If File Format is set to XAVC S and Record Setting is at the 30p setting, the slowest shutter speed in ordinary conditions is 1/30 second. If Auto Slow Shutter is turned on, the camera can use a shutter speed of 1/15 second.

If File Format is set to XAVC S and Record setting is at the 120p setting, the slowest shutter speed available is 1/125 second, and the Auto Slow Shutter option is not available.

There are a couple of limitations to this setting. First, even with this menu option turned on, the automatic use of a slower shutter speed will take place only when the RX100 III is set to a movie exposure mode in which the camera sets the shutter speed. The only movie exposure modes in which the camera sets the shutter speed are Program Auto and Aperture Priority. In addition, for the Auto Slow Shutter option to work, ISO must be set to Auto ISO.

The use of an unusually slow shutter speed can produce a slurred or blurry appearance because the shutter speed may not be fast enough to keep up with the motion in the scene. But, if you are recording in a dark area, this option can help you achieve properly exposed footage, so it is worth considering in that situation.

AUDIO RECORDING

This first option on screen 7 of the Shooting menu determines whether or not the RX100 III records sound with its movies. If you are certain you won't need the sound recorded by the camera, you can turn this option off. I never turn it off, because you can always turn down the volume of the recorded sound when playing the video, or if you are editing the video on a computer, you can delete the sound and replace it as needed, but you can never recapture the original audio after the fact.

MICREF LEVEL

The next movie-related option is Micref Level.

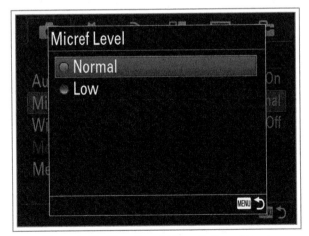

Figure 8-17. Micref Level Menu Options Screen

This option, whose screen is shown in Figure 8-17, can be set to Normal or Low. This setting controls how the camera records audio for movies using its built-in stereo microphone. With Normal, the default setting,

the camera uses an automatic gain control to boost the level of quiet sounds to an audible volume. However, it also boosts the level of ambient sounds from sources such as heating or air conditioning equipment. You might want to use this setting if you are recording a speech or a small, relatively quiet event, so the camera will not miss any important sounds.

The Low setting would be more appropriate when you are recording an event such as a concert, and you want to let the sound level vary according to the sound levels of the music without any artificial boosting or limiting.

WIND NOISE REDUCTION

This option, if turned on, activates an electronic filter designed to reduce the volume of sounds in the low frequencies of wind noise. I recommend not activating this feature unless the wind is quite strong, because it limits the sounds that are recorded. With video (or audio) editing software, you can remove sounds in the frequencies that may cause problems for the sound track, but using the camera's built-in wind noise filter may permanently remove or alter some wanted sounds.

Effects of Mode Dial Position on Recording Movies

The second type of setting that affects the recording of movies with the RX100 III is the position of the Mode dial. As I discussed above, you can shoot movies no matter what position this dial is set to (if the Movie Button menu option is set that way), and you can get access to many movie-related menu items no matter what position the dial is in. However, as I also noted above, the shooting mode does make some difference for your movie options.

First, as noted earlier, you cannot select the Movie option on the Shooting menu unless the camera is in Movie mode. The Movie option lets you select one of the 4 exposure modes for shooting movies: Program Auto, Aperture Priority, Shutter Priority, or Manual Exposure. In the last 3 of those modes, you can set the aperture, shutter speed, or both for movie recording. Also, in all 4 of these modes, you can see the size of the movie frame before you start recording, unlike the case with the still-shooting modes.

Second, the camera's shooting mode has an effect on what options are available on the Shooting menu and with the control buttons, as discussed in the next 2 sections. For example, if the Mode dial is set to Intelligent Auto, Sweep Panorama, or Scene, the Shooting menu options are limited. If the Mode dial is set to Program, Aperture Priority, Shutter Priority, or Manual exposure, the options are greater. This point is important for video shooting because, as discussed below, several important Shooting menu options carry over to movie recording. For example, if the camera is set to Program mode (P on the Mode dial), you can make several settings that will control the recording of videos while the Mode dial is in that position.

If the camera is set to Sweep Panorama mode, it will act largely as if it were set to Movie mode with the Program Auto exposure mode selected. If it is set to Scene mode, it will shoot movies as if it were set to Intelligent Auto mode, in which limited menu options are available. It will not recognize any specific scene settings, such as Portrait, Sports Action, or Sunset.

Effects of Other Shooting Menu Settings on Recording Movies

Next, I will discuss other Shooting menu options that have an effect on movie recording, beyond the options that are applicable only to movie recording, such as File Format, Record Setting, Auto Slow Shutter, and the others discussed earlier in this chapter.

One of the main reasons the shooting mode is important for movies is that, just as with still photography, some menu options are not available in some shooting modes. For example, in an advanced still-shooting mode such as Aperture Priority or Program, video recording will be affected by the settings for ISO, ND Filter, Metering Mode, White Balance, DRO, Creative Style, Picture Effect, Focus Magnifier, Lock-on AF, and Face Detection.

In some cases, you can adjust these settings while the video is being recorded. You cannot get access to the Shooting menu by pressing the Menu button; you have to use a control button or the Control ring to call up the item to adjust. Of course, you have to have that setting assigned to the button or ring ahead of time.

For example, you can adjust ISO while recording a video, but only if you have assigned ISO to the Control ring or one of the control buttons using the Custom Key Settings menu option on screen 4 of the Custom menu. Table 8-1 shows which of these settings can be adjusted while a video recording is in progress.

Table 8-1. **Shooting Menu Items that Affect Movies, and Items that Can Be Adjusted During Video Recording.**

Shooting Menu Item	Can Adjust During Video Recording
File Format	No
Record Setting	No
Dual Video Recording	No
Focus Mode	Yes
Exposure Compensation	Yes
ISO	Yes
ND Filter	Yes
Metering Mode	No
White Balance	No
DRO/Auto HDR	No
Creative Style	No
Picture Effect	No
Focus Magnifier	Yes
Center Lock-on AF	Yes
Smile/Face Detection	No
Movie	No
SteadyShot (Movies)	No
Auto Slow Shutter	No
Audio Recording	No
Micref Level	No
Wind Noise Reduction	No

There are built-in limitations with some of these settings. Exposure compensation can be adjusted to plus or minus 2.0EV only, rather than the 3.0EV range for still images. The ISO range is from 125 to 12800, omitting the lowest settings. Also, you cannot set ISO to Multi Frame Noise Reduction, which would cause the camera to take multiple shots. With Picture Effect, you can use some of the sub-settings, but not all. The settings that are unavailable for movie recording are Soft Focus, HDR Painting, Rich-tone Monochrome, Miniature, Watercolor, and Illustration.

There are some other options on the Shooting menu that have no effect for recording movies. Some of these settings are clearly incompatible with shooting movies, such as Drive Mode, Flash Mode, and Auto Object

Framing. Some are less obvious, including Focus Area, AF Illuminator, and Scene Selection.

There are 2 other points to make about using Shooting menu settings for movies in a still-shooting mode. First, you have a great deal of flexibility in choosing settings for your movies, even when the camera is not set to the Movie position on the Mode dial. You can set up the camera with the ISO, Metering Mode, White Balance, Creative Style, Picture Effect (to some extent), and other settings of your choice, and then press the Movie button to record using those settings. In this way, you could, for example, record a black-and-white movie in a dark environment using a high ISO setting. Or, you could record a movie that is monochrome except for a broad selection of red objects, using the Partial Color-Red effect from the Picture Effect option, with the red color expanded using the color axis adjustments of the White Balance setting.

Second, you have to be careful to check the settings that are in effect for still photos before you press the Movie button. For example, if you have been shooting stills using the Posterization setting from the Picture Effect menu option and then suddenly see an event that you want to record on video, if you press the Movie button, the movie will be recorded using the Posterization effect, making the resulting footage practically impossible to use as a clear record of the events. Of course, you may notice this problem as you record the video, but it takes time to stop the recording, change the menu setting to turn off the Picture Effect option, and then start recording again, and you may have missed a crucial part of the action by the time you start recording again.

One way to lessen the risk of recording video with unwanted Shooting menu options is to switch the Mode dial to the Intelligent Auto position before pressing the red Movie button. That action will cause the camera to use more automatic settings and will disable the Creative Style and Picture Effect options altogether. (Of course, you have to have the Movie Button item on the Custom menu set to Always for this approach to work.)

There is one more point to make about menu options when recording movies. For some reason, the RX100 III is programmed to use the Soft Skin Effect option whenever you record a movie with autofocus and Face Detection activated. You cannot turn this option off. If you don't want to have people's faces altered by the

Soft Skin Effect processing, you need to turn off Face Detection. If you find that the normal continuous autofocus does not keep faces in focus, you can use the Center Lock-on AF option. To do so, turn on that option on screen 5 of the Shooting menu and press the Center button to activate tracking. That option cannot be used with XAVC S video in the 120p 50M format.

Effects of Physical Controls When Recording Movies

The next settings that carry over to some extent from still-shooting to video recording are those set by the physical controls. In this case, as with Shooting menu items, there are differences depending on the position of the Mode dial. I will not try to describe every possible combination of shooting mode and physical control, but I will discuss some settings to be aware of.

First, you can use the exposure compensation button while recording movies when the Mode dial is at the P, A, S, M, Movie, or Sweep Panorama setting. The button has no effect in Auto or Scene modes. The range of exposure compensation for movies is plus or minus 2.0 EV, rather than the plus or minus 3.0 EV for still images. If you set exposure compensation to a value greater than 2.0 (plus or minus), the camera will set it back to 2.0 after you press the red Movie button to start shooting a movie.

Second, the Function button operates normally. For example, if the Mode dial is set to P for Program mode, then, after you press the Movie button to start recording a movie, you can press the Function button and the Function menu will appear on the screen. This menu will let you control only those items that can be controlled under current conditions, as seen in Figure 8-18.

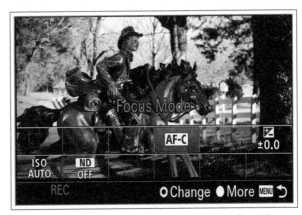

Figure 8-18. Function Menu During Video Recording - Program Mode

If you start recording a movie while the Mode dial is set to a mode such as Intelligent Auto in which most options on the Function Button menu are not available, the RX100 III will display the menu, but few items can be selected, as shown in Figure 8-19.

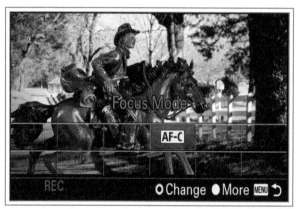

Figure 8-19. Function Menu During Video Recording - Intell. Auto

Third, if you assign the Custom, Center, Left, or Right button or the Control ring to carry out a particular operation using the Custom Key Settings option on screen 4 of the Custom menu, you can use that button or wheel to perform the operation while recording a movie if the action is compatible with movie recording in the current shooting mode.

For the Control ring, the functions that can be assigned and controlled during video recording are exposure compensation, ISO, zoom, shutter speed, and aperture. Although White Balance, Creative Style, or Picture Effect can be assigned to the ring and controlled before the recording starts, those listed above are the only items that can be controlled by the ring during the recording.

However, there are numerous options that can be assigned to a control button that will function during video recording, if the current context permits that control. For example, if the Left button is set to control ISO and you are shooting a movie with the Mode dial set to P, pressing the Left button will bring up the ISO menu and you can select a value while the movie is recording. If the Mode dial is set to Intelligent Auto, though, pressing the button will have to effect, because ISO cannot be adjusted in that shooting mode.

If the Center button is assigned its Standard setting through the Custom Key Settings menu option and the Center Lock-on AF option is turned on through screen 5 of the Shooting menu, you can press the Center

button during video recording to activate tracking focus. Of course, to use tracking focus, you have to have an autofocus mode selected using the Focus Mode menu option.

If you set the Right button (or some other button) to the AEL Toggle function, you can press that control while recording a movie to lock the exposure setting. This ability can be useful when recording a movie, when you don't want the exposure to change as you move the camera over different areas of a scene.

Following is a list of functions that can be assigned to one of the control buttons and that can be controlled during video recording by pressing the button:

- Focus Mode
- Exposure Compensation
- ISO
- ND Filter
- AEL Hold
- AEL Toggle
- Spot AEL Hold
- Spot AEL Toggle
- AF/MF Control Hold
- AF/MF Control Toggle
- Center Lock-on AF
- Focus Magnifier
- Zebra
- Grid Line
- Audio Level Display
- Peaking Level
- Peaking Color

Two more notes about physical controls: First, Program Shift does not function during video recording. If you turn the Control ring while the camera is set to Program mode, the exposure settings will not change while the camera is recording a movie.

Second, the Photo Creativity feature, described in Chapter 2, works during movie recording in a limited way. When the camera is set to Intelligent Auto or Superior Auto mode, you have to press the Down button before the recording starts, to put the Photo Creativity controls on the screen. Then, after you press the Movie button to start recording, you can control Background Defocus, but no other Photo Creativity settings.

Using External Microphones

One decision Sony made for the RX100 III that seems puzzling is the omission of a jack for plugging in an external microphone to record audio for movies. The previous model, the RX100 II, accepts external microphones through the Multi Interface Shoe, but the RX100 III has no such option.

The stereo microphone built into the RX100 III records good-quality sound, but, with the superior video quality available with this camera, you may want to record audio using higher-quality microphones.

Fortunately, it is not difficult to do this with the RX100 III, using current technology and software. The best solution I have found is to use a separate digital audio recorder and then synchronize the sound from the recorder with the video from the camera.

This system, often called double-system or dual-system sound recording, would have seemed more complex than I wanted to handle a few years ago. It probably would have involved using a clapper board to mark the first point of synchronization and a possibly laborious process to synchronize the audio and video tracks using time code.

Now, though, if you use good equipment and software, it can be easy to use this type of system. I'll outline the steps I used; you may find equivalent techniques that work as well.

1. Get a good digital recorder like the Zoom H1, the Zoom H6, the Shure VP83F, the Tascam DR-40, or the Tascam DR-100mkII, which is discussed in Appendix A.

2. Make sure the camera is set to record audio by turning on the Audio Recording option on screen 7 of the Shooting menu.

3. Set the audio recorder to record high-quality audio in a .wav file and place it, or one or more microphones connected to it, in a location to receive the sound clearly.

4. Start the audio recorder, then start the camera recording video and audio.

5. When the recording is done, load the video file and its attached sound track into a video-editing program such as Adobe Premiere Pro CC, Final Cut Pro, or others. You also can use Plural Eyes, a program from redgiant.com that synchronizes audio and video. The software will compare the waveforms from the camera's sound track and the external audio track to move them into sync. With Premiere Pro CC, which I use, the procedure is to select the video track and the 2 audio tracks, right-click on them, and select Synchronize-Audio-Mix Down. The software will move the external audio track into sync with the video track.

6. Once the external audio track has been synchronized with the video track, you can delete the audio track recorded by the camera.

Of course, this system introduces more complexity and expense into your video-recording process. But, if you want the highest quality audio for your movies, it is worth exploring this method.

Summary of Options for Recording Movies

As I have discussed, there is some complication in trying to explain all of the relationships among the controls and settings of the RX100 III for recording movies. To cut through that complication, here is a summary of your options for recording movies with the RX100 III.

To record a video clip with standard settings, set the Mode dial to an Auto or Scene position and press the Movie button. The camera will adjust exposure automatically, and you can use either continuous autofocus (set in this mode using the AF-S setting for the Focus Mode menu option) or manual focus (MF setting). In those shooting modes, you cannot adjust many shooting options, such as ISO, White Balance, DRO, Creative Style, or Picture Effect. You can use options such as Center Lock-on AF, Face Detection, and SteadyShot (Movies). You can choose File Format and Record Settings options to control the video quality.

For more control over video shooting, set the Mode dial to the P, A, S, or M position. Then you can control several additional Shooting menu options, including ISO, White Balance, Metering Mode, Creative Style, and Picture Effect, among others. You can choose continuous autofocus or manual focus in the same way as for the more automatic shooting modes. The camera will adjust exposure automatically.

For maximum control over movie recording, set the Mode dial to the movie film icon for Movie mode. Then select an option for the movie exposure mode from the Movie item on screen 6 of the Shooting menu. To control aperture, choose Aperture Priority; to control shutter speed, choose Shutter Priority; to control both aperture and shutter speed, choose Manual Exposure. Other options can be selected from the Shooting menu.

Control buttons operate during movie recording if the context permits, as discussed earlier. There are many possibilities for assigning settings to them. If you want a good set of functions tailored for video recording, use the list in Table 8-2 to start, and adjust it for your own needs:

Table 8-2.   **Suggested Control Assignments for Movie Recording**

CONTROL	FUNCTION
Control ring	ISO
Custom button	ND Filter
Center button	Standard
Left button	Zebra
Right button	Focus Magnifier

If you want the RX100 III to be ready to record good, standard video footage at a moment's notice without having to remember a lot of settings, I recommend that you set up one of the 3 registers (I use register 3) of the Memory Recall shooting mode with a solid set of movie-recording settings. Table 8-3 lists the settings I recommend. (Settings not listed here can be set however you like.)

Table 8-3.   **Suggested Shooting Menu Settings for Recording Movies**

SHOOTING MENU	
File Format	AVCHD
Record Setting	60p 28M (PS)
Dual Video Recording	Off
Focus Mode	AF-S
ISO	ISO Auto
ND Filter	Off
Metering Mode	Multi
White Balance	Auto White Balance
DRO/Auto HDR	Off
Creative Style	Standard

Table 8-3.   **Suggested Shooting Menu Settings for Recording Movies**

Picture Effect	Off
Center Lock-on AF	On
Smile/Face Detection	Off
Movie	Program Auto
SteadyShot (Movies)	Standard
Auto Slow Shutter	On
Audio Recording	On
Micref Level	Normal
Wind Noise Reduction	Off

Other Settings and Controls for Movies

There are several other points to be made about recording and playing back videos that don't concern the Shooting menu or the major physical controls. Here are brief notes about these issues.

The Step Zoom function is not available for video recording, even if the Zoom Function on Ring option is set to Step on screen 4 of the Custom menu. The zoom operates continuously for movies.

The Display button operates normally to change the information that is viewed during video recording. The screens that are displayed are controlled by the Display Button option on screen 2 of the Custom menu. However, the For Viewfinder screen does not appear for video shooting, even if it was selected through that menu option.

In playback mode, the Display button operates normally for movies. The screen with space for a histogram will display, but the spaces for histogram and other information will be blank.

The MF Assist option on screen 1 of the Custom menu does not operate for video recording, so the camera will not magnify the display when you turn the Control ring to adjust manual focus. However, you can assign the Focus Magnifier function to one of the control buttons and use that capability to enlarge the screen when using manual focus. After you press the assigned control button to put the orange frame on the display, press the Center button to enlarge the area within the frame to 4 times normal. (This is less than the 8.6x enlargement factor for still shooting.) Then turn the Control ring to adjust the focus. Half-press the shutter button to dismiss the Focus Magnifier frame.

The Setting Effect Off choice for the Live View Display option on screen 2 of the Custom menu does not function for video recording; the Setting Effect On choice is locked in. So, for example, if you are shooting movies in Movie mode using Manual Exposure for the Movie setting and you have the aperture and shutter speed set for strong underexposure, you cannot adjust this option to make the display more visible.

Movie Playback

As with still images, you can transfer movies to a computer for editing and playback or play them back in the camera, either on the camera's display or on a TV connected to the camera.

If you want to play your movies in the camera, there is one basic aspect of the RX100 III you need to be mindful of. As I discussed in Chapter 6, the View Mode option on screen 1 of the Playback menu controls what images or videos you will see in playback mode. If you don't see the video you are looking for, check to make sure this menu option is set to display all files from a certain date (Date View), Folder View (MP4), AVCHD View, or XAVC S View.

Once you have selected the proper mode to view your video, navigate to that file by pressing the direction buttons or turning the Control wheel. Once the first frame of the selected video is displayed on the screen, you will see a playback triangle inside a circle, as shown in Figure 8-20.

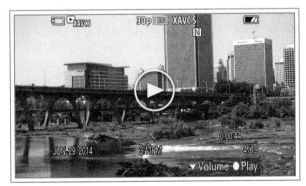

Figure 8-20. Movie Ready for Playback

In the lower right corner of the screen will be a Play prompt with a white circle icon indicating that you can press the Center button to play the video. (If you don't

see that prompt, press the Display button one or more times until it appears.)

After you press the Center button to start the playback, you will see more icons at the bottom of the screen, as seen in Figure 8-21.

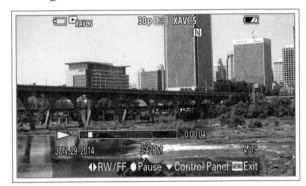

Figure 8-21. Initial Controls During Movie Playback

From the left, these icons indicate: Rewind/Fast Forward; Pause; Open Control Panel; and Exit. From this screen, you can press the Left or Right button repeatedly to play the movie rapidly forward or backward; multiple presses increase the speed up to 4 times.

One icon indicates that you can press the Down button to open the Control Panel. While the video is still playing, press the Down button, and you will see a new line of controls at the bottom of the screen, as shown in Figure 8-22.

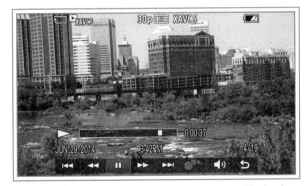

Figure 8-22. Detailed Controls During Movie Playback

When the movie is playing, these icons indicate, from left to right: Previous Movie; Fast Reverse; Pause; Fast Forward; Next Movie; Motion Shot; Volume; and Close Control Panel.

When the movie is paused, the icons change, as in Figure 8-23.

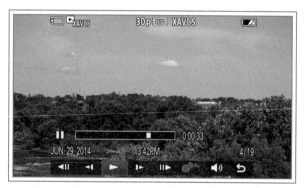

Figure 8-23. Detailed Controls When Movie Paused

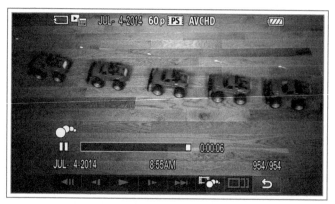

Figure 8-24. Illustration of Motion Shot Playback Effect

Those icons indicate, from left to right: Previous Frame; Reverse Slow; Normal Playback; Forward Slow; Next Frame; Motion Shot; Volume; and Close Control Panel. In either case, move through the icons with the Left and Right buttons, and press the Center button to select the function for that icon. When a movie is playing, you can fast-forward or fast-reverse through a video at increasing speeds by turning the Control wheel right or left or by pressing the Right or Left button.

MOTION SHOT FEATURE

Among the icons on the movie playback control panel is one that looks like a series of shrinking circles. That icon represents the Motion Shot feature. With this option, you can slow down the playback of part of a movie and display a motion sequence as a sequence of multiple exposures on the camera's screen, or on an HDTV screen if you have the camera connected to one.

This feature works only with AVCHD and MP4 movies; it does not work with movies recorded with the XAVC S format. To use the feature, start the movie playing and let it play up to the point where you want to start the motion-shot effect. For example, suppose you recorded some children playing basketball. You could play the movie up the point where a child shoots the ball toward the basket. At that point, or just before it, use the Right button to scroll to the Motion Shot icon, highlight it, and press the Center button to select it.

The camera will then play back the video as a series of multiple exposures tracing the path of the object in motion. For example, Figure 8-24 shows how the camera processed a video sequence of a model truck moving across the floor. If the images of the moving object overlap too closely on your first attempt, you can make an adjustment using the Motion Interval Adjustment option.

On the video control panel, once you have selected the Motion Shot icon, the line of icons will change, as shown at the bottom of Figure 8-24. The Motion Shot icon will change to an icon for exiting the Motion Shot mode. The icon to the right of that one, which looks like a set of overlapping rectangles, lets you adjust the interval between the images. Select that icon and adjust the scale to a lower number to place the images closer together and to a higher number to place them farther apart. You also can adjust the interval between images using the Motion Interval Adjustment option on screen 2 of the Playback menu.

You cannot save the results of your work with the Motion Shot feature unless you connect the camera to a video capture device using an HDMI cable, as I did for the sample image shown here. I view this feature as an interesting novelty that lets you examine the path of an object in motion in some detail. It might be helpful for checking your golf swing or it might be considered a good way to add some interest to a video demonstration.

If you like the general idea of the Motion Shot feature, you can purchase an application (app) called Motion Shot from the Sony website, http://www.playmemoriescameraapps.com. That app lets you save the composite image that shows the motion trail. I will discuss the use of in-camera apps in Chapter 9.

Editing Movies

The RX100 III camera cannot edit movies in the camera. (At least, not with the options that come with the camera. It may be that an application will be developed for in-camera movie editing in the future.) If you want to do any editing, you will have to do it with a computer. For Windows, you can use software such as

Windows Movie Maker. If you are using a Mac, you can use iMovie or any other movie editing software that can deal with MP4 and AVCHD files, and with XAVC S files, if you record movies using that format. I use Adobe Premiere Pro on my Mac, and it handles all 3 of these file types very well.

You also can use the PlayMemories Home software that comes with the RX100 III. To install PlayMemories Home on your computer, you need to download the software from the internet. For Windows-based computers, go to http://www.sony.net/pm. For Macintosh computers, go to http://www.sony.co.jp/imsoft/Mac/. This software is updated with new features periodically, so be sure to keep checking the website for updates.

One issue you may encounter when first starting to edit movie files from the RX100 III is finding the files. When you insert a memory card into a card reader, the still images are easy to find; on my computer, the SD card shows up as No Name or Untitled; then, beneath that level, there is a folder called DCIM; inside it are folders with names such as 100MSDCF, which contain the still images. (If you use the Folder Name option on screen 5 of the Setup menu to select Date Form, the folder names will be based on dates the images were taken; an example is 10040810 for images taken on August 10, 2014.)

The movie files are a bit trickier to find. The XAVC S files that you need to find and import into your software for editing have an .mp4 extension, but they are not the same as the more ordinary .mp4 files. Here is the path to a sample XAVC S file, assuming the file name at the level of the SD card is Untitled: Untitled\Private\M4ROOT\CLIP\C0007.MP4.

Here is the path to an AVCHD movie file: Untitled\Private\AVCHD\BDMV\Stream\0006.MTS. These files can be difficult to find on a Macintosh, because the Finder may not immediately show the contents of the AVCHD folder. You may have to right-click on the AVCHD item in the Finder and select Show Package Contents in order to view the BDMV folder. You may have to repeat that process to see the contents of the BDMV folder.

Here is the path to an ordinary MP4 movie file: Untitled\MP_ROOT\100ANV01\MAH00180.MP4.

You can avoid the complications of finding the movie files on a memory card by connecting the camera to your computer using the USB cable. With most video-editing software, the camera should be detected and the software should import the movie files automatically, ready for you to edit them.

Also, with the RX100 III, you can transfer your files to your computer using the Wi-Fi capabilities that are built into the camera, as discussed in Chapter 9.

CHAPTER 9: WI-FI, APPLICATIONS, AND OTHER TOPICS

Connections Using Wi-Fi and NFC

One useful feature of the RX100 III is its ability to connect to computers and other devices using a Wi-Fi network. As noted in Chapter 1, you can transfer images and videos wirelessly using an Eye-Fi card or other memory card that includes Wi-Fi connectivity, but having Wi-Fi circuitry built into the camera gives you features that are not available with a card. Also, with some devices, the RX100 III can use NFC technology to establish a Wi-Fi connection without going through the steps that are ordinarily required. In this section, I will describe these features and give examples of how you can use them.

First, here is one note to remember when using any of the camera's Wi-Fi features: The Wi-Fi menu has an option called Airplane Mode near the bottom of its first screen. If that option is turned on, no Wi-Fi features will work. Make sure that menu setting is turned off when using the Wi-Fi options.

SENDING IMAGES TO A COMPUTER

Although you can edit and print images and edit videos to some extent using a smartphone or tablet, the easiest way to work with them is to transfer them to a computer. The traditional ways to do this are to connect the camera to the computer with the camera's USB cable or to use a memory card reader. However, there are 2 methods you can use to transfer your images and videos to a computer over a wireless network, eliminating the need to use a USB connection or a card reader.

First, as discussed in Chapter 1, you can use an Eye-Fi card or a similar memory card with the capability to transfer your files wirelessly to the computer. This system works well, but it requires the purchase and use of this special type of memory card.

The other approach for wireless transfer is to use the Wi-Fi capability built into the RX100 III. Once you have the camera and computer set up to communicate over a wireless network, you can use the Send to Computer menu option to transfer images and videos from the camera's memory card over that network, regardless of what type of memory card is installed. Here are the steps to set up the camera and computer:

1. Install the appropriate Sony software on the computer. For Windows-based computers, the software is PlayMemories Home, available for download at http://www.sony.net/pm/.

   –or–

   For Macintosh computers, install Wireless Auto Import, available for download at http://www.sony.co.jp/imsoft/Mac/.

2. Run the software you downloaded in Step 1. Follow the program's prompts to connect the camera to the computer using the camera's USB cable, and select the option to designate this computer to receive images from the camera. (That step needs to be done only once, unless you later switch to a different computer.) Then disconnect the USB cable.

3. Make sure the camera is within range of a wireless access point, also known as a Wi-Fi router. Normally, this will be a private, secured network at your home or office.

4. If the router has a button labeled WPS (Wi-Fi–protected setup), use the button to connect the camera to the network. Select the WPS Push option on the first screen of the Wi-Fi menu, and the camera will display the screen in Figure 9-1.

5. Within 2 minutes, press the WPS button on the router. Figure 9-2 shows an example of that sort of button.

6. If the setup is successful, the camera will display a message saying the access point has been registered. Proceed to Step 10.

–or–

If the router does not have a WPS button, or if pushing the button does not work, proceed to Step 7.

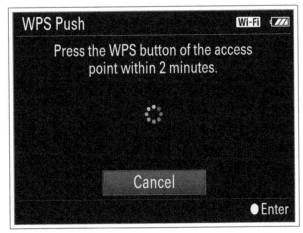

Figure 9-1. WPS Push Menu Screen

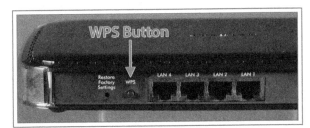

Figure 9-2. WPS Button on Router

7. Locate the name of the network and its password. (This information may be on a label on the router or modem.)

8. Select the Access Point Settings option on the second screen of the Wi-Fi menu, as shown in Figure 9-3.

9. If the name of your network appears on the camera's screen, as shown in Figure 9-4, enter the network's password, as shown in Figure 9-5. The camera will display a virtual keyboard to let you enter the necessary characters.

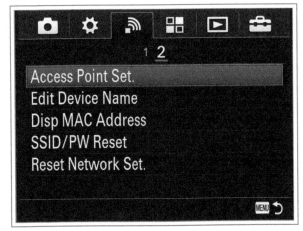

Figure 9-3. Access Point Settings Item Highlighted on Menu

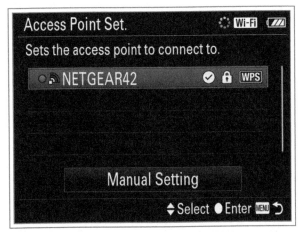

Figure 9-4. Screen Showing Available Access Points

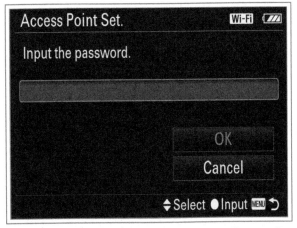

Figure 9-5. Screen for Entering Access Point Password

–or–

If the access point does not appear on the camera's screen, enter its SSID (network ID), using the Manual Setting option on the menu screen, as shown in Figure 9-6, and then enter the network's password, as shown in Figure 9-5.

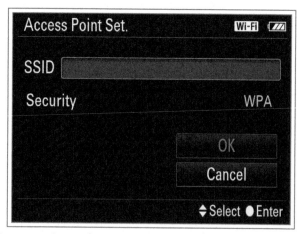

Figure 9-6. Screen for Entering Access Point Network ID Manually

10. On the Wi-Fi menu select Send to Computer, as in Figure 9-7.

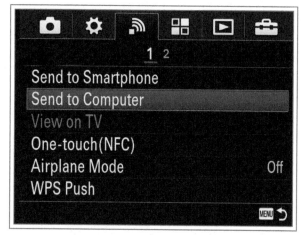

Figure 9-7. Send to Computer Item Highlighted on Menu

11. The camera will display a screen like that in Figure 9-8, reporting the name of the computer it is connecting to.

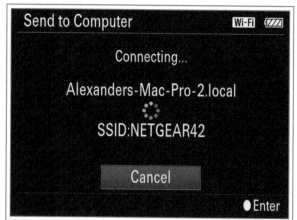

Figure 9-8. Screen When Camera Connects to Computer

12. The computer will display an Importing dialog box. The images and videos will be uploaded to

the appropriate folder on your computer. You can designate that folder using the software installed in Step 1. On my Macintosh, the default folder is the Pictures folder; the computer places the images and videos in a sub-folder bearing the date of the transfer.

The camera will only transfer images and videos that have not previously been transferred wirelessly to the computer, but there is no way to select which items will be transferred. The transfer may take a long time, especially if the transfer includes AVCHD and XAVC S videos. In fact, Sony does not recommend transferring XAVC S videos using the Send to Computer option, though it did work as expected when I tried it.

I have not found this option to be as useful as transferring images and videos using a card reader or a USB cable, because of the time it takes for the transfer. However, if you have only a few items to transfer, it can be convenient to have this option available.

SENDING IMAGES TO A SMARTPHONE

If you don't need to print your images or do heavy editing, you may want to transfer them to a smartphone or tablet so you can send them to social networks, display them on the larger screen of your tablet, or otherwise share and enjoy them.

You can transfer your images and MP4 videos (not XAVC S or AVCHD videos) wirelessly from the RX100 III to a smartphone or tablet that uses either the iOS (iPhone and iPad) or Android operating system. These 2 systems have different capabilities. With iOS devices, you have to use the camera's menu system to connect. With many Android devices, you can use NFC technology, which establishes a Wi-Fi connection automatically when the camera is touched against the smartphone or tablet.

Here are the steps for connecting using the menu system, using an iPhone as an illustration:

1. Install Sony's PlayMemories Mobile app on the phone; it can be downloaded from the App Store for the iPhone (or from Google Play for Android devices).

2. Put the camera into playback mode and select an image or MP4 video to be transferred to the phone.

3. On the Wi-Fi menu, select Send to Smartphone, and from that option choose Select on This Device, as shown in Figure 9-9. On the next screen, you can

choose to transfer This Image, All Still Images (or All Movie (MP4)) on Date, or Multiple Images.

4. On the next screen, as shown in Figure 9-10, the camera will display the SSID (name) of the Wi-Fi network it is generating.

5. On the phone, go to the Settings app, select Wi-Fi, and select the network displayed on the camera's screen, as shown in Figure 9-11. The first time you connect to that network, you will have to enter the password displayed on the camera's screen. After that initial connection, you can connect to that network without entering the password.

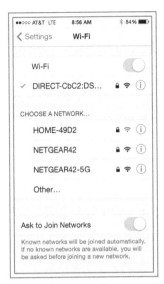

Figure 9-11. Camera's Network Shown on iPhone Screen

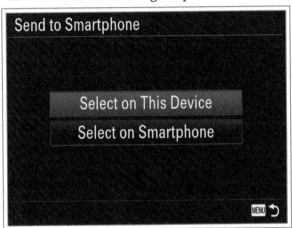

Figure 9-9. Send to Smartphone Menu Options Screen

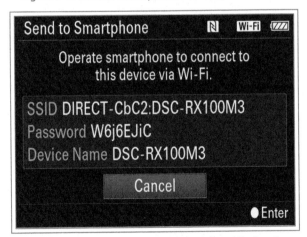

Figure 9-10. Camera's Network ID Displayed for Send to Smartphone Option

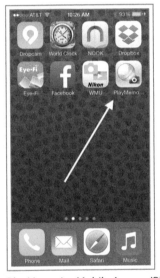

Figure 9-12. PlayMemories Mobile App on iPhone Screen

7. The phone will display a message saying it is copying the images or videos from the camera, and will confirm the copying with a screen like that in Figure 9-13. The images or videos will appear in the Camera Roll area on an iPhone.

6. The camera will then display a message saying "Connecting." At this point, start the PlayMemories Mobile app, shown by the arrow in Figure 9-12 on the iPhone.

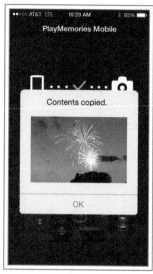

Figure 9-13. iPhone Screen Showing Image Transferred Successfully

CONNECTING WITH NFC

If you are using an Android phone or tablet that has NFC capability built in, the steps for connecting that device to the RX100 III are considerably easier. I tested the procedure using a Google Nexus 7 tablet, but the same process should work with many Android devices that have NFC included. Here are the steps:

1. On the Android device, go to the Google Play Store and find and install the PlayMemories Mobile app, as shown in Figure 9-14.

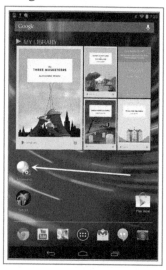

Figure 9-14. PlayMemories Mobile App on Nexus 7 Tablet Screen

2. On the Android device, go to the Settings app, and under the Wireless and Networks area, choose More. On the next screen, make sure there is a check mark next to the NFC item, as shown in Figure 9-15.

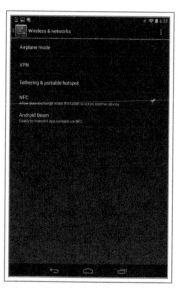

Figure 9-15. NFC Settings Screen on Nexus 7 Tablet

3. Put the RX100 III into playback mode and display an image that you want to send to the Android device.

4. Find the NFC icon on the left side of the camera, which looks like a fancy "N," as shown in Figure 9-16.

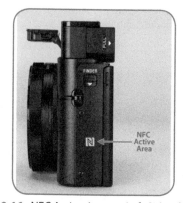

Figure 9-16. NFC Active Area on Left Side of Camera

5. While both devices are active, touch the N on the camera to the NFC area on the Android device. (On the Nexus 7, this area is on the back, as shown in Figure 9-17.) Be sure the 2 areas touch; you cannot have the 2 NFC spots separated by more than about a millimeter, if that.

6. Hold the devices together, and within a couple of seconds you may hear a sound, depending on settings, and the camera will transfer the image to the Android device; you should see a display saying the transfer is complete, as in Figure 9-18.

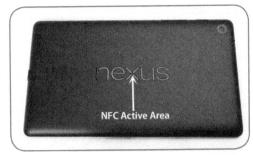

Figure 9-17. NFC Active Area on Nexus 7 Tablet

7. The image will appear in the Photos app on the Android device.

8. If you want to transfer multiple images, just select that option from the camera's menu before touching the camera to the Android device to start the transfer.

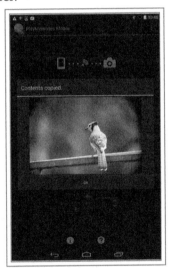

Figure 9-18. Message on Nexus 7 Tablet Showing Image Copied Successfully

By default, when you transfer images to a smartphone or tablet, the maximum image size will be 2 MP. That is, if the image originally was larger than that, it will be reduced to that size. You can change this setting to send the images at their original size or at the smaller VGA size, if you want. To do that on your device, find the settings for the PlayMemories Mobile app. (On an iPhone, go to Settings, then scroll to find PlayMemories Mobile. On an Android device, open PlayMemories Mobile, then tap the Settings icon.) If the images were taken with Raw quality, they will be converted to JPEG format before being transferred to the smartphone or tablet, even if the device is set for transfer at the original size.

USING A SMARTPHONE OR TABLET AS A REMOTE CONTROL

You can use a smartphone or tablet as a remote control to operate the RX100 III from a distance of up to about 33 feet (10 meters), as long as the devices are in sight of each other. Here are the steps to do this with an iPhone:

1. Go to the camera's Application menu, marked by an icon with white and black blocks. Select the first item, Application List. Press the Center button to display the list of applications, or apps, currently loaded into the camera.

2. Use the direction buttons or the Control wheel to highlight the app called Smart Remote Embedded, as shown in Figure 9-19. (If you have downloaded an updated version of this app, it may be called Smart Remote Control instead of Smart Remote Embedded.)

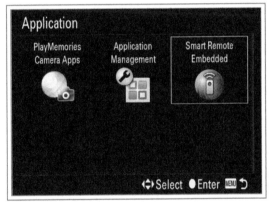

Figure 9-19. Smart Remote Embedded App on Camera's Screen

3. Start the app by pressing the Center button, and the camera will display a screen with the identification information for its own Wi-Fi network, as shown in Figure 9-20.

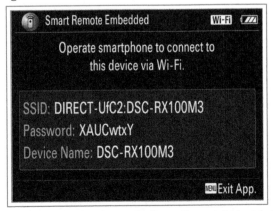

Figure 9-20. Connection Screen for Smart Remote Embedded App

4. On the phone, go to the Wi-Fi tab of the Settings app and select the network ID displayed by the camera, as shown in Figure 9-21. If this is the first time you are making this connection, you will have to enter the network password on the phone; you will not have to enter the password for future connections unless the network ID is changed.

5. Set up the camera on a tripod or just place it where you want it, aiming at your intended subject.

6. Open the PlayMemories Mobile app on the iPhone.

7. The camera will display a screen like that shown in Figure 9-22, with an icon in the upper left corner showing that the camera can now be controlled from the phone.

8. The phone will display a screen like that in Figure 9-23, with the view from the camera's lens and several control icons.

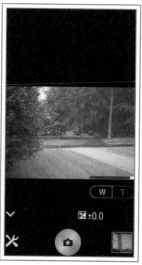

Figure 9-23. Camera Controls on iPhone Screen

9. Using these controls, you can zoom the lens and control exposure compensation. You can press the wrench-and-screwdriver icon to get access to settings for the self-timer, image review, and save options, as shown in Figure 9-24. You also can adjust several menu options using the camera's controls. For example, you can use the Mode dial to change the shooting mode and you can use the Creative Style menu option. If you want to record a movie, you have to turn the Mode dial to the Movie mode position, at which point the camera icon on the iPhone app will change to a red button for starting a video recording. If you download the updated version of the app, you can focus by touching the screen with your finger and adjust exposure settings more fully.

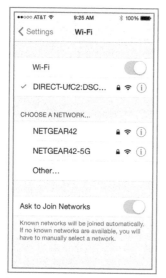

Figure 9-21. Camera's Network Displayed on iPhone Screen

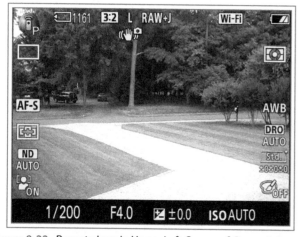

Figure 9-22. Remote Icon in Upper Left Corner of Camera's Screen

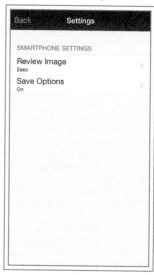

Figure 9-24. iPhone Settings Screen for Smart Remote Embedded App

By default, images saved to the phone will be resized down to 2 MP unless they already were that small or smaller. Movies will be saved only to the camera; they cannot be displayed or shown on the phone.

When you have set up the shot as you want it, press the camera icon on the iPhone app to take the picture or start the video recording.

If you are using an Android device with NFC capability, you should be able to connect to the camera by touching the device to the camera, as discussed above in connection with transferring images. To do this, though, you first have to register the Smart Remote Embedded (or Smart Remote Control) app using the One-touch (NFC) menu option on screen 1 of the camera's Wi-Fi menu. Once the connection has been made, you can separate the devices to the standard remote-control distance of up to about 33 feet (10 meters). If you have difficulty making an NFC connection, start the PlayMemories Mobile App on the Android device before touching the camera to that device. The camera can then be controlled using the PlayMemories Mobile app on the Android device, as noted in the numbered steps above.

The features of the remote control app are likely to change as Sony updates this and other apps; you can download updated versions at www.playmemoriescameraapps.com.

You can use the remote-control setup if you want to place your camera on a tripod in an area where birds or other wildlife may appear, so you can control the camera from a distance without disturbing the animals. (The wireless remote will work through glass if you are indoors behind a window.)

Also, you can try pole aerial photography, which involves attaching the camera to a painter's pole or other pole about 10 to 16 feet (3 to 5 meters) tall, as shown in Figure 9-25, to get shots from a higher vantage point than would otherwise be possible.

I took the image shown in Figure 9-26 using this pole, which allowed me to get a shot from the ceiling looking straight down at a bed. You can see a part of the pole and my hand holding the iPhone in this image.

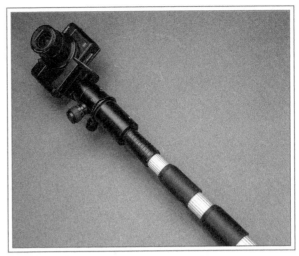

Figure 9-25. Camera Attached to Pole

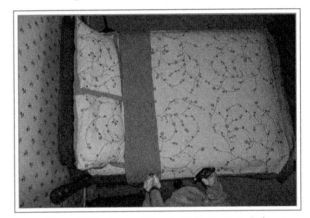

Figure 9-26. Image Taken with Camera on Pole

With this system, I could see exactly where the camera was being aimed. It was difficult holding the pole steady while using the iPhone, but if you have another person to help, this setup can be useful for higher-angle photos of properties being sold, viewing above crowds, and other applications. Being able to control the camera remotely also might be useful in other situations in which you want to have the camera set up unattended, such as when you want to capture images in a classroom or other group setting without calling attention to the camera.

Wi-Fi Menu

I have discussed some of the options on the Wi-Fi menu, whose first screen is shown in Figure 9-27, but there are several other options that I need to discuss. Following is information about each of the items on this menu.

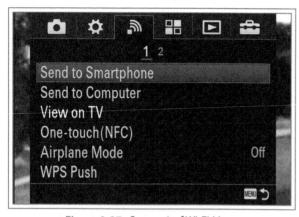

Figure 9-27. Screen 1 of Wi-Fi Menu

SEND TO SMARTPHONE

This first Wi-Fi menu option is what you select to transfer images or MP4 videos to a smartphone or tablet. I discussed the steps for using this option earlier in this chapter.

SEND TO COMPUTER

This next option lets you send your images and movies directly from the RX100 III to your computer via a Wi-Fi network. I discussed the steps for this process earlier in this chapter.

VIEW ON TV

This option sets up the RX100 III to transmit still images (not movies) wirelessly to a Wi-Fi–enabled TV, such as a Sony Bravia TV. The procedure will vary with the TV set you are using. Once the connection is established, you can browse through the images using the controls on the camera or the remote control of the TV if the TV is compatible with this setup.

This is a useful option once it is working properly, but I found it difficult to set up. After many hours of trying various approaches with little or no success, I finally got it to work using a device called WD TV Live, a media player made by Western Digital. I connected that device to an HDTV using an HDMI cable, and configured the device to connect to my home network. Then I connected a laptop computer running Windows 7 to the same network. I configured the Windows Media Player software on the computer to allow streaming of media over the network, and I also downloaded a program called Serviio from http://serviio.org and configured this system to work as a DLNA streaming

media server on my network. (DLNA stands for Digital Living Network Alliance; see www.dlna.org.)

Once everything was working together, I selected the View on TV menu option and the camera displayed the screen shown in Figure 9-28 as it connected to the WD TV Live device.

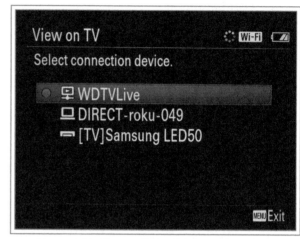

Figure 9-28. View on TV Device Selection Screen

Then the camera began sending still images to the TV through the wireless network. The camera displayed the screen shown in Figure 9-29, with a few control icons at the bottom. Once this screen appeared, I pressed the Center button to pause the transmission, and pressed the Down button to display the screen shown in Figure 9-30, with additional options.

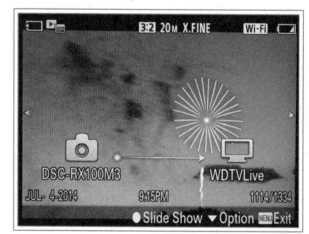

Figure 9-29. Screen When Camera Sends Images to TV

If you are familiar with setting up a DLNA server, this option may be great for you. Otherwise, I recommend that you view your images on a TV using an HDMI cable, a USB flash drive, or some other direct connection.

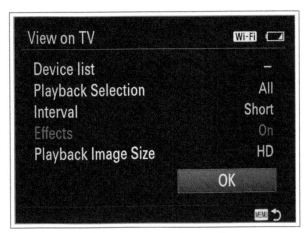

Figure 9-30. View on TV Options Screen

ONE-TOUCH (NFC)

The RX100 III has built-in near field communication (NFC) functionality, which means it can establish a wireless connection just by touching a smartphone or tablet that also has NFC built in. As of this writing, many Android phones and tablets have this feature, but Apple devices, such as iPhones and iPads, do not.

To use the NFC feature to start a camera app, you first have to use this menu option to register that app. Then, with the smartphone or tablet turned on and the camera in shooting mode, touch the N mark on the left side of the camera to the NFC area on the smartphone or tablet. (It may be marked by an X, and not necessarily by an N.) The 2 devices should immediately start to establish a connection, and the application you registered using this menu option should launch. For example, you might want to register the Smart Remote Embedded application or another application that you have downloaded from Sony's site.

You don't have to use this option before connecting the camera to a phone or tablet to transfer images.

AIRPLANE MODE

This option is a quick way to disable all of the camera's functions related to Wi-Fi, including Eye-Fi card activity and the camera's own internal Wi-Fi network. As indicated by its name, this option is useful when you are on an airplane and you are required to disable electronic devices. In addition, this setting can save battery power, so it may be useful to activate it when you are on an outing with the camera and you won't need to use any Wi-Fi capabilities for a period of time.

If you are trying to use any of the camera's built-in Wi-Fi functions such as Send to Smartphone or Send to Computer and notice that the menu options are dimmed, it may be because this option is turned on. Just turn it back off and the Wi-Fi options should be available again.

WPS PUSH

The WPS Push option gives you an easy way to set up your camera to connect to a computer over a Wi-Fi network. Ordinarily, to connect to a wireless network, you have to use the Access Point Settings option and then enter the network password into the camera to establish the connection. The WPS Push option gives you a shortcut if the wireless access point or wireless router you are connecting to has a WPS button. That option, if it is present, is likely to be a small button on the back or top of the router, and it is likely to have the WPS label next to it or on it. For example, one router I connect to has the button shown in Figure 9-2.

If the router has a WPS button, you will not have to make any manual settings or enter a password. All you have to do is select the WPS Push menu option on the RX100 III, and then within 2 minutes after that, press the WPS button on the router. If the operation is successful, the camera's display screen will show that the connection has been established, as shown in Figure 9-31.

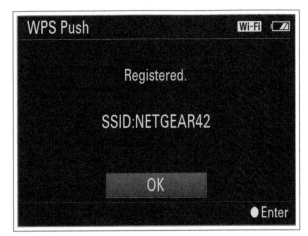

Figure 9-31. Message After WPS Push Option Succeeds

Once that connection has been made, you will be able to connect your camera to a computer on that network in the future to transfer images using the Send to Computer option. If the connection does not succeed using WPS Push, you will need to use the Access Point Settings option. That option is the first item on screen 2 of the Wi-Fi menu, which is shown in Figure 9-3.

ACCESS POINT SETTINGS

This option is for connecting the camera to a router if WPS Push, discussed above, is not available or does not work. I discussed the use of this option earlier in this chapter, in connection with sending images and videos to a computer wirelessly.

EDIT DEVICE NAME

This next option, shown in Figure 9-32, lets you change the name of your camera as it is displayed on the network. The default name is DSC-RX100M3, and I have found no reason to change it, especially because doing so would require me to use the camera's laborious data-entry system. This option could be useful, though, if you are in an environment where other RX100 III cameras are present and you need to distinguish one camera from another by using different names.

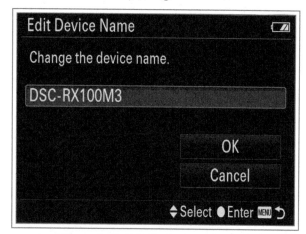

Figure 9-32. Edit Device Name Screen

DISPLAY MAC ADDRESS

If you select this menu option, the camera will display a screen like that seen in Figure 9-33, which provides the MAC address of your camera. MAC stands for media access control. The MAC address is a string of characters that identifies a physical device that can connect to a network. In some cases, a router can be configured to reject or accept devices with specified MAC addresses. If you are having difficulty connecting your camera to your Wi-Fi router using the options discussed above, you can try configuring your router to recognize the MAC address of your camera, as reported by this menu item. I have not had to use this option, but it is good to have it available in case it is needed.

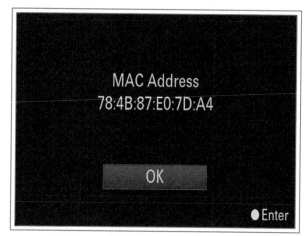

Figure 9-33. Display MAC Address Screen

SSID/PW RESET

When you connect your RX100 III to a smartphone or tablet, either to transfer images or to control the camera remotely with the other device, the camera generates its own Wi-Fi network internally. With this option, whose main screen is shown in Figure 9-34, you can force the camera to change the SSID (name) and password of its own wireless network.

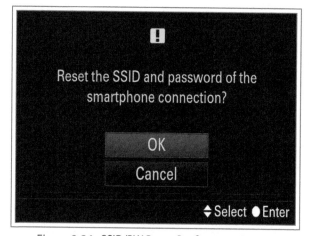

Figure 9-34. SSID/PW Reset Confirmation Screen

You might want to do this if, for example, you have attended a conference where you allowed other people to connect their smartphones to your camera, and now you want to reset the camera's network ID so they will no longer have access to the camera's network.

RESET NETWORK SETTINGS

This final item on the Wi-Fi menu lets you reset all of the camera's Wi-Fi network settings, not just the SSID and password. This option is useful if you are having problems and need to get a fresh start with the wireless functions, if you are switching to a new wireless network where you use the camera, or if you are selling the camera and want to erase these settings.

Applications and Application Menu

The one menu system I have not yet discussed in any detail is the Application menu, represented by an icon with white and black blocks, to the right of the Wi-Fi menu's icon. This menu system opens the door to expansions of the RX100 III's features through applications, or apps, that you can download from a Sony website. I will give a brief introduction to this capability, which undoubtedly will continue to develop after this book is published.

The apps available from Sony are similar to apps for smartphones and tablets. Each camera app provides a separate function or set of functions, and is represented by a name and an icon. The apps are found on the RX100 III by going to the Application menu and selecting the first item, Application List, shown in Figure 9-35.

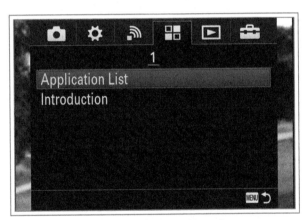

Figure 9-35. Applications Menu Screen

When you highlight that item and press the Center button, you will see a screen like that in Figure 9-36, with icons for all apps currently loaded into the camera. (This screen image includes the Time-lapse app, which I purchased from Sony; that app does not come with the camera.) If you highlight any of those icons and press the Center button, you will activate that app.

Although I think it is likely that the set of initial apps will change over time, when my camera was new it came with just one actual camera app installed—Smart Remote Embedded, which lets you use a smartphone or tablet to control the camera. (The camera included 2 other apps that involve downloading and management

of camera apps.) Not long after I purchased my camera, Sony updated that app to add new features, and I won't be surprised if it is updated further as time goes by.

Besides the app that came pre-installed, Sony has, as of this writing, made available several other apps, some free and some for prices up to $9.99. These apps include My Best Portrait (free); Photo Retouch (free); Picture Effect+ (free); Star Trail ($9.99); Motion Shot ($4.99); Time-Lapse ($9.99); and Bracket Pro ($4.99), among others. You can read about these apps at Sony's site, mentioned in the next paragraph. Some of them, like Picture Effect+, add enhancements to features that already exist in the camera, and others, like Time-lapse, add new features.

In order to install and use any of these apps, you first have to go to Sony's site at www.playmemoriescameraapps.com and create an account. Then you can obtain information about the apps and download them. Once the account is set up and you have your camera registered with a Wi-Fi access point, you can also download an app directly to your camera. The camera has about 100 MB of capacity to install apps, and each of the ones I have downloaded so far has used about 5 MB, so you may be able to have about 20 apps installed altogether. To manage installed apps, you use the administrative app called Application Management, whose icon is shown in Figure 9-36.

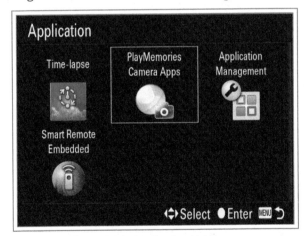

Figure 9-36. Application List Screen

To purchase an app from the camera, use the PlayMemories Camera Apps icon, also shown in that illustration.

Once you have installed an app and activated it by selecting its icon, press the Center button and follow the on-screen instructions to use it. If you press the camera's Menu button while the app is running, the camera may display a special menu with options that apply while that app is in use. For example, when the Smart Remote Embedded app is running, if you press the Menu button you will see one of the 5 menu screens for that app, as shown in Figure 9-37.

The other 4 menu screens for this app display standard camera options that can be controlled when the app is in use, such as Image Size, Quality, ISO, and the like. In other cases, an app may just use icons to let you choose various functions.

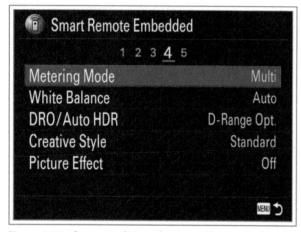

Figure 9-37. Screen 4 of Menu for Smart Remote Embedded

If you expect to use in-camera apps regularly, you can assign the Application List menu item to the Custom, Center, Left, or Right button so the list can be called up quickly.

The second line of the Application menu, Introduction, provides some general information about applications.

Other Topics

ASTROPHOTOGRAPHY AND DIGISCOPING

Astrophotography involves photographing sky objects with a camera connected to (or aiming through) a telescope. Digiscoping is the practice of using a digital camera with a spotting scope to get shots of distant objects such as birds and other wildlife.

There are many types of scope and several ways to align a scope with the RX100 III's lens. I will not describe all of the methods; I will discuss the approach I have used and hope it gives you enough guidance to explore the area further.

I used a Meade ETX-90/AT telescope with the RX100 III connected to its eyepiece. To make that connection, you need a filter adapter, such as the one sold by Sony, model number VFA-49R1, or a similar one sold by Lensmate, as discussed in Appendix A, as well as adapter rings that let you connect the filter adapter to the telescope's eyepiece. You can get the proper adapter rings for the Sony filter adapter by purchasing the 49mm Digi-Kit, part number DKSR49T, from the online site telescopeadapters.com. That is the setup shown in Figure 9-38.

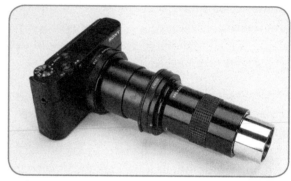

Figure 9-38. Camera Attached to Telescope Eyepiece

I took the image in Figure 9-39 with the RX100 III connected to an eyepiece on the telescope using adapter rings. I set the camera to Manual exposure mode with settings of 1/100 second, f/4.0, and ISO 800. I used manual focus, adjusting the telescope's focus control until the image appeared sharp on the camera's LCD. At first I used the MF Assist option, so I could fine-tune the focus with an enlarged view of the moon's craters. After experimenting, I found I got better results using the Peaking Level function, with Peaking Color set to red. When focus was sharp, I saw a bright, red outline on the outer edge of the moon, which made focusing much easier than relying on the normal manual focus mechanism, even with MF Assist activated.

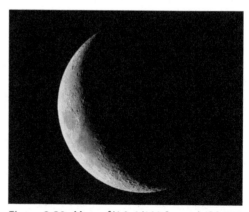

Figure 9-39. Moon, f/4.0, 1/100 Second, ISO 800

I set the self-timer to 2 seconds to minimize camera shake. I set Quality to Raw & JPEG so I would have a Raw image to give extra latitude in case the exposure seemed incorrect. As you can see in Figure 9-39, the RX100 III did a good job of capturing the crescent moon. Because of the large sensor and relatively high resolution of the RX100 III, this image can be enlarged to a fair degree without deteriorating.

You can use a similar setup for digiscoping. I attached the RX100 III to a Celestron Regal 80F-ED spotting scope, shown in Figure 9-40, using the same eyepiece I used with the telescope.

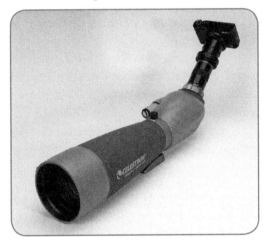

Figure 9-40. Camera Attached to Celestron Spotting Scope

Figure 9-41 is a shot of a cardinal at a feeder, taken with the RX100 III through this scope. I used Program mode at 1/200 second, f/4.0, and ISO 1600. I turned on continuous shooting to catch various views of the bird. I used manual focus with Peaking at its mid level set to red, and that worked well.

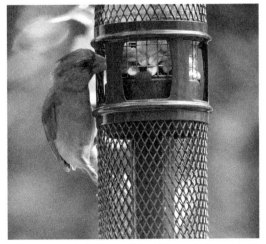

Figure 9-41. Example Image Taken Through Spotting Scope

Figure 9-42 is a shot I took from the same location as the digiscoping image using the full optical zoom of the RX100 III to show how much magnification the Celestron scope provided. The feeder is barely visible to the left of center of the image.

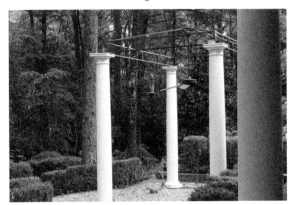

Figure 9-42. Digiscoping Comparison Image Taken with Full Optical Zoom

INFRARED PHOTOGRAPHY

Infrared photography involves recording images illuminated by infrared light, which is invisible to the human eye. The resulting photographs can be spectacular, producing scenes in which green foliage appears white and blue skies appear eerily dark.

To take infrared photographs, you need a camera that can "see" infrared light. Many modern cameras include internal filters that block infrared light. However, some cameras do not, or block it only partially. (You can do a quick test of any digital camera by aiming it at the light-emitting end of an infrared remote control and taking a photograph while pressing a button on the remote; if the remote's light shows up as bright white, the camera can "see" infrared light at least to some extent.)

The RX100 III is quite capable of taking infrared photographs. To unleash this capability, you need to get a filter that blocks most visible light but lets infrared light reach the camera's light sensor. (If you don't, the infrared light will be overwhelmed by the visible light, and you'll get an ordinary picture based on visible light.)

The infrared filter I use is the Hoya R72. As discussed above in connection with astrophotography and in Appendix A, you can obtain a filter adapter for the RX100 III that lets you attach various filters and other accessories. When you attach the very dark red R72 filter to the RX100 III, a great deal of the visible light from the scene is blocked. I have found that this reduction in light causes some problems for the camera's ability to set automatic exposure and white balance. With experimentation, though, you can get an interesting result.

For the image in Figure 9-43, I aimed the camera at green trees in bright sunlight to set a custom white balance that would yield the characteristic white appearance of green grass and leaves. The camera displayed an error message for setting the white balance each time I tried, but it still appeared to set a usable white balance.

For exposure, I first tried Aperture Priority, but the camera underexposed the images heavily. I eventually used Manual exposure mode and adjusted the shutter speed until I could see the image clearly on the LCD display. I ended up with an exposure for 10 seconds at f/5.0 with ISO set at 800.

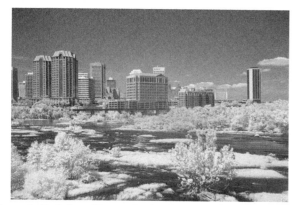

Figure 9-43. Infrared Image, f/5.0, 10 Seconds, ISO 800, Hoya R72 Filter

This sort of infrared photography often is most successful in the spring or summer when there is a rich variety of green subjects available outdoors.

CONNECTING TO A TELEVISION SET

The RX100 III can play back its still images and videos on an external television set, as long as the TV has an HDMI input jack. The camera does not come with any audio-video cable as standard equipment, so you have to purchase your own cable, with a micro-HDMI connector at the camera end and a standard HDMI connector at the TV end. These cables are available through online retailers.

To connect the cable to the camera, you need to open the little flap marked HDMI on the right side of the

camera and plug the micro-HDMI connector into the port underneath that flap, as shown in Figure 9-44.

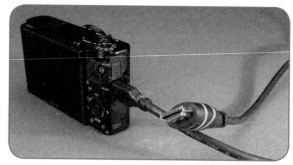

Figure 9-44. HDMI Cable Attached to Camera

Then connect the large connector at the other end of the cable to an HDMI input port on an HDTV set.

Once you have connected the camera to the set, the camera not only can play back images and videos; it also can record. When the RX100 III is hooked up to a TV while in recording mode, you can see on the TV screen the live image being seen by the camera. In that way, you can use the TV as a large monitor to help you compose your photographs and videos.

You also can use this port and cable to output a "clean" video signal to another device, such as a video recorder. To do that, you have to turn off the HDMI Information Display option under the HDMI Settings item on screen 3 of the Setup menu, as discussed in Chapter 7.

As noted in Chapter 7, the RX100 III also has an option on the Wi-Fi menu, View on TV, that is intended to let you view your images on a Wi-Fi–enabled TV. As I discussed in that chapter, I have found this option to be difficult to use effectively. Unless you are familiar with setting up the special type of network that is needed for this sort of connection, I recommend that you stick to using an HDMI cable for the connection.

APPENDIX A: ACCESSORIES

When people buy a new camera, especially a fairly expensive model like the Sony RX100 III, they often ask what accessories they should buy to go with it. I will discuss several options, with an emphasis on items I have used personally.

Cases

The RX100 III is such a small camera that you may find you don't need a case. There is no separate lens cap to deal with as there is with some models in this class, and when the camera turns off and its lens retracts, the RX100 III is ready to stow easily in your pocket, purse, or other handy location. But I do use a case with my RX100 III, and I know that other users do also, so I will provide some suggestions.

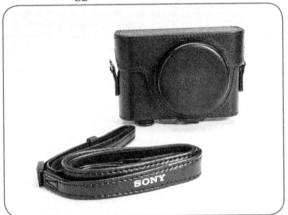

Figure A-1. Sony Jacket Case LCJ-RXF and Strap

The first case I will mention is the Sony case made for the RX100, RX100 II, and RX100 III cameras, model number LCJ-RXF, shown in Figures A-1 and A-2. This case is similar to an earlier version that was made for the original RX100 camera. The older version may not fit the newer camera, so be sure to check the model number of the case. This case is roomy enough to hold the RX100 III with its tilting LCD.

This is a very attractive case made of synthetic material that looks like leather. It holds the camera securely and comes with a matching shoulder strap.

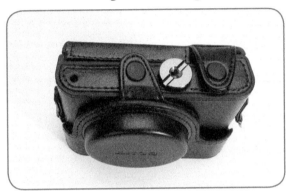

Figure A-2. Sony Jacket Case, LCJ-RXF, Bottom

It will hold the camera with the filter adapter attached, but not with the add-on grip installed. It does not have room for holding an extra battery or other items.

A less expensive option is the Camson case, shown in Figures A-3 and A-4. This brown leather case comes with a matching strap and can hold the camera with filter adapter, but not much else. It has a nice appearance and feel and does not display the Sony label, so it may provide a degree of security because it does not reveal the brand of your camera. I purchased this case from Wall Street Photo in New York.

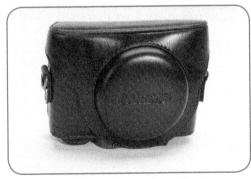

Figure A-3. Camson Case, Closed

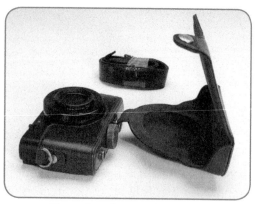

Figure A-4. Camson Case, Open

If you want a case with room for other items besides the camera, there are many choices. The smallest one I have tried is the Sony LCM-CSVH case, shown in Figure A-5. This "semi-hard" case can hold the camera with grip and filter adapter, and has a small pocket for an extra battery, memory card, or other small item. It comes with a shoulder strap and can attach over a belt. It provides fairly good protection against bumps and short drops.

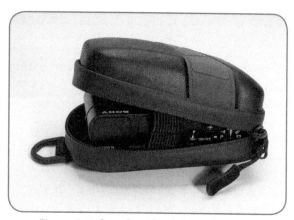

Figure A-5. Sony Semi-hard Case, LCM-CSVH

When I am going on a day trip to take photos, I often use a larger pack, such as the Lowepro Inverse 100 AW waist pack, shown in Figure A-6.

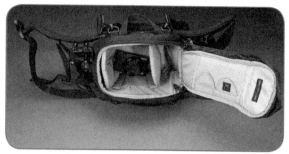

Figure A-6. Lowepro Inverse 100 AW Waist Pack

You can strap this case around your waist or use its shoulder strap. It easily holds the camera along with water bottles, batteries, chargers, and other items. One of the features I appreciate most is that it has straps for attaching a tripod. In the image shown here, the Manfrotto BeFree tripod is strapped to the bottom of the case.

Batteries and Chargers

This is a category of items that I recommend you purchase along with the camera or soon after getting the camera. I use the camera heavily, and I find it runs through batteries fairly quickly. You can't use disposable batteries, so if you're out taking pictures and the battery dies, you're out of luck unless you have a spare battery (or an AC adapter and a place to plug it in, as discussed below). The model number of the Sony battery is NP-BX1. You can get a spare Sony battery for about $50 as I write this. It won't do you a great deal of good by itself, though, because the battery is designed to be charged in the camera.

There is an easy solution to this problem. You can find generic replacement batteries, as well as chargers to charge the batteries outside the camera, inexpensively from online sellers. I purchased a package including a generic replacement battery and a charger for about $20 on eBay. You also can get the official Sony external charger, model number BC-TRX. Besides charging a battery externally, the Sony charger can be used with its included USB cable to charge a battery inside the camera. Both the Sony charger and a generic charger are shown in Figure A-7, along with a generic battery and a Sony battery.

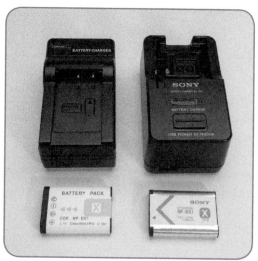

Figure A-7. Generic Charger with Battery, Sony Charger with Battery

While I am on the subject of power, I should mention one other aspect of the power supply for the RX100 III. The AC adapter that comes with the camera (in the United States), model number AC-UB10, cannot be used to power the camera when it is in operation; it only serves to charge a battery inside the camera. If you want to use an adapter that provides power so you can operate the camera for long periods of time while recording videos, transferring images, or for other applications, you need to use a different Sony adapter, model number AC-UD10 or AC-UD11. The AC-UD11 charger is shown in Figure A-8.

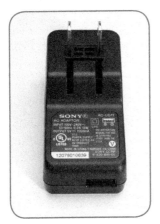

Figure A-8. Sony AC Adapter, AC-UD11

You use this charger by plugging one end of the camera's USB cable into the camera's USB port and the other end into this charger. You then plug the charger into a standard electrical outlet, and it will supply power to the camera indefinitely.

Actually, model AC-UD11 is the AC adapter that came with the original RX100 camera. So, if you happen to own that camera and its power adapter, you can use that adapter to power the RX100 III, even when no battery is installed in the camera.

Add-On Filters and Lenses

There is no way to attach a filter or other item, such as a closeup lens, directly to the RX100 III's lens, as you can with DSLRs and other cameras whose lenses are threaded to accept filters and auxiliary lenses. With the RX100 III, to add such accessory items you need to get an adapter. Sony provides an adapter designed for the RX100 and the RX100 II, model number VFA-49R1. This adapter was not designed for use with the RX100 III, but it works fairly well with this camera, with a couple of caveats.

The adapter has 2 parts. The first part, shown already attached to the lens in Figure A-9, is a plastic ring called the "base ring" that you glue onto the front of the lens barrel. This piece stays in place and does not interfere with the lens or the automatic lens cover. Because the lens barrel of the RX100 III is different from that of the RX100 and RX100 II, the installation guide provided with the filter adapter is not the right size for the RX100 III. Therefore, you have to be careful to install the base ring so it is centered on the lens barrel, without using an installation guide. I did not find that process to be difficult.

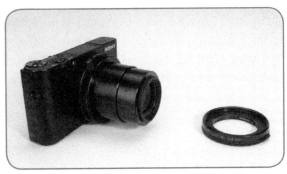

Figure A-9. Sony Filter Adapter, VFA-49R1

To use a filter, you attach a larger piece, the actual "filter adapter," at the right in Figure A-9, which bayonets onto the base ring as shown in Figure A-10. Then you can screw any 49mm diameter filter or other auxiliary lens into the holder. One problem with this system is that I detected a very slight amount of vignetting at the corners of the images, because the adapter is not sized exactly right for the newer model of camera. The problem can easily be fixed by zooming in slightly or cropping the image later. But, if you don't want to have to deal with that issue, there are other options, discussed below.

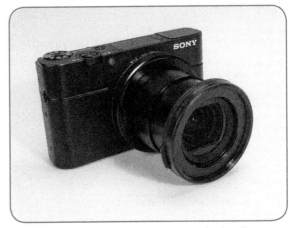

Figure A-10. Sony Filter Adapter Attached to Camera

The base ring is removable if you later want to take it off the lens; Sony includes a "remover," which is a pair of plastic rings attached to a thread; you work the thread under the base ring and pull it through to remove the ring from the lens.

As you might expect, this system is not as sturdy as the natural screw-on capability of other cameras because everything depends on a plastic ring that is glued in place. So don't expect to attach large items like teleconverters or anything heavier than a standard 49mm filter. Having the ability to attach filters, however, enhances the usefulness of the camera greatly. You can use infrared filters, neutral density filters, polarizers, or any of a wide assortment of closeup lenses, among others. Also, as discussed in Chapter 9, I used this system to attach the RX100 III to the eyepiece of a telescope and spotting scope to take pictures through the scopes. You have to be careful not to put too much stress on the adapter in that situation, but the adapter worked well for that purpose.

There is a similar system sold for the RX100 III by Lensmate, a company that developed this system before Sony used it. Lensmate sells an adapter for use with 52mm filters. Details are at lensmateonline.com.

There also is at least one other option available for attaching filters to the RX100 III—the "Magfilter" system, which involves gluing a thin metallic ring to the front of the lens and then attaching a magnetic filter holder to that ring. I have not tried this system myself, but I have read good things about it. You can get more details at www.carryspeed.com.

Grips

Some users find it difficult to get a firm grasp of the RX100 III because it is small and has a smooth front surface with no place to take hold of it. Lensmate, which provides the filter adapter discussed above, also offers a solution to this issue—the custom-made grip designed by Richard Franiec, shown in Figure A-11.

The Franiec grip is well crafted from aluminum and contoured to fit on the camera's body with a low profile. It is attached with a strong adhesive supplied by Lensmate. This grip offers you a solid ridge for keeping a tight hold on the camera. I do not find it necessary, but this is a matter of personal taste.

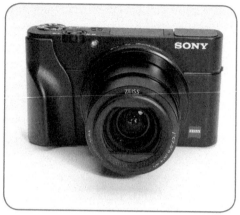

Figure A-11. Richard Franiec Grip on Camera

Here again, as with the filter adapter, Sony later adopted the technology sold by Lensmate, and now offers a grip of its own, model number AG-R2. I didn't purchase this grip myself, but Figure A-12 shows the previous model, AG-R1, which seems to fit reasonably well on the camera.

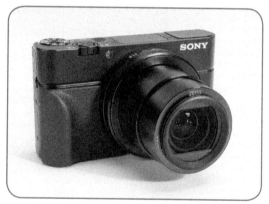

Figure A-12. Sony AG-R1 Grip on Camera

This grip has a different shape, appearance, and texture from the Franiec grip, and it is less expensive. There also are other grips available, but I have not tried any of them. Again, I do not use an add-on grip myself, but it is good to have these options available.

Remote Control

In several situations, it is useful to control a camera remotely. For example, when you are using slow shutter speeds, holding the shutter open with the BULB setting, doing closeup photography, or taking pictures through a telescope, any camera motion during the exposure is likely to blur the image. If you can control the camera remotely, you can lessen the risk of blurred images from moving the camera as you press the shutter button.

As I discussed in Chapter 9, the RX100 III has a built-in Wi-Fi capability for connecting a computer, smartphone, or tablet to the camera wirelessly. Besides using that feature to transfer images from the camera to the other device, you can use a smartphone or tablet as a wireless remote control. However, it can be tricky to establish and maintain the connection between the camera and the phone or tablet.

Fortunately, with the RX100 III, Sony has included another option for remote control, shown in Figure A-13.

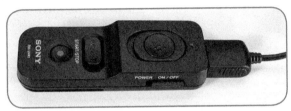

Figure A-13. Sony Remote, RM-VPR1

You can connect a Sony wired remote, model number RM-VPR1, to the Multi port on the right side of the camera. With this device, you can turn the camera on and off, use the autofocus system, zoom the lens in and out, take a still image, lock the shutter down for a long exposure, and start and stop video recording.

The remote control comes with 2 cables—one for cameras with a Remote terminal and one for cameras like the RX100 III, which has the Multi terminal. Take the cable that has identical connectors at each end, and plug the end with the smaller plastic housing into the camera. Plug the other end of the cable, which has a larger housing, into the remote. You also can attach the included clip to the underside of the remote, if you want to clip the remote to a tripod or other support.

You can half-press the shutter button to cause the autofocus system to operate (if the camera is in an autofocus mode), and press the button fully to take a still picture. You can press the shutter button down and then slide it back toward the other controls to lock it in place. This locking is useful when you are taking continuous shots using the Drive Mode settings, or when you want to hold the shutter open using the BULB setting in Manual exposure mode. Press the shutter button back up in its original direction to release it.

The red button labeled Start/Stop is similar to the Movie button on the RX100 III camera. Press it once to start recording a movie and press it again to stop the recording.

The power button on the side of the remote control can be used to turn the camera on and off, and to wake it up from power-saving mode. Press the switch back toward yourself as you hold the control to power the camera either on or off.

External Flash

When Sony designed the RX100 III, they included the desirable feature of a built-in viewfinder that pops up, but, probably because of that feature, they omitted a hot shoe where you can attach an external flash unit. So, if you want to use an external unit to supplement the light from the camera's small pop-up flash, you have to use an optical slave.

An optical slave is a flash unit that includes a sensor that triggers the flash when it senses the light from the camera's built-in flash. (You also can use a separate optical slave that can be attached to any compatible flash unit.)

One problem with using this system is that the RX100 III fires one or more pre-flashes before it fires the main flash burst to expose the image. The camera uses the pre-flashes to measure the amount of light being reflected from the subject so the image can be exposed properly. If the optical slave is not set to ignore the pre-flashes, it will fire as soon as it "sees" a pre-flash, and the external flash will not be synchronized with the actual exposure.

The solution to this problem is to use an optical slave that can be set to ignore the pre-flashes. One of the best ones I have found for use with the RX100 III is the LumoPro LP180, shown in Figure A-14. This powerful unit has a head that swivels and rotates, a built-in diffuser, variable power, and settings that allow it to ignore a variable number of pre-flashes. I have had good success using this flash with the RX100 III by setting the flash to its S2-1 mode.

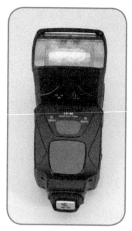

Figure A-14. LumoPro LP180 Flash

With this flash, as with any other optical slave, you have to use Manual exposure mode on the camera and determine the proper exposure by trial and error or by using a light meter. You can set up the external flash on a light stand or tripod at any location where it can sense the light from the camera's built-in flash.

Another good unit for use as an optical slave is the Yongnuo YN560 III, shown in Figure A-15, which also has a built-in optical slave capability. I had success using this unit with the RX100 III with the flash set to its S2 mode. As you can see in Figure A-15, you can attach this, or any, external flash to the RX100 III using a standard flash bracket with a tripod socket. With this flash, I found it necessary to use a piece of electrical tape to cover the flash shoe on the bracket, because the contacts on the shoe evidently interfered with the firing process.

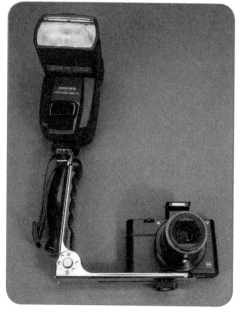

Figure A-15. Yongnuo YN560 III Flash with Camera on Bracket

There is one other issue to be aware of when using an external flash unit. When you set the camera to Manual exposure mode, the camera's display screen (or electronic viewfinder display) is likely to be black or very dark because the exposure settings would result in a dark image if you were not using flash, and the camera will not "know" about the effects of the external flash. Therefore, it may be difficult to compose the shot. The solution is to go to Screen 2 of the Custom menu on the camera, and set the Live View Display option to Setting Effect Off. With that setting, the camera's display will not darken to show the effects of the manual exposure settings, and you will probably be able to view the display clearly enough to compose the image.

You may want to consider one other accessory for use with any external flash unit—a softbox, like the one shown in Figure A-16.

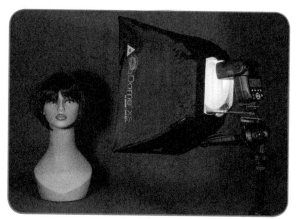

Figure A-16. Photoflex Lite-Dome XS Softbox Attached to Yongnuo Flash

A softbox is an enclosure that surrounds a flash unit and diffuses the light through a white, translucent surface, enlarging the area that lights up the subject. The effect of using a softbox is to soften the light because the larger the light source, the less harsh the light will be, with softer shadows. This softbox is a Photoflex Lite-Dome XS, whose enclosure is about 12 by 16 inches (30 by 40 cm).

As you can see in Figure A-16, I placed the softbox on a tripod over the Yongnuo YN 560 III flash unit. I set up the Yongnuo flash in its S2 slave mode, so it would fire when I pressed the shutter button on the RX100 III, with the camera's flash mode set to Fill-flash. With this setup, you can achieve more indirect and pleasing lighting effects than with on-camera flash.

External Sound Systems

As I discussed in Chapter 8, the Sony RX100 III has excellent video features but has no provision for connecting an external microphone for high-quality audio. Although the built-in microphone records good-quality audio, you can get better results if you use an external audio recorder and synchronize the audio track from that recorder with the sound recorded by the camera.

One excellent piece of equipment for this purpose is the Tascam DR-100MkII recorder, shown in Figure A-17.

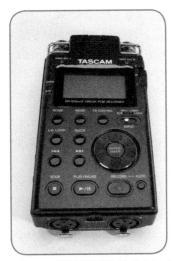

Figure A-17. Tascam DR-100MkII Digital Audio Recorder

This recorder includes 2 sets of high-quality microphones, one set that is omnidirectional for recording lectures or classes, and another that is directional for recording concerts or other performances. The recorder also has 2 XLR inputs where you can connect high-quality microphones of your choice. There are many other options that will work for this purpose, depending on your budget and needs, including the Shure VP83F, the Tascam DR-40, the Zoom H1, and the Zoom H6.

Appendix B: Quick Tips

In this section, I will list some tips and facts that might be useful as reminders. I have tried to include points that you might not remember from day to day, especially if you don't use the RX100 III constantly.

Move the focus point quickly. To adjust the focus point for single-shot autofocus, choose Flexible Spot from the Focus Area menu and Standard for the Center Button option of the Custom Key Settings item on screen 4 of the Custom menu. Then, when the camera is in shooting mode, just press the Center button to put the movable focus frame on the screen. Use the direction buttons to move it and the Control wheel to resize it.

Use Auto ISO with Manual exposure mode. This is a new feature for the RX100 III that the earlier RX100 models did not have. With these settings, you can set a shutter speed and aperture and let the camera set the ISO to produce a good exposure. This is like having a new shooting mode that lets you stop action and control depth of field at the same time.

Use continuous shooting. Consider turning burst shooting on as a matter of routine, unless you are running out of storage space or battery power, or have a particular reason not to use it. Even with portraits, you may get the perfect expression on your subject's face with the fourth or fifth shot. Press the Left button (or use the menu system) to call up Drive Mode, scroll to Continuous Shooting, and turn it on. Continuous Shooting is not available when the camera is set to Sweep Panorama mode or to any Scene mode setting other than Sports Action.

Use shortcuts. Speed up access to many settings by placing them on the Function menu for recall with a press of the Fn button. In some cases, as with flash settings and Drive Mode, you can press a button (the Right and Left buttons, respectively) to get access to the features you need. Speed through the Shooting menu using the Control wheel to move rapidly through the items on a screen. Use the Right and Left buttons to move through the menus a screen at a time by highlighting the icons at the top of the screen.

Take advantage of the help system. The RX100 III does a good job of advising you about conflicts between settings. If a menu option is unavailable for selection, you can still highlight it and press the Center button. The camera will display a message telling you what setting is causing the highlighted item to be unavailable.

Use the Memory Recall shooting mode. The MR position on the Mode dial lets you save 3 favorite groups of settings. You also can use it for more specific purposes. I like to have one slot set up to remove all "special" settings, such as Creative Style, Picture Effect, and self-timer, so I can quickly set up the camera to take a shot with no surprises. You can use one slot to set the camera at a particular zoom range, such as, say, 50mm. To do this, press the zoom lever to move the lens, so you see the desired range below the zoom scale in the upper right corner of the display. When the range is set as you want it, save the settings to one of the MR slots. (You also can use the Step Zoom feature to set a particular zoom amount; to do that, set the Zoom Function on Ring option on the Custom menu to Step.)

Remember the extra settings for White Balance and Creative Style. When you set White Balance, even to Auto White Balance, you can press the Right button and use the amber-blue and green-magenta axes to further adjust the color of your shots. Remember to undo any color shift when you no longer need it. Also, you can press the Right button after selecting a Creative Style option and then adjust the contrast, saturation, and sharpness settings. (Saturation is not adjustable for the Black and White and Sepia settings.)

Play your movies in iTunes, and on iPods, iPhones, and iPads. If you record movies using the MP4 format, you can use iTunes to copy the MP4 files to an iTunes-compatible device, such as an iPad. After transferring the files to your computer, open iTunes on the same computer and drag an .mp4 file from the computer's Explorer or Finder window to the Movies panel in iTunes. You can then play the movie from iTunes. To play it on an iPod, iPhone, or iPad, select the video in iTunes, and, on the iTunes menu, select File—Create New Version—Create iPod or iPhone version, or Create iPad or AppleTV version, as appropriate. Then you can sync iTunes with your device, and the converted movie will play on that device. (If you have trouble locating the .mp4 files on your computer, see the last part of Chapter 8.)

Explore the RX100 III's creative potential. Use Manual exposure mode with shutter speeds as long as 30 seconds or the BULB setting to take nighttime shots with trails or other patterns of lights from automobiles, flashlights waved in the air for "light painting," and other sources. Use shutter speeds as fast as 1/2000 second to freeze moving motorcycles, athletes, and other subjects in mid-motion. Try panning or otherwise steadily moving the camera during a multi-second exposure. Use long exposures (on a tripod) to turn night into day. Take HDR images with partly blurred subjects, such as blowing flags.

Diffuse your flash. If the built-in flash produces light that's too harsh for macro or other shots, try using translucent plastic pieces from milk jugs or broken ping-pong balls as homemade diffusers. Hold the plastic between the flash and the subject. When using Fill-flash outdoors, use the Flash Compensation setting on the Shooting menu to reduce the intensity of the flash by -2/3 EV. You can bounce the light from the built-in flash off of the ceiling or a wall by holding it back gently with a finger.

Use the self-timer to avoid camera shake. The self-timer is not just for group portraits; you can use the 2-second self-timer whenever you use a slow shutter speed and need to avoid camera shake. It also is useful for macro photography. Don't forget that you can set the self-timer to take multiple shots, which can increase your chances of getting more great images.

Use DMF for focusing. The direct manual focus option combines the camera's autofocus ability with your own manual focus adjustments, to achieve precision for critical focus tasks. You can use the MF Assist option, which enlarges the display when you turn the Control ring to adjust focus, but, with DMF, you have to half-press the shutter button as you turn the Control ring for MF Assist to work.

Try time-lapse photography. With time-lapse photography, a camera takes a series of still images at regular intervals, several seconds, minutes, or even hours apart, to record a slow-moving event such as the rising or setting of the moon or sun or the opening of a flower. The images are played back at a much faster rate to show the whole event unfolding quickly. The RX100 III does not have this feature built in, but you can purchase the Time-lapse app from Sony through playmemoriescameraapps.com for $9.99 as of this writing. This app includes several preset options for capturing sunsets, night scenes, miniatures, and other traditional time-lapse subjects.

Appendix C: Resources for FurtherInformation

Books

There are many excellent books about photography. Rather than trying to compile a long bibliography, I will list a few especially useful books that I consulted while writing this guide.

C. George, *Mastering Digital Flash Photography* (Lark Books, 2008)

C. Harnischmacher, *Closeup Shooting* (Rocky Nook, 2007)

H. Horenstein, *Digital Photography: A Basic Manual* (Little, Brown, 2011)

H. Kamps, *The Rules of Photography and When to Break Them* (Focal Press, 2012)

J. Paduano, *The Art of Infrared Photography* (4th ed., Amherst Media, 1998)

S. Seip, *Digital Astrophotography* (Rocky Nook, 2008)

Websites and Videos

Since websites come and go and change their addresses, it's impossible to compile a list of sites that discuss the RX100 III that will be accurate far into the future. One way to find the latest sites is to use a good search engine, such as Google or Bing, and type in "Sony DSC-RX100 III." I just did so in Google and got more than 23 million results.

I will include below a list of some of the sites or links I have found useful, with the caveat that some of them may not be accessible by the time you read this.

Digital Photography Review

Listed below is the current web address for the "Sony Cyber-shot Talk" forum at Dpreview.com. Dpreview. com is one of the most useful sites for reviews, discussion forums, technical information, and other resources concerning digital cameras.

http://www.dpreview.com/forums/1009

For a useful compilation of tips and tricks for effective use of the RX100 and RX100 II, many of which apply for the RX100 III, see the following thread in this forum:

http://www.dpreview.com/forums/post/51991398

Reviews of the RX100 III

The links below lead to reviews or previews of the RX100 III by dpreview.com, photographyblog.com, and others, as well as some YouTube videos with useful demonstrations.

http://www.dpreview.com/reviews/sony-cybershot-dsc-rx100-m3

http://www.imaging-resource.com/news/2014/07/23/sony-rx100-iii-shooters-report-iii-steadyshot-video-flash-and-more-you-aske

http://www.cameralabs.com/reviews/Sony_Cyber-shot_RX100_III/index.shtml

http://www.pcmag.com/article2/0,2817,2460983,00.asp

http://gizmodo.com/sony-rx100-mark-iii-the-point-and-shoot-champ-takes-it-1577110556

http://www.pocket-lint.com/review/129428-sony-cyber-shot-rx100-iii-review

http://www.ephotozine.com/article/sony-cyber-shot-rx100-iii-full-review-25485

http://www.amateurphotographer.co.uk/reviews/
compacts/129520/1/sony-cyber-shot-dsc-rx100-iii-
review

http://www.whatdigitalcamera.com/equipment/
reviews/compactcameras/129803/1/sony-cyber-shot-
rx100-iii-review.html

http://www.photographyblog.com/reviews/sony_
cybershot_dsc_rx100_iii_review/

Finally, my own site, White Knight Press, provides
updates, offers support for download of PDFs and
eBooks, and provides a way to contact me with
questions or comments.

http://whiteknightpress.com

THE OFFICIAL SONY SITE

Sony provides resources on its websites, including the
downloadable user's manual for the RX100 III and
other information.

http://esupport.sony.com

http://helpguide.sony.net/dsc/1410/v1/en/print.pdf

https://docs.sony.com/release/2014_DSCRX_series_
accessories_mat.pdf

https://docs.sony.com/release/specs/DSCRX100M3_
mksp.pdf

http://support.d-imaging.sony.co.jp/www/disoft/int/
playmemories-mobile/en/operation/index.html

Index

CPSIA information can be obtained
at www.ICGtesting.com
Printed in the USA
BVOW05s0351170917
494790BV00018B/121/P